TEACH TRUTH TO POWER

TEACH TRUTH TO POWER

HOW TO ENGAGE IN EDUCATION POLICY

DAVID R. GARCIA

THE MIT PRESS   CAMBRIDGE, MASSACHUSETTS   LONDON, ENGLAND

The MIT Press would like to thank the anonymous peer reviewers who provided comments on drafts of this book. The generous work of academic experts is essential for establishing the authority and quality of our publications. We acknowledge with gratitude the contributions of these otherwise uncredited readers.

This book was set in Stone Serif and Avenir by Westchester Publishing Services. Printed and bound in the United States of America.

ISBN: 978-0-262-54322-4

10 9 8 7 6 5 4 3 2 1

To Lori, Lola, y Olivia

CONTENTS

ACKNOWLEDGMENTS

Thank you to my students over the years who trusted in me as I developed and tested the lessons for the book in my course on "Translating Research for Educational Change" at Arizona State University. Thanks, Anabel for being my Zuko. Dick Foreman, I listened and learned from your insight along with my students during the class discussions. Ian Danley, thank you for inspiring me to take the political journey that brings a unique perspective to my scholarship. Alex Molnar, I appreciate your guidance on how to be a public scholar. Kris Gutierrez, thank you for providing me a space at the American Educational Research Association (AERA) annual conference years ago to seed these ideas. I am also grateful to have received a National Education Association/Spencer Post-Doctoral Fellowship and for the national experiences that reinforced for me the importance of research utilization. Emily Ackman and Stacey Long-Genovese for their early work on this topic. I appreciate the feedback from Gustavo Fischman, Keon McGuire, and George Diaz. And always, Lori.

1

SETTING THE CONTEXT

Aaron Wildavsky wrote *Speaking Truth to Power: The Art and Craft of Policy Analysis* in 1979—over thirty-five years before this book was written. It is not only an inspirational title; it remains the oft-cited rallying cry of academics searching for a higher purpose for their scholarship. Yet, if one reviews the state of affairs on research utilization in education policy, it becomes clear that the book's insightful lessons and productive orientation toward the role of evidence in policymaking remain largely unfulfilled. Academics may be "speaking truth to power," but few are listening.

Why? Because Wildavsky's perspective on policy analysis is applicable to those who have access to the policy process, but very few academics have such access. It is most applicable when you are at the table or within earshot, close enough to policymakers so that there is a chance that someone in power will listen. Wildavsky's book describes how to make the most of the opportunity to "speak truth to power"—once you get in the room.

Academics, however, are *not* in the room. They stand on the outside of the policy process—by design. Education research and education policy happen in very different places and are undertaken by very different actors. Being on the outside is not the same as being on the margins, though. Academics and academic research are, or at least should be, necessary parts of the policymaking process. Academics can be extremely influential as outsiders who engage in education policy—if they shift their perspectives and learn how to function best from that position, outside the legislative process, in what is a highly productive and influential space.

To learn to engage in education policy effectively, academics and researchers must shift the way we think about the nexus of research, policy, and politics. Like other professional staff who work with politicians from inside government and legislative circles, Wildavisky's insights are largely applicable to those tasked with carrying out policy, but whose ability to influence policy creation is constrained (chapter 2). Academics and researchers, on the other hand, can provide the frameworks to help set education policy when research has been conducted with an eye to the future, it is brought into the policy process with an awareness of the pressures facing politicians, and it is translated to a policy context (chapter 6).

Teach Truth to Power: How to Engage in Education Policy is written for academics and researchers who are ready to engage in the policy process to influence education policy. You have research that you believe is important. You believe that your research should be heard by policymakers and that it should be considered in making future education policy decisions. You may have conducted original research, or you may have conducted a literature review to inform a policy change that you believe is important. Now, you are ready to "speak truth to power" and want to learn how to engage in policy most effectively.

You may be under the impression that your research is either of high quality, politically "neutral," or so compelling that it can transcend politics. You think that if it can only it could get a fair hearing, both sides will certainly agree with your evidence. In your mind, the quality of your research is beyond reproach. You are convinced that your research is important and can make a difference (hopefully for the better) for the communities that you value. At the end of this book, you will be politically astute enough to know that your research, regardless of its merits, enters a policy context where the political lines have been drawn before you walked in the door. But when you walk in the door, where many voices and other ways of knowing also clamor for attention from busy politicians in a pressure-packed environment (chapter 5), you will be armed with a strategy to translate your research to a policy context so that politicians can take action.

Here, I begin our departure from much of the existing literature on research utilization. First, there is no causal relationship or generalized theory of either the policymaking process or research utilization that you can follow methodically. *Engaging in education policy is not a science—it is a craft.* It is a combination of acquired knowledge and intuition, and similar to learning other crafts, it can be practiced and learned. This book will guide you in developing a strategy to hone your craft to engage effectively in your local policy context.

Second, engaging in education policy is an interpersonal process that cannot be accomplished from the safe confines of your educational setting, even in the social media era (Goodwin 2013). *Engaging in education policy means getting face to face with politicians.* Yes, politicians. This is an uneasy proposition for many academics who want their research to speak for itself without direct political engagement. As Weiss (1977, 531) astutely observed about academics, "They want their work to be so cogent and intellectually compelling that it cannot fail to affect the outcome of policy. Herein lies much of the lure of the policy research enterprise. But hereto arise many of its frustrations." Rest assured, however, as academics we do not have to compromise our strengths, lose the objectivity of our research, or "get political" to be heard.

Third, academics should understand the dynamics of research utilization from a politician's perspective. Most politicians have professional skillsets that are very different from those of academics. Politicians also have requisite electoral demands, and multiple policy actors, including academics, seek to influence their decisions with information. Also, politicians must face the public, by name, to explain and defend their policy positions, while academics remain relatively anonymous. The sweet spot for you to "teach truth to power" involves understanding the political realities and interpersonal dynamics facing politicians, as well as how you, as an academic, are best positioned in a policy context to leverage your expertise to influence policy.

Lastly, academics should set realistic expectations about their involvement in the policymaking process. Academics should not expect to "make" policy (Gluckman 2014). The process of making policy, meaning writing specific legislative provisions or the text of a motion that is considered by a school district governing board, is an intense and detailed process left to professional staff who work close enough to politicians to keep pace with the up-to-the-minute maneuvering that occurs in the process. Academics should expect to influence policy through research. But academics should not expect politicians to adopt their policy recommendations wholesale. Politicians are most likely to adopt as much and as many policy recommendations at any one time as they can support and "champion" on their own to *their* people.

WHAT IS THE RESEARCH AND POLICY GAP AND WHY IS IT IMPORTANT TO BRIDGE IT?

The gap between research production and policy implementation is a perplexing and ongoing quandary facing nearly all scholarly research in the field of education. The problem is that not enough education research is used in the formation of education policy, despite the commonly held belief among academics that research should be used to inform policy.

Almost every academic book or journal in education counts policymakers among its intended audience, and academic journal articles routinely close with policy implications or recommendations for policymakers. Too often, however, these thoughtful suggestions remain hidden from the very policymakers they are intended to reach. While academics criticize education policies, lamenting the fact that too few policymakers use research evidence to guide their decisions, policymakers complain that education research is neither relevant enough nor timely enough to suit their purposes. The copious number of books and journal articles on education that should inform education policy decisions go unread by those who make those decisions.

This is not to say that policymakers do not value research. There is an abundance of knowledge that is worthy of sharing and could be helpful in the formation of sound education policy, if presented in a way that politicians can use it to take action. Today's education issues have historical roots, meaning that there is an accumulation of knowledge available in *the* research literature to inform policy solutions (chapter 9). By and large, education stakeholders expect politicians to be consistent and hold that education is better served when the policies that influence students' lives and school conditions are made on the best available evidence. Where, then, does the disconnect between research and policy lie?

Scholars of research utilization have identified four points along the progression between research production and its utilization in a policy context where the disconnects occur: in research production itself; in the dissemination of research; in the "soft tissue" or space where research is available for use by policymakers (Hess 2008); and in its utilization in a policy context.

Those scholars who focus on research production argue that academics may not be producing research that is accessible or helpful to policymaking. Academics may not be asking the "right" questions, as viewed from politicians' perspectives, or the research products may be difficult to read or understand—as in academic articles that are overly theoretical, written in abstruse language, or conducted via highly technical research methods that require advanced training to interpret the results. Academics have suggested remedies such as "use-inspired" research that is better connected to the real-world challenges facing policymakers and research articles written in language that is accessible to lay audiences.

Research dissemination, also referred to as "knowledge mobilization," is concerned with how research is made available to nonacademic audiences. Some academics have taken a critical view of traditional means of knowledge sharing, such as publishing in academic journals that require paid subscriptions. Knowledge mobilization research looks at how individuals and institutions can expand opportunities for sharing academic knowledge with broader communities in nontraditional ways and how institutional incentives either reward or restrict efforts to communicate research evidence (Fischman et al. 2018). From a knowledge mobilization lens, strategies to close the research and policy gap include open-access journals, more sophisticated uses of social media (e.g., podcasts, and blogs), direct interactions with practitioners, and organizational commitments through the creation of knowledge mobilization centers or institutes.

The space between research production and its use in the policy process, where research is available and policy decisions are being made based on ways of knowing that may (or may not) include academic research, is the "soft tissue" of research utilization (Hess 2008). It is at this point that other intermediaries enter the policy space in addition to academics to provide politicians with information, including research. Organizations from think tanks to advocacy organizations package and present research to facilitate use by politicians and to influence policy toward their preferred goals. Philanthropic organizations provide funding for the dissemination of research that meets their strategic objectives. Lobbyists, who are often overlooked as intermediaries, provide individual politicians with localized information on the politician's specific constituents. Constituents bring their own evidence and stories to persuade politicians. Professional staff, such as legislative aides and agency heads, engage with the research literature in their role as gatekeepers, who search for, screen, synthesize, and present information to politicians.

The last point of connection is the use of research in the policymaking process. What does it mean to "use" research in a policy context? One can think about research utilization along a continuum from instrumental to conceptual. The most concrete use is instrumental, which can be understood as "the direct impact of research on policy and practice decisions. It identifies the influence of a specific piece of research in making a specific decision or in defining the solution to a specific problem" (Nutley, Walter, and Davies 2007, 36). Instrumental uses include cases where specific research products have been applied in a specific policy decision, directly influenced practice in the field, or have had an impact that can be shown through measurable outcomes. By contrast, conceptual uses introduce a "more wide-ranging definition of research use, comprising the complex and often indirect ways in which research can have an impact on the knowledge, understanding, and attitudes of policymakers" (Nutley, Walter, and Davies 2007, 36). In these cases, research is regarded as "creeping" into and "enlightening" the policymaking process over time (Weiss 1977; 1980).

The consumption side of research utilization also places a spotlight on politicians themselves. Politicians are criticized for either ignoring the research evidence or using it for political purposes. Politicians are faulted for a lack of training in research methods and the inability to discern quality research from shoddy research. Here, some academics have called for more politicians to educate themselves in research or for more collaborations between academics and politicians to co-create educational policies (Ball 2012; Edelstein 2016).

Nearly all the literature in the field of research utilization contributes to an understanding of the research and policy gap but offers little insight on how to bridge it for those who aspire to engage in policy (Oliver and Cairney 2019). This book is filling a prominent void in the existing literature by contributing concrete strategies that academics can use to engage in education policy effectively.

WHY HASN'T A "HOW-TO" BOOK LIKE THIS BEEN WRITTEN YET?

Many have pointed to the idea that research and policy reside in separate "worlds" or communities as the reason why the research and policy gap persists. "Authors who hold this view attempt to explain the nonutilization in terms of the relationship between the researcher and the research system and the policymaker and the policymaking system. They argue that social scientists and policymakers live in separate worlds, with different and often conflicting values, reward systems, and languages. The social scientist is often concerned with "pure" science and esoteric issues. By contrast, politicians are action-oriented and practical, concerned with immediate issues" (Caplan 1979, 459). More recently, Bogenschneider and Corbett (2010, 15) advanced the "community dissonance theory" to argue that knowledge producers and knowledge consumers function "within a discrete number of disparate communities that find it difficult to communicate with each other."

The two worlds/communities metaphors mean that academics and policymakers hold very different perspectives on which characteristics of social science research they find most valuable, their modes of inquiry for accessing and processing information, how they characterize policy problems, the organizational constraints and structures under which they operate, and the ways in which research should be communicated (Dunn 1980).

The concept of two worlds or communities is also the primary reason why a book like *Teach Truth to Power* has not been written to date. Due to the gulf between research and policy, there are very few academics who have worked extensively in both worlds. There are even fewer who have been trained, or have trained themselves, in both worlds. Repeated experiences and concerted inquiry in both worlds are essential if one is going to teach others how to engage in education policy.

By and large, those who study education and education policy are content experts. For the bulk of their career, they have been academics with a focus on advancing the theory and knowledge base of a particular topic or academic discipline, and most of their professional interactions have occurred in academic settings with other content experts or students who are invested in learning. These highly educated and well-meaning experts, either willingly, or often unwillingly, find themselves in the position of working with politicians. They are confronted with people who do not have the same expertise and, probably most difficult for academics to fathom, they neither share the same respect for research nor value the acquired knowledge of experts. What grates academics further is that "policymakers," while having little to no experience in education or education research, are in positions of influence to make important decisions that dictate resource allocations and school conditions.

For the junior academic, it can be career suicide to engage in education policy during the pressure-packed years as an assistant professor. During this time the professional pressures to "publish or perish" require one to focus almost exclusively on publication in academic journals and developing a reputation among other academics. There are few or no incentives in the first years of an academic career to engage in policy. In fact, such activity could be considered as counterproductive, insofar as influencing education policy does not count in traditional metrics of tenure and promotion. In addition, academics who work directly with politicians who hold power and the purse strings risk becoming too political (Henig 2009; Cairney and Oliver 2017) and could jeopardize public funding for their home institutions.

The disincentives to engage in education policy continue throughout one's academic career. For one thing, academics must invest time and energy into learning how to engage in policy (Weible et al. 2012), and many academics choose not to incur the transaction costs of acquiring the skills and knowledge to engage with politicians (Landry, Amara, and Lamari 2001). This decision is reasonable because promotion in academia remains based largely on scholarly production, which is itself based on professional interactions with other content experts and not concerned with influencing policy. Those with content expertise who could inform education policy, therefore, are encouraged to "stay in their lane" within established academic confines for the bulk of their career, communicating their research largely with academic audiences. Even in universities with expressed institutional goals to disseminate research to broader nonacademic audiences, academics still value traditional forms of dissemination, such as publishing in journals and presenting at professional conferences, over engagement activities that bring them face to face with communities outside the university environment (Zuiker et al. 2019).

In many cases, academics wait until later in their careers to engage in policy. While these career academics may have done extensive scholarly work on education or education policy, they would not consider themselves as experts in *engaging in* education policy, and many have little to no experience working with politicians directly. In a policy context, they are novices who often engage under one of two conditions. First, they may have developed a substantial research record and their scholarship has risen to politicians' attention. These entries into the world of education policy are generally viewed as success stories because academics are receiving attention for their research. But when bridging the two "worlds" directly, many academics are faced with frustrations:

Professors are not necessarily naive, but neither are they prepared for precisely how politicized the political process can be, and how far it can stray from public interests. Academics hoping to promote social welfare can frequently be frustrated by the petty personal concerns and partisan agendas that stand in the way. Those steeped in the pursuit of knowledge also may be insufficiently sensitive to the limits of their usefulness in policy arenas: their data may not be definite, uncontested, or able to resolve complex value trade-offs. And academics who are hoping for power, status, and recognition can be discomfited by the low esteem and inadequate influence that their advice commands among politicians. (Rhode 2006, 128)

Or, as Weiss (1977, 534) noted, "If they come into the game expecting that research will have an obvious and immediate impact and nothing happens—nothing to the naked eye—they may prematurely give up on the whole business. They have been known to go home and write scathing diatribes for professional journals criticizing bureaucrats and politicians for their neglect of important research evidence."

Second, when academics assume administrative positions, as deans, for example, their elevated public profiles pull them out of their university offices into the broader community and in front of politicians.

Administrative positions, however, can be highly constrained. A dean, for one, represents the university and does not necessarily speak with the full voice of their acquired academic expertise. University administrators have many obligations, including to funders, faculty, and community groups. Thus, like many other policy actors, university administrators, particularly public university administrators, must remain agreeable to diverse groups so they are at the table to represent the university.

Overall, one gets the impression that policy engagement is not the academic's preference. They describe their entry as being "pulled" or "forced into" doing policy, and policy engagement is treated like a sacrifice that is carried out for the greater good. After a public stint in policy, most professors return back to their research and may not clamor to return back to working with politicians directly. Most academics would rather be left to conduct their research and teach, the reasons for which they became academics in the first place.

Often, when professors write about their policy experiences, they tell of blunt confrontations with dimwitted politicians, being in the room as the deal went down, or dueling with reporters, all narrated with the kind of wounded glory that one would associate with war stories. To audiences of wide-eyed graduate students, they tell of how their research was disregarded offhand by a politician or junior legislative aide, while showing off the battle scars with a martyr's pride for having engaged in the front lines of policymaking. To the junior scholar, or the student who wants to learn from their experiences, these accounts serve as cautionary tales that discourage similar behavior. No, don't go there, don't do that. Yet, "doing something" or "making a difference" is a primary motivation for many who toil in education research.

Very few academics write about their policy experiences as part of a sustained research agenda. While some of the "how-to" advice for academics to engage in policy is located in the "grey" literature (blogs, editorials, commentaries, and the like), the practical knowledge base for individuals to learn how to engage in education policy is thin (Oliver and Cairney 2019). There is scant advice on what to expect or what one should do when engaging in a policy context. And, the how-to advice that does exist is incomplete, vague, safe, or naive to the realities of the policymaking process (Cairney and Oliver 2020).

I can't help myself. I will also recount my own war stories throughout the book for context and color. In these sections, I will present personal stories and conversational perspectives of the research literature beginning with the first seeds of this book. In 2008, I was selected as a National Academy of Education/Spencer Foundation postdoctoral fellow, a prestigious honor that included networking opportunities in Washington, DC, with some of the most influential scholars in education. Prior to my leaving for DC, the chairman of the Arizona State Senate Education Committee forwarded me a bill with a request to let him know my impressions of it. During the trip, I received a flood of emails from lobbyists, many of whom I knew from my time at the legislature. I learned that the chairman's decision to bring the bill to committee (or not) was based on my input. The policy implications were substantial. The bill shifted the training of all school principals from the state colleges of education to business schools.

One of the NAE/Spencer sessions was on making an impact in policy. The panel members, most of them influential senior scholars, were relating their personal war stories about the times that they testified before legislative committees with a mix of martyrdom and pride, all the while warning the room full of junior scholars to keep our heads down and write for tenure. I mentioned that testifying before committees rarely impact policy. The votes are counted before the hearings start. One senior scholar called my view "pessimistic." I pulled out the bill, explained to the senior scholar the policy implications riding on my input, and mentioned that the "work" of influencing policy is interpersonal, decidedly low-profile, and certainly would not "count" on my tenure application.

Why? Because most academics, while being content experts, are policy novices who learn "on the job" how to engage in a policy context (chapter 3). In general, they write about their policy work as singular experiences based on their particular personalities, scholarship, and the policy actors that they encountered at the moment. When academics present the actors, policy issues, and interactions in a manner that is not easily generalizable, their experiences come across as idiosyncratic events that impede a collective understanding from one policy context to another. Certainly, not all policy contexts are alike, but there is still much that can be learned and applied across policy contexts (Bogenschneider and Corbett 2010). Academics who dabble in policy, however, do not have the expertise to compare their experiences against others and, most important, to predict future circumstances for the educational benefit of others.

A few academics are trained well enough to forge a career in both the research and policy worlds. Their real-world experiences shine through in their research, writing, and continued engagement in the policy process. Academics who have worked in both worlds are coveted in policy context, not only for their content expertise but precisely because they know how to communicate with politicians. Manna and Petrilli (2008, 74) analyzed those who contributed to No Child Left Behind as witnesses in formal hearings. They found that 17.4 percent of all witnesses came from the research profession. Notably, researchers who testified most frequently in legislative hearings also had prior experience working in federal government either in the executive or legislative branches (they included, for example, Maris Vinovskis, Chester Finn, and Diane Ravitch). These researchers were selected because of their familiarity with Washington, DC and their relationships with members of Congress and staff, and because they have the ability to communicate with politicians effectively. Researchers from think tanks (such as the Heritage Foundation) or professional research firms (such as Mathematica or SRI International) were also popular because they were able to identify trends in *the* research and communicate them in jargon-free language. Unlike academics who work in narrow niches and speak in limited scholarly circles, those who work with think tanks are expected to translate research in a manner that eases the cognitive challenges and time constraints that confront politicians.

LET'S GET POLITICS OUT OF THE WAY

This book is about politicians but not politics, per se. The book is not concerned with how politicians learn about or engage in political activities related to campaigning, winning elections, influencing voter behavior, or the horse trading that is characteristic of the policymaking process.

The book is centered on how politicians learn about education, education research, and education policy and takes a broad view of the knowledge and actors that politicians utilize to inform themselves and make policy decisions.

The entire process is political, including gathering and evaluating evidence (Parkhurst 2017). But as a content expert, you will not be expected to engage in the political part. Nearly all of the overtly political activity (fundraising, campaign events, and so on) occurs away from the policy process. You will stay close to your strengths and connected to the research evidence. The policymaking process is filled with predefined roles, and the content expert is one such role. This book will help you operate effectively as a content expert. You will encounter politics, which is ever-present, but you should not let politics deter you from engaging in policy.

You can expect that politicians will look at your contributions with a political or ideological eye (Miller and Fredericks 2000). The omnipresent pressure of getting elected means that it may be more difficult to engage with those politicians who are making policy decisions with electoral consequences, rather than research evidence, in mind. Or, you will encounter dogmatic politicians, those who are almost completely devoted to party ideology when making policy decisions. Is it a waste of time for academics to engage with "hyper-political" or dogmatic politicians? No. Lobbyists, an important informational source for the book, would counsel academics to prepare their best presentation and bring it to whoever will listen, and you may be surprised who is willing to listen if your presentation is tailored to policymaking. This book is about how to create the best presentation possible and to bring it to politicians as effectively as possible so that it gets heard.

ABOUT ME

This is the point in the book where I convince you that I am one of those rare academics with sufficient experience in and understanding of both worlds to teach others how to engage in education policy. My experience stems from being trained to engaging in policy, forging a successful academic career, and jumping into politics myself. Unlike many of my academic colleagues, I became a professor and earned tenure after working in the highest levels of state education policy. I was the lead analyst for the Arizona State Senate Education Committee and served as the Associate Superintendent of Public Instruction for the state of Arizona while completing my dissertation at the now defunct graduate school of education at the University of Chicago. After co-founding a state-based research and policy think tank and working as a peer consultant for the US Department of Education during the early implementation stages of No Child Left Behind, I got the opportunity to fulfill my professional dream and join the faculty at the College of Education at Arizona State University.

As an academic in the field of education policy, I have published in the areas of school choice and accountability. I have also engaged in public scholarship during my entire academic career, even during the pressure-packed years as an assistant professor, when I was writing for tenure. I maintained a public profile outside of academia to remain connected to Arizona education policy. I released reports for public audiences, directed a research and policy center that contributed to education policy from the city to the state level, presented frequently to community groups in an effort to engage with politicians *before* they become politicians, and remained a media contact for education-related stories. I have authored two book chapters on closing the research and policy gap; these introduce the ideas that will be unpacked thoroughly in the book (Garcia 2018a; Garcia 2018b).

I went to the "dark side," running for state office twice and losing both times. In 2014, I ran for Arizona State Superintendent of Public Instruction, losing by less than half a percentage point. In 2018, as the Democratic gubernatorial candidate for the state of Arizona, I became only the second Latino candidate in Arizona history to win the gubernatorial nomination of a major party. My experience as "the candidate" is the lynchpin that connects the two worlds of research and policy for this book. Through my political experiences, I realized that academics must go through politicians to influence policy, a perspective that is largely missing in the academic literature on the research and policy gap.

These formative experiences forged this book. At the Arizona state senate, I learned quickly that in order to interject research evidence into policymaking, I had to become astute at translating research into frameworks that could be digested quickly and easily by those who were veteran politicians but education research and policy novices. I remember my first committee hearing and being tasked with providing on overview of the status of education in Arizona. I stood before the committee with my back to a room full of lobbyists, educators, and everyday citizens, and proceeded to speak from a set of colorful slides that I had created for the presentation. In the opening sentences, I indicated that I had "triangulated" multiple sources of data. One outspoken senator, raised her hand

and asked me, "What's triangulated?" I offered my best off the cuff definition after which she said, "Mr. Garcia I don't get it, and I ask that you not
use big words like that before the committee." I was dumbfounded. All of
my graduate training had been cut off at the knees. I finished—doing my
best not to use any more "big words."

Working with the Arizona state legislature, I learned that engaging
in policy is a local, personal, and (more or less) predictable process that
can be learned (and taught). In fact, every year, in state houses across
the country and at the federal level, legislative interns and staffers learn
about the policymaking process. I will pass these essential lessons on to
you as they relate to research utilization in policymaking starting with
the recognition that bridging the research and policy gap is accomplished
through people. Academics must leave the familiar confines of university offices to engage with politicians directly. Blogging from a distance
is insufficient to engage effectively. Yes, technology has changed how
information is exchanged in policy contexts, but those who are paid to
understand and influence policy, namely lobbyists, know that the real
work still gets done face to face.

I served as the director of research and policy under Superintendent
Lisa Graham Keegan, a highly visible school choice advocate and controversial political figure (Maranto et al. 1999), and as associate superintendent for standards and accountability under Jaime Molera, who was
appointed after Keegan resigned to accept a post in Washington, DC.
During this time, I turned around a troubled state assessment system and
developed Arizona's first school accountability system. While these were
certainly high-profile public positions, I was only one of several public
officials who were communicating with the public through the media,
large gatherings, and face-to-face meetings. To maximize my potential
to communicate with the public, I had to teach others, most of whom
were not well versed in assessment or statistical methods, to communicate complex ideas to *their* people in applied settings. I communicated
in words and phrases that others could use verbatim as their own. Most
importantly, I focused on frameworks, rather than on minute details and
research methods, to help others understand the education landscape
around them and to predict future policy outcomes. In this book, these
experiences are transformed into shifting academic's perspectives from

teaching politicians to understand a given body of research to coach politicians in their role as policy champions, enabled and empowered to bring the research forward themselves to the people and networks of their choosing—without the academic in the room.

My appointment as an assistant professor was the ideal moment to leave the applied policy work behind me. But I couldn't. My professional experiences in state policy had shaped me. Even during the hours toiling over academic publications as a junior professor, I knew that writing in a journal or presenting to other academics did not influence education policy. I understood that the larger policy world was functionally detached from our scholarship. So, during my years as an assistant professor, I remained engaged in policy, despite the fact that these applied experiences would not "count" for the purpose of getting tenure and could have counted against me at times. During this period, I worked to educate my academic colleagues about how to engage in education policy. Thank you, Kris Gutierrez, who during her tenure as president of the Annual Education Research Association (AERA) gave me the professional space to explore these ideas through a session at the annual conference entitled, "Interacting with Policy Makers: A Strategic Approach." Kris understood that we, the academic and research community, must take the lead to leverage our collective expertise and experiences to educate our colleagues on how to "teach truth to power" most effectively.

Beginning in 2014, my experiences as the candidate exposed a completely different aspect of the connection between research and policy—the grinding reality of politics. I ran for office because I came to the conclusion that the most direct way for me to influence policy through research was to become a politician myself. It was a sobering realization that the path to use my academic expertise to influence policy went through politics. Like other academics, I was apprehensive about "getting political" for professional and personal reasons. The process of getting political itself, however, was surprisingly easy: it started humbly with gathering a few friends around my kitchen table and announcing that I was running for office. In big picture terms, being the candidate and working with so many passionate people made for an amazing experience. The day-to-day activities of campaigning, however, were soul-crushingly monotonous.

As an academic engaged in two statewide campaigns and working with many other candidates and politicians in Arizona and in settings across the country, I was struck that research was (almost) never mentioned in the formative period when, as candidates, politicians establish the agendas that will guide their policy ideas once elected, or re-elected. One example from the campaign trail illustrates how much work lies ahead of academics to influence policy through research and serves as my motivation to improve research utilization. The term "segregation," a common topic in the academic literature, yields 2.15 million hits in 0.04 seconds using Google Scholar (April 11, 2019, 10:11 a.m.). By contrast, in over four years of either preparing for or running for statewide office—the formative time for developing a policy agenda for me and many other candidates—segregation was brought up once. Just once.

Lastly, my political experience erased any mystique that I held about politicians. I learned that politicians are essentially members of the public who are brave (some would say crazy) enough to run for office (and win).

WHAT TO EXPECT FROM THIS BOOK

Teach Truth to Power: How to Engage in Education Policy is unlike any other book, report, or academic article on research and policy gap: this book will teach you how to engage in education policy rather than fall into a familiar academic tendency of taking an overly analytical approach that leaves readers stranded to apply the findings on their own (Nathan 1985). After making the case for reconceptualizing the relationship between research and policy, the book includes concrete strategies that you can use to develop your own plan of action to engage in education policy. The book is an ambitious effort to make explicit the hidden curriculum of engaging in education policy, and it has broader applicability to other social science fields.

This book is for educators, researchers, graduate students, classroom teachers, and university professors (I will collectively refer to this group as academics), who aspire to "do something" with what they have learned in education to make a difference in education, but who remain frustrated that education programs fail to teach "how" to take what they know and make a difference in education policy.

At its core, the book is a how-to manual with straightforward advice that readers can apply to influence education policy in their local context. In this way, it can be used to design and deliver a course on engaging in education policy. In addition, the chapters include a detailed treatment of the literature on the research and policy gap and thus contribute to the fields of research utilization, knowledge mobilization, and public scholarship. Finally, this book is a resource that you can turn to for guidance when you are ready to "teach truth to power."

The book is organized into two parts. Part I, "The Shift," challenges many of the fundamental findings in the literature on the research and policy gap to orient the reader toward thinking about engaging in education policy as a localized and interpersonal endeavor that involves politicians, specifically. Part II, "Learning the Craft," teaches specific strategies that will help you engage in education policy.

PART I: THE SHIFT

Part I prepares the reader to engage in education policy by clarifying the actors who engage in the policymaking process, challenging long-held assumptions in the academic literature about how research is used in a policymaking context, and rethinking the very nature of research itself as a source of policy-relevant information. The shift toward thinking about research utilization as direct engagement in a local policy context is based on the tools available to the education policy analyst: a critical review of the academic literature combined with personal experiences in education policy.

Chapter 2: Who Sets Policy?—Politicians, consisting of elected officials and their appointees, set policy, and professional staff establish the options to carry out policy. Politicians and professional staff have disparate background knowledge and carry out very distinct roles in the policymaking process. Academics should approach politicians and professional staff differently. Using Kingdon (2003) as a frame, I reexamine the academic literature and conclude that much of what we know about the use of research in policy derives from studies involving professional staff who carry out policy rather than the politicians who set it. The confusion comes from the misapplied and overused term "policymaker" in the academic literature in a way that does not discriminate between different policy actors, regardless of their role. I also discuss other influential policy actors, including prospective politicians; laypersons who are involved in their local communities and who are among those whom politicians are likely to appoint to positions of authority in education policy or who may become politicians themselves; individuals and organizations who package and present their own research to politicians; lobbyists whose job of influencing politics includes providing information to politicians; and politicians themselves who act as intermediaries when they champion a policy issue and bring research into the policymaking process to persuade their colleagues.

Chapter 3: Politicians and Knowledge—Politicians are education research and policy novices—by design—and become generalists, at best. They function with half-knowledge, intentionally filtering out surplus information, so that they can take action. Not only do academics possess more knowledge about education than politicians, but they also recall information, apply knowledge, and approach problems very differently than politicians. To guide academics in how to interact with politicians, who are likely education policy novices or generalists or something in between, I apply literature on skill acquisition borrowed from the field of nursing (Benner 1982). I also introduce the theory of "half-knowledge," which refers to how politicians are aware of policy problems but screen out surplus information, seeking and using research that helps them fulfill a specific purpose—to take action.

Chapter 4: Problems with Research—There is sufficient research available at any time to inform any policy idea brought forth by politicians. But of the formal products used in a policy context (audits, analyses, evaluations, and research), research is the only product with no direct application in a local policy context. Context is king in the use of research to influence policy. Among the formal products used in the policymaking process, however, research is the least context-specific. Yet, it has the longest shelf life and is the most useful information source to influence policy over time. In this chapter, I examine the criticisms leveled against academic research and conclude that, despite its many shortcomings, the research enterprise itself does not have to undergo a dramatic overhaul to be relevant to politicians. Why? Because, there are very few entirely "new" problems in education. So, there is sufficient research on any topic to address any policy issue at any time. The research may be hard to find. It may be difficult to under-stand. And it certainly requires translation to a local policy context to be applicable—but it's available.

Chapter 5: Research Use in Policymaking—Research evidence is one of many ways of knowing in policymaking. Academics are one of many types of actors in the policymaking process. And neither research nor academics hold a privileged position. In this chapter, I review Weiss's models of research utilization and side with the interactive model, which recognizes many sources of information—ranging from informal sources, such as social media, to for-mal sources, such as academic research, and many actors, most of whom are not experts—as being influential in the policymaking process. Given the interactive nature of policymaking, the most effective method to influence policy is to engage directly with politicians despite the fact that the policy context is foreign to most academics. In addition, since there are many ways of knowing that influence policy decisions, ranging from concrete to abstract, I suggest how to recognize when politicians rely on a specific way of knowing and the implications of each way of knowing for academics who are engaging in policy.

Chapter 6: Asked, Brought, Inside, Outside—Politicians have the least control over and least inherent trust in unsolicited research that is brought to them by outsiders. Academics are outsiders who bring unsolicited research to politicians. I introduce the asked/brought/inside/outside (ABIO) framework to help aca-demics understand their position relative to politicians and other actors in a policy context. The matrix reveals the dynamics associated with research from the politician's perspective. The major implication for academics is that politicians have the least amount of inherent trust in unsolicited research and no control over how it is framed and released publicly.

PART II: LEARNING THE CRAFT

The second part of the book teaches the reader the craft of engaging in education policy in their local context.

Chapter 7: Building Relationships with Politicians before They Are Politicians—The most opportune time to build trusted relationships with politicians is before they get elected, not after. The quiet time before politicians begin electoral campaigns, when they are forming their policy agendas, is when they are most inclined to listen to diverse perspectives on education issues. Readers will learn how to identify the places where they can connect with prospective politicians to build trusted relationships to put themselves in influential positions over time.

Chapter 8: The Influence of Unexpected Allies—Your research is likely to stand out if brought to politicians by unexpected allies. The common advice in the research utilization literature is to leverage issue networks or advocacy coalitions to bring research to politicians. From one legislative session to the next, however, issue networks repeatedly tout the same types of evidence (particularly those that put their policy issues in the best light), creating a repetitive message that mutes the influence of individual research products because hearing about research from the usual suspects is exactly what politicians expect. To disrupt the political dynamics, academics should enlist unexpected allies, people or organizations outside the expected issue networks or advocacy organizations, who are willing to bring your research to others, including politicians. The enlistment of unexpected allies is also a stringent test of public interest in your research. If your research is of public interest, then you should be able to convince someone who is not one of the usual suspects or in academia to bring your research to *their* people.

Chapter 9: Leveraging the *Research to Predict Policy Outcomes—Academics can distinguish themselves from other lay voices in a policy context by leveraging* the *research to predict future policy outcomes.* Academics can be most relevant in a policy context by serving as intermediaries of *the* research, defined as the cumulation of evidence available in the academic literature. With a mastery of *the* research, academics can serve as education policy experts who are able to predict future policy outcomes, distinguishing themselves from lay voices in a policy context who do not possess the expertise to provide this coveted perspective.

Chapter 10: From Practical Problems to the Ask—To engage with politicians most effectively, academics must translate research to a local policy context by restructuring how they present their research in order to make the most compelling case for its applicability to policymaking. When presenting research to politicians, academics should begin with a practical problem to capture the politician's attention, present the key policy-relevant elements of their research, and end with the ask to the politician. *The ask* is a direct and specific request for politicians to take action. Those who are uncomfortable with the ask will be both relieved and empowered to learn that an "ask" is not only common in a policy context—it's commonplace.

Chapter 11: The Research One-Pager—Academics must translate research to a policy context in a manner that communicates the key policy-relevant details required for politicians to take action. All in 20 seconds. Academics recognize that research should be communicated to politicians in accessible language and abbreviated formats. There is a lack of guidance, however, on exactly how succinctly and directly academics should write for politicians. This chapter introduces the research one-pager, which is modeled on the legislative one-pager that is ubiquitous in policy contexts and is a different product written specifically for politicians to understand how they can take action. The research one-pager connects politicians to research through the practical problem, gleans those findings that are most applicable to specific policies, tells politicians exactly what they can do to take action, and does it all in twenty seconds. Yes, twenty seconds.

Chapter 12: Answers, Advocacy, Activism, and Frameworks—When asked to contribute in a policymaking context, academics can answer questions, advocate for a policy change, engage in activism, or present a framework. Frameworks are best. Readers will learn the advantages and disadvantages of the four basic ways to respond to politicians in a policy context. They will learn to scaffold their answers to politicians from practical responses to complex concepts. The utility of advocacy as a response is diminished over time because advocates respond predictably and become marginalized sources of new information. Also, activists tend to get to the table through political pressure, not expertise, and may be excluded from participation in controversial or emerging issues. Frameworks are the most effective because they help novice politicians make sense of new conditions and guide future policy decisions based on research. Fortunately, academics are experienced at developing and communicating frameworks given their work with simplifying complex ideas for students.

Chapter 13: Teach to Champion—Teaching to champion entails enabling and empowering politicians to bring research forward themselves to the people and networks that they choose—without the academic in the room. I introduce the crucial role of politicians as champions of policy change who expend political capital to achieve desired policy outcomes, on their own accord.

Why go through the hassle of engaging in education policy? It is time consuming, fraught with pitfalls, and the institutional rewards are few. You should engage in education policy because it's immensely rewarding. In danger of sounding overly idealistic, you can make a tangible difference. You will experience education research in a way that is more interactive and captivating than any academic presentation because, to me, policy engagement completes the study of education policy. Policy engagement animates education research. You will learn that policy actors have names, faces, personalities, and vulnerabilities. You will recognize that individual policies have a backstory; how they emerge from the context in which they were drafted, with many factors—big, small, intended, and unforeseen—affecting the course that policies take. You will realize that policies are not unalterable and understand what it takes to change their trajectories. When you engage, you will learn firsthand that there is a vital purpose for a research perspective at the table to teach "truth to power."

Political champions bring information, including research evidence, to others, including their colleagues and influential external networks, to generate support for their preferred policy outcomes. In this role, politicians are intermediaries. The academic's role in this process is to not to teach politicians to understand research, but to enable and empower politicians to bring research evidence to others on their own.

Chapter 14: A Renewed Role for Academics—Academics are optimally positioned to influence education policy. Thus, a well-rounded faculty of education should include a professor of impact whose job requirements include translating research to influence policy. Teach Truth to Power culminates in two sweeping implications that bookend the research utilization process. First, because academics' skillsets include predicting policy outcomes in an ever-changing education landscape and are thus tailor-made to influence policy. In order to bridge the research and policy gap, the academic field of studying education policy should be reimagined so as to value influencing education policy. Thus, the well-rounded education faculty should include a dedicated professor of impact, who is compensated and professionally recognized for advancement accordingly.

I

THE SHIFT

2

WHO SETS POLICY?

Politicians, consisting of elected officials and their appointees, set policy. and professional staff establish the options to carry out policy. Politicians and professional staff have disparate background knowledge and carry out very distinct roles in the policymaking process. Academics should approach politicians and professional staff differently.

For our purpose, we will define policy as a "plan or course of action carried out through a law, rule, code, or other mechanism in the public or private sector" (Bogenschneider, 2006, 57). Thus, learning to engage in education policy begins with separating those who set policy from those who carry it out. In this chapter, I distinguish politicians, the elected or appointed officials who set policy, from the professional staff who are tasked with carrying it out. At the school district level, elected officials include locally elected school board members. At the state level, elected officials include governors, state senators and representatives, and elected state school superintendents or commissioner who are elected, while the remainder are appointed by politicians. At the federal level, elected representatives include US senators and members of Congress. Professional staff, as described by Kingdon (2003, 19), are the "hidden cluster of specialists in the bureaucracy and in professional communities" who influence the selection of policy options that are put forth to carry out policy.

This large and influential group includes state administrators, agency officials or heads, legislative staff, and research staff. Professional staff serve at the discretion of politicians. I separate politicians from professional staff to concentrate on the former for the remainder of the book, while mentioning the latter only when it is important to distinguish my perspective on closing the research and policy gap from that of the bulk of the academic literature on research utilization.

Distinguishing between politicians and professional staff is also helpful for putting the lessons from the academic literature on research utilization in proper perspective. Much of the academic work on research utilization has been conducted with professional staff who implement policy, not the politicians who set it. In the academic literature, politicians and professional staff are repeatedly co-mingled under the label "policymaker" or "decision-maker." In a policy context, however, policymakers and decision-makers are elusive. There are politicians and professional staff. The commingling of politicians and professional staff has also distorted our view of how to engage in the policy process because politicians and professional staff have disparate background knowledge and carry out very distinct roles in policymaking. Politicians and professional staff are fundamentally different. Academics should approach politicians and professional staff differently.

Professional staff are much more likely to share a common knowledge base with academics, making it easier for academics to approach and work with professional staff. The ability of professional staff to influence policy, however, is highly constrained because their actions cannot get ahead of the policy positions held by the politicians who employ them. Politicians, on the other hand, are likely novices with respect to education research and policy. Academics should not walk in the door with the expectation that they share a common knowledge base with politicians. To the contrary, novice politicians may not understand or even value research. In some cases, politicians may even hold a negative view of the potential of research to influence policy, creating a potentially oppositional relationship between themselves and academics.

The separate treatment of elected official from professional staff is not intended to discount the importance of professional staff in the policy process. To the contrary, professional staff are consistent sources of institutional knowledge in the policy process as term limits and political winds change the composition of legislative bodies. Professional staff are also key gate-keepers to politicians, and they are often regarded by politicians as more credible sources of research than academic experts, even though staff are not necessarily experts themselves. Anyone taking research into the policy context should be aware of the influential role that professional staff play in the process. As insiders, professional staff are trusted and valued by politicians.

Four other key actors in the policy process should also be considered: prospective politicians, a pool of laypersons who are involved in their local communities and whom politicians are likely to appoint to positions of authority in education policy or who may become politicians themselves; intermediaries, in the form of individuals and organizations that package and present research to politicians; lobbyists who in their professional role of influencing political decision-making also provide information to politicians; and politicians themselves who, act as intermediaries when they use research to persuade their colleagues and people in *their* networks.

POLITICIANS SET POLICY

Politicians are the key drivers who set public policy. As Kingdon (2003, 44) concludes about the role of politicians in the policymaking process, "To the extent that anybody is important it is elected officials and their appointees." Elected members of Congress set federal education policy, which is implemented by the US Department of Education under the leadership of the secretary of education, who is appointed by the president of the United States and confirmed by the Senate. State legislators set state education policy that is administered by departments of education and state boards of education, which are led by either elected or appointed officials. Locally elected school board members are involved in implementing state and federal policy at the district level but also have considerable discretion to set school-level policies, particularly with respect to curriculum, instruction, and personnel decisions.

Politicians announce their policy positions via policy agendas, defined as "the list of subjects or problems to which governmental officials, and people outside of government closely associated with those officials, are paying some attention at any given time" (Kingdon 2003, 3). The policy agenda is where policy problems are defined, and research evidence competes with other influences such as values, metaphors, symbols, and different ways of knowing to influence problem definition (Stone 2012). For our purpose, there are two key points about policy agendas that are relevant to influencing policy. First, policy agendas are distinct from and precede policymaking. Second, policy agendas are created outside the legislative process.

Policy agendas are short and general. In determining the contents of their policy agenda, candidates select a few broad issues that can resonate with a wide audience. Policy agendas are intended to persuade, not inform, and they are not detailed enough to be implemented. They may be filled with emotionally ridden buzzwords intended to move voters to action. Also, policy agendas are not expected to evolve or change through the course of a campaign. Once these agendas have been established, politicians are directed to "stay on message," communicating the content of their policy agenda ad nauseam to different audiences while on the campaign trail. Sometimes, politicians release multi-point plans to provide the details of their policy agenda, and while each point may communicate a defined direction or principle to guide policy once the candidate is elected, the points are not stand-alone policies. Policy agendas require considerably more detail and interpretation to be adopted and implemented as policies.

McDonnell and Weatherford's (2013) study of the enactment of the Common Core State Standards (CCSS) demonstrates the difference between the policy agenda and implementing policy. The authors traced the seeds of the policy agenda that would eventually become the CCSS back two decades to the influence of a small group of policy entrepreneurs who defined the scope of a policy problem as the need to improve the United States' global competitiveness—and worked directly with politicians to forge political acceptance of possible solutions—namely the need for national standards. The implementation of the CCSS, on the other hand, involved content experts (legislative staff, national teacher organizations, academics, practitioners) who used research evidence to ground decisions. Yet, the content experts were required to work within the parameters set by the policy agenda and not to stray from the larger political goal of getting the CCSS adopted by individual states. As they worked through specific proposals, they were unable to question the merits of the overarching policy agenda, such as the very desirability of national standards.

In models of policymaking, agenda setting is described as a separate step that precedes policy formation and is conducted outside the legislative process. For politicians, policy agendas are developed while they are candidates to indicate the specific policies that they will pursue once elected. Politicians include issues on their policy agenda that they believe the public considers to be important at a given time. Not all of the problems at a given moment are on the policy agenda, and a problem may persist for some time before making it to a politician's policy agenda. An event, such as a natural disaster or accident, can focus public attention on a problem and lead to placing the problem on a policy agenda. Or politicians may "soften the ground" by discussing issues publicly in an effort to influence public opinion. Likewise, constituents, an important source for problem identification for politicians, may highlight issues that they want included on policy agendas.

POLITICIANS USE GENERAL INFORMATION TO COMMUNICATE WITH GENERAL AUDIENCES

In fast-paced campaigns, politicians communicate their message via a policy agenda that is short and general in nature, of which education is one of many important issues. Or, when interacting with the public, politicians stick to talking points that highlight the general policy goals, leaving out the minute details that could cloud the communication of the main ideas. The information that politicians need to develop and communicate with the public is more general and direct than the detailed and nuanced evidence of most academic research.

The content and wording of most policy agendas are developed using research on public perceptions to influence voter behavior. For this reason, candidates and campaign staff rely heavily upon poll results rather than academic research to develop policy agendas. Politicians adopt "poll-tested" words and phrases that the public understands and that can resonate with as many people as possible. The academic discourse is more specialized, nuanced, and technical than the public discourse at any given point in time. Most academic journal articles are based on research questions that are complex, and their findings must be translated into a direct, "publicly consumable" format that is qualitatively different from a journal article or a synthesis of the literature (chapter 11).

Once candidates develop a policy agenda, they spend most of their time at public events filled with lay audiences, such as town halls, rallies, and fundraisers where candidates are encouraged to "stay on message" and are likely to repeat poll-tested phrases to reinforce their message. Communicating to the public, either via the media or in direct interactions with large groups of constituents, is not conducive to nuanced policy discussions. For academics, the lesson is that once politicians develop the content and wording of their policy agenda, it is highly unlikely that they will search for any additional information, particularly the type of detailed content that is characteristic of academic research. Candidates embark on the campaign trail, communicating their policy agenda over and over again to different audiences in general terms. And, once they are elected, the agenda becomes the framework for crafting proposals that become the policies that professional staff implement,

In my 2014 run for Arizona superintendent of public instruction, the Common Core Standards (Common Core) was a controversial policy issue. I supported the Common Core, along with the business community and broad swaths of the education community, which is one reason why I received bipartisan support that included the endorsement of the Republican-leaning Arizona Chamber of Commerce. My opponent had no education policy experience and opposed the Common Core. I viewed the Common Core as an issue of school accountability. I focused on the accountability consequences that were attached to assessment results, arguing that state assessments and consequences associated with them were more detrimental to teaching and learning in the classroom than the standards themselves. My perspective was not how the public viewed the Common Core, however. The public viewed the Common Core as a states' rights issue, an infringement by the federal government on Arizona's ability to govern their schools. My opponent won the election, vowing to repeal and replace the Common Core, with standards that were "developed by Arizonans for Arizona students" (Staff 2016). The policy impact was negligible. The "new" Arizona standards amounted to little more than minor wording changes to the original Common Core Standards (McGrady 2017).

while politicians stick to communicating the big ideas through talking points.

MOST OF WHAT WE KNOW ABOUT RESEARCH UTILIZATION IN POLICY COMES FROM PROFESSIONAL STAFF, NOT POLITICIANS

In almost all of the literature on the research and policy gap, politicians who set policy are either missing entirely or they are commingled with professional staff who work within government and who support the policy process. Usually, when academics study research utilization they include only professional staff in the sample. For example, in the foundational literature on research utilization, Weiss and Bucuvalas (1977) based their work on 150 mental health decision-makers, a sample that included fifty-one top federal officials "in the highest tier of positions" and fifty-two local decision-makers who administered health centers and hospitals. The sample did not include politicians. Caplan's (1979) study that yielded the two worlds metaphor, which is still in use to frame the research and policy gap, was based on an investigation of research use among 204 persons holding important positions in departments and agencies of the executive branch, not politicians. In more recent reviews of the research utilization literature, politicians are either completely absent (Petkovic, Welch, and Tugwell 2015), continue to be combined with policymakers (Wiseman 2010), or the term "policymaker" is left undefined (Oliver et al. 2014). Furthermore, while the William T. Grant Foundation sponsors scholarship to improve the use of research evidence, in a search of its funding from 2003 to 2020, I found thirty-seven grants of which only two focused on research use among politicians explicitly.

In the few studies that do include politicians, elected and appointed officials often constitute only part of the sample of those under study, and the opinions of politicians are rarely disaggregated from the opinions of professional staff. The commingling of politicians and professional staff is so pervasive that it is nearly impossible to review the literature and separate politicians' perspectives on research utilization from that of professional staff. For example, Seashore Louis (2005, 220) combined politicians and professional staff under the label of "policymakers" and

described them as "a group, including not only those who actually propose or vote on laws and regulations, but also advisors, advocates, or
other participants in the policy process." Nelson, Leffler, and Hansen (2009)
studied the conditions under which research evidence is used by policymakers and practitioners. Their sample of sixty-five participants included
a combination of professional staff and elected/appointed officials from
all levels of the public education system. The professional staff included
deputy state superintendents, congressional staff, school district superintendents, and school employees (curriculum coordinators, principals,
and teachers). The sample also included eighteen state and district-level
politicians. The findings for professional staff and politicians are combined throughout the report.

There are exceptions, however. Hird (2009), for example, conducted a
study of a nationally representative sample of state legislators. Ironically,
his research question pertained to politicians' use of research generated
by professional staff. His focus was on the role and influence of nonparti-
san research agencies located within state legislatures. Bogenschneider and
others have conducted surveys on research use based on separate samples
of three policy actors—legislators, legislative staff, and agency officials—
disaggregating the results to determine how each type of policy actor seeks,
values, and uses research differently and finding that agency officials, not
politicians, were the most enthusiastic users of research (Bogenschneider,
Little, and Johnson 2013; Bogenschneider and Corbett 2010; Bogenschneider, Day, and Parrott 2019).

Logistically, one can understand why academics would resort to supple-
menting their samples to include professional staff. Politicians are a very
small and extremely busy group, making it very difficult to include them in
research samples. They may also decline participation in research because
they assume the legitimate risk of "saying the wrong thing and falling
victim to a freewheeling online public sphere" (Marland and Esselment
2018, 2) with little political payoff in the form of direct benefit to their
constituents or of electoral advantages. For academics, working directly
with politicians who hold power and the purse strings may come with the
risk of becoming too "political" (Henig 2009), and getting athwart with
politicians could jeopardize public funding for their home institutions.

I once asked an Arizona-based professor who was involved in policy bodies in other states why he refused to get involved in Arizona policy. The response: "I don't pee where I sleep." The professor was concerned with the ramifications for their home institution if they found themselves crossways with their home-state politicians. In other states, where there was no threat of political retribution, the professor was free to serve as a critical voice.

Why is it important that the perspectives of politicians and professional staff on research utilization not be commingled? As I discuss in more detail in the following sections, professional staff's background knowledge and roles differ from those of politicians. In the course of carrying out their responsibilities, professional staff are more likely than politicians to interact with content experts and to understand and engage with research. Politicians, on the other hand, serve a more public role than professional staff and use more general information to communicate a more general message to a more general audience. When making policy decisions, politicians need evidence that is localized to their jurisdiction and can demonstrate how policies impact their constituents specifically. Because of their differences, the findings from research on professional staff are largely not applicable to politicians since these two groups should be treated differently when engaging in education policy (Newman, Cherney, and Head 2016; Shonkoff 2000).

ABOUT PROFESSIONAL STAFF

My rationale for separating elected officials from staff is based on three considerations : (1) Most professional staff have either academic or professional knowledge in research or policy, or both, (2) the ability of professional staff to impact policy is constrained by the public positions held by politicians, and (3) professional staff serve as gatekeepers of information and access to politicians.

Professional staff are expected to have some academic or professional knowledge in education or public policy and stay abreast of the research in their field (Wye et al. 2015). Typically, professional staff have attended universities or graduate schools and hold degrees in an education-related or public policy field. As former education or policy students, they likely completed courses in research methods or policy analysis. Professional staff have read academic articles, know how to use a search engine to find research, and may have written a review of the literature or carried out policy research themselves or in collaboration with a professor. Through the course of their education and training, professional staff have likely become familiar with academic research and even the work of specific academics. In fact, some university academics may find former students or students of another university colleague in the role of professional staff. Either way, when approaching professional staff, academics are able to use their shared academic and professional knowledge to discuss policy matters with little to no requirements to start from the beginning, simplify concepts, or even defend the legitimacy of the research enterprise itself.

Despite having training and exposure to academic research, professional staff are constrained by the public positions of elected and appointed officials, and they do not set policy. At best, professional staff can take advantage of whatever latitude is available to them to influence the range of policy options available *after* the policies have been set. As Kingdon (2003, 41) noted in his study at the federal level, staffers must work "within limits that are set by the senators and representatives who hire and can fire them. Even respondents with the highest estimates of staff importance frequently refer to the staff's need to 'sell their boss' on an idea."

Professional staff serve at the discretion of politicians or work in agencies that are charged with carrying out policies set forth by elected bodies. This dynamic has not changed in the forty years since Weiss's seminal research on research utilization. When suggesting or implementing policies, professional staff can go only as fast and as far as politicians are willing to go and when politicians are ready to move. Thus, professional staff do not view themselves as setting policy. Rather, they see their work as responding to mandates from their elected bosses or to the policies that are set by them. For professional staff, even at the highest echelons of government, "the job often looks like rubber-stamping decisions already made" (Weiss 1980, 400).

Certainly, street-level bureaucrats can have considerable discretion in policy implementation, but in situations where professional staff disagree with political leaders, it is a delicate, even perilous task, for professional staff to get out in front of the public positions held by elected and appointed officials. If the present administration is not receptive to the ideas of professional staff, the staff is wise to shelve the ideas and wait for a change in leadership. Likewise, when professional staff embark on dramatic shifts in policy, their doing so is contingent on the permission of their politician bosses (Hart-Tervalon and Garcia 2014).

Therefore, when one reads about how school district officials use research (Coburn, Honig, and Stein 2009; Coburn and Talbert 2006), one recognizes that their actions are limited by the policies set forth by locally elected school boards who hire and fire them. Research use by state agency officials is limited by the policy positions of state-level politicians who make decisions with electoral implications in mind (Barnes, Goertz, and Massell 2014); McDonnell 1988). Even an appointed chief state school officer (CSSO) must carry their duties "within the constraints and expectations of legislators who have strong views about the CSSO's proper role and who are quite willing to undermine one who takes initiative 'improperly'" (Marshall, Mitchell, and Wirt 1985, 97).

Professional staff and politicians also work in drastically different professional circles. Professional staff may be found behind the scenes with other staff and content experts, remaining largely anonymous. In addition, professional staff are likely to attend informational sessions on research and policy where "ideas from academic literature are regularly discussed" (Kingdon 2003, 54).

Moreover, professional staff are not affected by election results in an absolute sense. Professional staff may continue in the same or a similar role, regardless of which politicians win or lose elections. Politicians, however, have electoral responsibilities and accountability that precede their role in setting education policy. Compelled by electoral forces, politicians are responsible for fundraising, maintaining political allegiances, and they are required to explain and defend policy ideas to the public and through the media. As public figures, they are not anonymous. Their names and faces become associated with policy ideas.

Politicians who are bombarded with information and often find themselves overwhelmed. In response, they create systems and strategies to cope with information overload (Huang et al. 2003). These "lines of defense" are dependent on professional staff, along with trusted confidants, who help politicians determine which information merits their attention at any given time. Professional staff are charged with preparing and presenting research to politicians who count on them as "a kind of life memory of facts and figures to be mobilized any time" (Walgrave and Dejaeghere 2017, 236).

Lastly, professional staff fulfill a key role as gatekeepers who are influential in determining which research products and academics get an audience with politicians. For example, department heads who run major federal or state agencies and are responsible for directing, synthesizing, or presenting research for use by politicians in a policy context. Legislative staffers, positions that are largely filled by early career professionals or interns who rotate on a regular basis, screen the information that comes before politicians. At the school district level, school district administrators are professional staff who determine what information and research are presented to elected school board members.

PROSPECTIVE POLITICIANS

Prospective politicians are involved members of the public whom, either politicians appoint to serve in public roles, such as ad-hoc task forces, commissions, and boards, or who are interested in or are running for office themselves. Prospective politicians often come from organizations such as chambers of commerce, philanthropic organizations, and civic or community groups. Once appointed to a board or commission, prospective politicians leap from their standing as members of the public with no direct role in public education to influential policy positions in which they become responsible for the direction of education policies that affect the professional lives of educators and student educational experiences.

From an academic perspective, there is virtually no research on how prospective politicians use or view education research. This oversight is understandable—after all these people are not in formal decision-making positions within the traditional education system, yet. Still, when engaging in policy, academics should pay attention to prospective politicians, and for four reasons. First, prospective politicians are an election away from becoming politicians. Second, during the period which prospective politicians "gear-up" to run for office is when they develop their own agendas that will eventually guide policy. Third, prospective politicians may have the ear of current politicians, so ignoring prospective politicians means ignoring a potentially influential advisory group that may inform future education policies. Fourth, prospective politicians can become unexpected allies who can advocate for your research in the public sphere, open up opportunities in nonacademic spaces, or bring public and/or media attention to your work.

THE ROLE OF INTERMEDIARIES

Recent work on research utilization confirms what academics observed almost forty years ago: Academics rarely bring research to politicians directly; rather, research is most often brought to politicians through intermediaries. Despite the emergence and growth of online platforms such as websites and social media to "push out" research (Goldhaber and Brewer 2008), one consistent finding in the research utilization literature is that personal contacts are the most common means by which research is communicated to politicians (Nutley, Walter, and Davies 2007). To complicate matters further, the "soft tissue" (Hess 2008) between research production and research use in policy is squishy precisely because at the point where research meets policy neither academics nor politicians may be involved directly. Most often, they are both represented by intermediaries, individuals and organizations that package and present research to politicians but may not have conducted original research themselves or that connect with professional staff to get research before politicians. In many cases, politicians do not interact with original research; instead, they receive filtered and synthesized versions of research evidence provided by professional staff. This indirect relationship between academics and politicians contributes to the diffuse nature of research use and is a major reason why it is difficult to track the connections between research and policy.

The importance of intermediaries in research utilization has emerged as a consistent finding in much of the academic literature. As Nelson, Leffler, and Hansen (2009) note, "While not originally intended to be a focus of the study, one factor that emerged as a central feature to the research utilization process was the role of intermediaries" (Nelson, Leffler, and Hansen 2009, 52). They continue, "What is clearly apparent from our study is that intermediaries (in one form or another and including peers) are the most commonly sought out source of research evidence for decision making by policymakers and practitioners. Intermediaries are seen as the most important component in the process of accessing, understanding, and applying research to decisions related to policy and practice" (Nelson, Leffler, and Hansen 2009, 49).

For our purpose, an intermediary is a person or organization that works in the space between research production and research use. Intermediaries access original research, but in most cases, intermediaries do not conduct original research. They "package" research for politicians by finding, synthesizing, and presenting research conducted by subject-matter experts and academics in a way that is helpful to politicians and can be used in a policy context. The most effective intermediaries are highly skilled at providing information in a concise form when policy agendas are being developed or when legislation is being considered.

Sundquist (1978) provided an early description of the academic intermediary that remains largely applicable today. He recognized that most academics are not naturally suited to work in a policy context: "Most academics do well not to try to be their own interpreters and marketers; they do those tasks badly and, when they attempt to do them, they waste time that could be better spent on research" (Sundquist 1978, 128). Those who engage well communicate with a "flair" for interpreting technical language that borders on marketing or public relations; they are sought by policymakers not "necessarily because they know more but because they can explain it better" (Sundquist 1978, 128). Yet, academic intermediaries face institutional resistance among their own colleagues who both envy those who can move between the academic world and policy life and scorn those who popularize academic research among politicians.

The number, scope, and influence of intermediaries have changed dramatically since Sundquist's conceptualization of academic intermediaries. In the current policy environment, university-based research centers and academic intermediaries compete as one of many intermediaries in the ever-changing policy landscape. The list of non-university intermediary organizations includes advocacy groups, civil rights organizations, professional trade organizations, and think tanks (Hird 2009). Foundations, media outlets, and school reform organizations have also come to play significant intermediary roles that shape the contours of education policy. While think tanks have long been part of the policy landscape, having arisen out of a concern among mostly conservatives about the influence of university-based academics on policy (Rich 2005), the number of ideological think tanks has also burgeoned in recent years, particularly at the state level (Ness and Gándara 2014).

More recently, a "third-wave" of think tanks occupy the policy research landscape, that "unlike their contract-driven predecessors, advocacy think tanks actively sought to involve themselves in policy debates and influence 'the direction and content of foreign and domestic policy.' This influence is achieved in part through 'aggressive marketing techniques' that promote the think tank's specific interests among policymakers and the general public" (McGann 2016, 28). Intermediary organizations are expanding their role to "blur the lines between research, policymaking and political advocacy" (Scott et al. 2014, 70), by not only providing research to guide politicians, but also managing public perception and promoting specific policies. For example, in the area of school choice, market-based reforms are advocated through an interconnected network that includes philanthropic organizations and foundations that fund intermediary organizations to produce research evidence on the desirability of these reforms and then promote the evidence to policymakers (Scott and Jabbar 2014).

LOBBYING AND LOBBYISTS

Lobbyists are omnipresent and influential policy actors. The National Council of State Legislatures (2017) defines lobbying as "an attempt to influence government action through either written or oral communication" and a lobbyist as someone who is "lobbying on behalf of another for compensation." When people think of lobbyists, they often think that lobbyists influence politicians through monetary incentives. Certainly, lobbyists do engage in such transactional relationships with politicians. Those outside of political spheres, however, are often unaware of how lobbyists also use information to influence politicians (Felgenhauer 2013; Cotton and Li 2018). Specifically, lobbyists are sources of coveted information on the impact of specific policies in specific political jurisdictions. This localized information allows politicians to weigh the costs of specific policy decisions on their constituents. When lobbyists provide information to politicians, they function as intermediaries for the purpose of influencing policy.

In a policy context the roles and goals of intermediaries, academics, and lobbyists often overlap as they all seek to influence policy. While academics may not meet the formal definition of a lobbyist, largely because they are not compensated for their efforts (National Conference of State Legislatures 2020), academics engage in lobbying when they provide information to politicians in order to influence policy, even though academics may be hesitant to think of themselves as "political" (Henig 2009). When academics take a position on a policy or recommend a course of action, they are competing in the same space with others who are seeking the same ends, including lobbyists and other intermediaries. While some distinguish academics from lobbyists or advocates (McGann 2016), the line is blurred in a policy context because the differences between the type of information that each actor provides are more a matter of degree than kind. While academics may regard their research as being in a separate and higher category, and although lobbyists may not provide "scholarly" research, both actors use information to persuade politicians.

POLITICIANS AS INTERMEDIARIES

When a policy idea becomes a reality, it is highly likely because a politician "championed" the issue to get it passed. As champions, politicians must persuade their colleagues, and research evidence is part of their arsenal (Bogenschneider, Day, and Parrott 2019). In this exchange, politicians become the ultimate intermediaries. Politicians must present and explain research evidence in support of their policy ideas to the public and their fellow colleagues. To do so, they must understand and explain the relevant research well enough to not only defend their positions but also to motivate others to action.

Politicians are most challenged to act as effective intermediaries when the research evidence is complex or involves findings that are counter to the prevailing public discourse. As I discuss in the following chapter, politicians are novices with respect to education research and policy, so how are they expected to be well-enough versed to stand behind research evidence that may place them in a contradictory position relative to their colleagues or constituents? To support politicians as intermediaries, academics should teach to champion, presenting their work in a manner that enables and empowers politicians to bring research to *their* people on their own accord—without the academic in the room (chapter 13).

SUMMARY

Professional staff and politicians have different background knowledge and are very different policy actors with distinct responsibilities. As elected or appointed officials, politicians are responsible for setting policy. Politicians interact directly with the public, and they are ultimately held accountable to the public for policy outcomes. Professional staff, on the other hand, are likely versed in research and are more apt to interact with academics, but they remain largely anonymous. Politicians rely on the expertise of professional staff to develop detailed options to carry out policy. Yet, most of the existing literature on research utilization either has been conducted with professional staff or does not disaggregate politicians specifically. As a result, academics know much more about how professional staff use research than how politicians use research.

I would not advise academics who are motivated to engage in education policy to walk in the door with the assumption that how professional staff use research in policy is applicable to politicians. Academics would be set up to fail in their engagement with politicians, particularly in cases where the academics are introducing either complex research or research that is contrary to the prevailing public discourse. Similarly, academics would be at a strategic deficit if they did not appreciate that they are one of many others seeking to influence politicians with evidence, including lobbyists, organizations, and politicians themselves. In the next chapter, we take a closer look at politicians, their levels of expertise, and how they use knowledge to take action to address practical problems.

3

POLITICIANS AND KNOWLEDGE

Politicians are education research and policy novices—by design—and become generalists, at best. They function with half-knowledge, intentionally filtering out surplus information so they can take action.

In chapter 2, I looked at politicians and prospective politicians. In this chapter, I examine politicians more closely to argue that politicians are education research and policy novices—by design. Unlike academics or even professional staff, politicians need not become experts in education research or policy to get elected or fulfill their duties to set education policy. Then, I apply the literature on how novices learn to become experts as a guide on how to approach, advise, and teach novice politicians. Lastly, I incorporate Marin's (1981) concept of half-knowledge to describe how politicians use research in policy contexts.

WHAT'S WRONG WITH POLITICIANS?

"Much that is wrong with educational policy research could be improved by the discovery of an authoritative, rational policy maker. However, . . . no such event is likely" (Hill, 132). I would amend Hill's comment to read that not only is such event not likely; it is not expected to occur in a democracy comprised of citizens in policymaking roles and in environments where political parties may find it advantageous to select mediocre candidates (Mattozzi and Merlo 2015).

According to academics, the list of politicians' shortcomings with respect to how they view and use research, assuming that they do, can be condemnatory. Politicians are viewed as

1. closed-minded or set in their ways, and therefore resistant to new perspectives;
2. untrained in understanding and making use of research;
3. lacking the commitment to seek out research evidence and reflect on their decisions;
4. committed to a dominant political ideology and dogmatic about not accepting research findings that cross the party line (Hammersley 2005, 320).

This list of criticisms describes not only elected officials, but also how the public views research. That is, for our purpose, how the public views research is instructive for learning how politicians' view and use research to set the policy. Why? Because politicians are essentially involved members of the public who won an election. After navigating the electoral process, these citizens find themselves in positions of authority to set policy. The primary difference between citizens (pre-election) and politicians (post-election) is that politicians have a duty to create policy, often in areas where they have little expertise, and they must gather knowledge in a highly public, pressure-filled, and political environment. For academics, it is informative to understand how politicians view research *before* they are politicians (i.e., as members of the public), which is the formative stage for developing policy (chapter 7).

First, the public does not read academic journals or attend professional conferences. "Citizens receive very little information about academic research in any form" (Howell 2008, 138). Second, much of what the public knows about education research and policy is limited to what they encounter in the media. And, while the public is intensely interested in education and holds strong opinions about education policies, "they lack the time, inclination and training . . . to formulate independent judgements about the quality of research itself" (Howell 2008, 140). Third, as a shortcut, citizens may look to the organization that produced the report or the media outlet that reported it to determine its credibility because individuals find those with similar worldviews to be more credible than those with different worldviews. Fourth, if research evidence confirms citizens' prior views, then it may do little to change public opinion and may even reinforce entrenched opinions. When research evidence contradicts existing views, it is most influential when it "offers citizens a good reason to abandon their current beliefs and adopt altogether new ones" (Howell 2008, 140). And finally, politicians and the public are alike in another way: They are both education research and policy novices.

POLITICIANS ARE EDUCATION RESEARCH AND POLICY NOVICES—BY DESIGN

Politicians tend to be novices in education. Their formal academic training and professional experiences are more than likely not in education or in education research or policy. For example, Hird (2009) in a study that included a nationally representative sample of politicians, found that 48 percent of politicians identified their profession as "legislation," 21 percent included medicine and law, and only 8 percent identified their profession as education. With regard to level of education, 51 percent of legislators earned a postgraduate degree, while an additional 23 percent were college graduates. Among school board members nationally, 27 percent worked in education (Hess and Meeks 2010). Furthermore, there is no requirement that politicians be experts in all the areas in which they set policy. There is simply too little time and too many commitments for politicians to develop a thorough expertise in all policy areas.

While politicians may not have expertise in education research or policy, they have educational, personal, and professional experiences in some area prior to becoming politicians, which are likely to be distinct from the training and professional culture of academics (Bogenschneider and Corbett 2010). They leverage their prior education and experiences to inform themselves in policy areas in which they have little expertise or experience and they have a tendency to look to others to understand what and how they should learn, providing an opportunity for academics to leverage their expertise in a policy context.

What constitutes "expertise" for politicians? Kingdon (2003, 37) provides a succinct summary at the federal level:

> With some notable exceptions, Congress is not the place to find the detailed, technical types of expertise found in the bureaucracy, in the community of academics and consultants, or among the interest groups that are occupied with the detailed impacts of programs and new proposals on the operations of their members. Certainly, among senators and representatives themselves, again with some exceptions, "expertise" in the congressional context is really a system in which generalists learn enough about a given subject matter to help other generalists, their colleagues.

Or, as a veteran legislator describes expertise among his colleagues at the state level, "We have about an inch of knowledge. I always say we're an inch deep and about a mile wide: We know a little bit about a lot of things. And so what we really do, we research as much on a topic as we want to" (Bogenschneider and Corbett 2010, 55). According to a 1985 study, even the legislators who were considered "education specialists" among their colleagues "openly stated that their staffs were the ones who really knew education policy" (Marshall, Mitchell, and Wirt 1985, 106).

Let me present a hypothetical example to illustrate my claim that politicians are research and policy novices—by design. If I were to get elected to public office, such as state representative, it would be logical for me to sit on the education committee. I have two advanced degrees in education. I am a published author and teach education policy at the university level. In the education committee, I would be an expert because my academic training and professional experiences would be directly applicable to my work in setting education policy. Those wishing to bring new education research to my attention could rely on my previous academic training to make their case. They could assume that I understand quite a bit about education policy, and they would not need to sell me on the fact that education research is important—with me, it's a given.

But, as an elected official, I would have many other committee responsibilities in addition to education. I would also sit on other legislative committees, such as the health committee, for example. There my academic training and professional experiences would not be directly applicable to my responsibilities to set health policy. I would be a novice in health policy. I have not read health literature, and I have not attended any health conferences. Even the most junior health analyst out of graduate school would be more knowledgeable about health policy than I. Furthermore, I would find myself in the challenging position of learning about health policy at the same time that I am setting healthy policy—a major reason why politicians describe legislative sessions as "drinking water from a firehose."

Those seeking to influence my health policy positions through research should not walk in the door and assume that we share the same academic knowledge base. Health academics who are engaging in policy must translate research in a simplified manner that I can understand and use. But, with me, the health academics would at least find someone versed in research methods. Simplification would not require dumbing-down the research. In addition, I hold a positive orientation toward the role of research in policymaking, a perspective that the health academics should not assume when working with other politicians who do not have an academic background.

Let's consider another example. Many legislators come from the business community, and so their academic training and professional experiences are not in education. The businessperson who is assigned to the

Even veteran politicians are routinely placed in the position of content novices, insofar as they make decisions in many different policy areas. During nearly every legislative session, politicians can expect to address a specific policy issue with intensity. One year the issue could be healthcare, another year the issue could be prison reform, and so on. For me, the year was 1998, and the issue was school finance. The state legislature was under a deadline to resolve a long-standing court mandate to equalize school capital construction. This meant that newly elected legislators needed to be brought up to speed—to "drink" school finance from a "firehose" to catch up. I learned that there were also vast differences in the amount of attention that veteran legislators had paid to school finance up to this decisive point. Those veteran legislators whose policy interest and content expertise were invested in other policy issues were effectively novices in school finance and also needed to be "caught up." Given the intensity of the school finance issue, along with the pending deadline, politicians used many of the aforementioned strategies of the novice and advanced beginner stages to learn a lot and quickly. They turned to experts to direct their learning and to filter information to focus on what they "really" needed to know and from whom.

education committee, which is a common occurrence in legislatures across the country, would likely be a novice in education research and policy. In attempting to learn about education research and policy at the same time as beginning to set education policy, the businessperson turned politician would rely on a few available resources. The first is personal experiences in education, as well as the experiences of others close to them, such as their children or grandchildren. These personal experiences, regardless if they occurred years ago, serve as the basis of their working understanding of the present state of education. What is most important for the academic to realize is that any issues that the novice politician encountered through their personal experiences or through the experiences of others will likely be perceived as continued problems in education, until the politician learns otherwise. The inverse situation is also applicable: That is, those issues that the novice politician did not experience personally or learn about through other personal accounts are unlikely to be perceived as pressing educational issues, until the novice politician learns otherwise.

Novice politicians will also leverage their academic training and professional experiences as a foundation for learning about education issues, filtering research, and screening potential policy options. Thus, the businessperson turned politician will leverage what they learned in business school and their professional experiences working in the business sector. For this reason, one could assume that our hypothetical politician likely enters their position in the education committee with an understanding of business principles, a high tolerance for risk, an understanding of markets, and an appreciation for competition. It is unlikely that the novice politician has consulted the education literature in a meaningful or sustained manner. Thus, they are likely to be unfamiliar with education issues such as equity, intersectionality, segregation, and institutionalized racism, which are prevalent in academic literature.

To learn about the issues facing the schools and constituents in their district, the novice politician will be inclined to turn to others with expertise for help. The most immediate resource is legislative staff who are knowledgeable and whose interactions with politicians are held in confidence and remain private. Lobbyists are another readily available resource, and they are likely to introduce themselves to newly elected officials in the course of their jobs. Lobbyists learn about issues of importance to newly elected politicians and offer to make information available on education issues, particularly as it relates to the schools and constituents in the politician's jurisdiction. Next, newly elected politicians listen to constituents who are making their case for the education issues of importance to them, often with evidence of their own. Politicians also turn to trusted advisors for information and as a guide to filter resources.

Where do academics fit in the novice politician's inquiry process? If the academic is a trusted advisor, the novice politician, or their staff, may connect with the academic directly. It stands to reason that novice politicians are likely to connect with academics with whom they have an existing relationship or who share a common political philosophy. If the academic is bringing research to the novice politician without an established relationship, then the academic is effectively indistinguishable from the lobbyists, constituents, or intermediary organizations that are also vying for attention on their issues. If the academic is bringing evidence for the purpose of influencing the novice politician's policy positions, they are lobbying. If the academic is bringing informational research that does not take a position on a specific policy or side with an issue, then the next logical question the academic should consider is, how does *my* research help the novice politician learn to carry out *their* duties to make decisions on education policy issues?

In both hypothetical situations described above—my experiences on the health committee and the businessperson's on the education committee—the politician is a novice, and one who must acquire the knowledge necessary to carry out their policy duties at the same time that they are charged with making policy decisions. There is very little time to learn before politicians must begin making policy decisions; only a few months separate an election and when a politician is inaugurated into office. In this compressed timeframe and in the rush of the legislative session, novice politicians will rely on the most accessible resources, such as trusted advisors and political party positions, to find their footing. Over time, politicians evolve from novices to competent legislators with respect to education research and policy. In the next section, I introduce academic literature on how novices acquire expertise to show how knowledge is viewed and used at each stage so as to help academics understand and approach politicians most effectively.

School choice is one of my academic areas of study. If one views school choice policy from the perspective that novice politicians bring their past educational and personal experiences to their duties in office, it is not surprising to me that legislators whose professional background is in business or the private sector would embrace choice, lean toward market-based solutions, and largely ignore issues such as segregation. As such, these politicians likely appreciate and may have benefited directly from market choice in many aspects of their lives. As politicians, one can expect them to bring their penchant for market choice to how they view education policy decisions. These politicians likely have a working knowledge of markets as driving change, while other mechanisms to address education issues, such as equity, may be foreign to them.

With respect to some social outcomes associated with school choice, such as segregation, the public likely has little to no perspective on these issues outside their lived experiences. What the public understands about segregation, particularly outside their schools and neighborhoods, is derived largely from media reports. When engaging in education policy, academics may be presenting evidence on segregation that is counter to the politician's worldview or outside the politician's lived experiences. In response, the academic must connect the school segregation research to the real-world conditions facing the schools in the politician's jurisdiction and inform the novice politician about the relationship between school choice policies and segregation so that the novice politician can champion an actionable policy response.

FROM NOVICE TO EXPERT

If politicians are novices who are learning about education research and policy, then it is instructive to understand the characteristics of how novices learn in order to gain insight into how to inform novice politicians with research. In addition, given that most academics are experts, it is also wise to understand how experts access and view knowledge. The difference between political novices and academic experts is not just a matter of degree, such that experts know more about education research and policy than novices. Rather, the experts approach, access, and apply research to policy in a way that is fundamentally different from the way that novices do. This is an important consideration for those seeking to influence policy through research. To be successful in a policy context, academic experts cannot bring what they know to politicians in a form(at) that is understandable to other experts. Rather, they must translate their knowledge into a format that communicates best to laypersons so that novice politicians can champion research evidence to other lay audiences.

Dreyfus and Dreyfus (1980, 5) created a model of skill acquisition that incorporated everyday experiences "as a pervasive and essential feature of human intelligence behavior." Benner (1982) applied the five-step Dreyfus model of skill acquisition to professional learning contexts in nursing to develop a generalizable theory that can be applied to other fields outside of health. While Benner's application of the Dreyfus model is not the only theory of skill development or learning (Gobet and Chassy 2009), it provides a useful framework to describe how politicians use knowledge to evolve from novices to gain more competent levels of understanding of education and education policy for the purpose of making policy decisions.

In this section, I summarize the key characteristics of each stage of the model with a focus on how politicians learn the content of education research and policy. The stages also illuminate how politicians use knowledge (including research evidence) at different stages to influence policy decisions.

The first three stages (novice, advanced beginner, and competent) are largely applicable to politicians in their capacity to set education policy, but they are not applicable to academics or researchers who study education. The final two stages (proficient and expert), on the other hand, are applicable to academics, but not necessarily to politicians. I present the advanced stages to discuss the challenges that experts in particular face in presenting research to politicians and to demonstrate how academics must adjust their orientation toward research to communicate most effectively with education policy novices.

NOVICE
The first stage is novice. Novices

- are beginners with no experience;
- rely on existing rules to perform tasks;
- engage in "other-directed" learning;
- understand issues in isolation.

Novices assimilate information by connecting it to past experiences and make decisions based on the "best-fit" even if they knew such fit is not the most appropriate or correct. They begin to learn as they "acquire information and link that information in unique ways" (Daley 1999, 139). Novices are hesitant to use trial and error as a learning technique for fear of making a mistake, and they look for validation from experts to affirm their decisions. Novices understand issues in isolation and are unable to connect specific instances to a broader context. Furthermore, novices do not have a solid understanding of their learning process and may be unable to describe their learning process well.

There are several implications for how novices learn that are applicable to academics bringing research to politicians. First, the heavy reliance on past experiences to guide learning helps explain why novices make decisions based on what appears to be anecdotal evidence, a tendency among politicians that experts find shortsighted and frustrating. One can expect novice politicians to leverage their past educational and professional experiences to make sense of new content. For academics, it is essential to locate examples of the politicians' experiences in the research to establish heuristics to help politicians learn in the future. Academics who bring research that is counter to the politician's past experiences or information that introduces the politician to an issue with which they have no prior experience should contextualize *the* research to help the novice learner to recognize meaningful patterns in new experiences.

Second, since the novice stage is when learners look to others for direction on what and how to learn, it stands to reason then that the novice politician is likely to rely on staff and trusted advisors to understand what they need to learn, for assistance in how to acquire new knowledge, and to filter both information and informants. For academics approaching politicians, the novice stage would be a good time, except that novice politicians are bombarded by other policy actors who approach them with "ready-made" reports and information to help them learn the landscape of a new policy area. For this reason, a more opportune time to approach politicians is *before* they become politicians.

Third, novices rely on existing rules to perform tasks. Novice politicians may look to political party platforms or the policy guidance provided by

As legislative staff, some of my most eye-opening experiences involved working with novice politicians. Novice politicians became overwhelmed by the deluge of information brought to them. On occasion, exasperated by the efforts to filter the volumes of information and countless policy recommendations brought to them, novice politicians would to turn to me and say, "just tell me what I should do here." Or, novice politicians would cite a singular, personal experience as sufficient evidence to support their policy position. Sometimes they cited the singular experience because it left a lasting impression on them, and other times they cited the previous experience as a coping mechanism to stem the rush of information coming their way. Novice politicians are challenged to contextualize their experience in a broader setting to understand the extent to which their personal experiences were an anomaly (or not), if the experiences are still applicable in schools today, or if the experiences also occur in different kinds of schools or educational contexts.

I was in the delicate position of acknowledging the politicians' personal experiences while tactfully encouraging novice politicians to consider alternatives or to place their singular experiences in context. At times, novice politicians made broad sweeping statements that countered the prevailing findings in the academic literature, dismissing offhand well-developed theories and empirical results because they personally had never witnessed a real-life example of the theory or they had experienced one memorable counter-example. This behavior negated any potential for research to help them in future decision-making situations. I had to find a way to respond to statements such as, "segregation is no longer an issue" or "poor families don't care enough about student achievement." At this stage in my career, I was not an expert in education research and policy, but I was certainly proficient, meaning that I had an appreciation that educational policies influenced actions and outcomes in local education contexts and that larger societal forces influenced the implementation of education policies. I appreciated how education research could proactively influence policy decisions. For these reasons, I had to give concerted thought into how I would respond to these unversed comments in a way that helped politicians carry out their duties, even in cases where my comments were counter to their positions, while not offending politicians. How I learned to translate what I learned from education research to teach novice politicians is an important foundation of the book.

ideological think tanks for existing rules that they can use to guide learning and decision-making in this early stage. Once novices begin to follow a set of existing rules, they are unlikely to stray from them until they learn and experience enough to predict the consequences of taking contrarian actions. For academics, one potentially productive approach to teaching novice politicians is to introduce them to frameworks that help novice politicians to recognize (and predict) meaningful patterns in educational contexts and build heuristics to guide future actions (chapter 12).

Last, novices understand specific experiences in isolation, without an understanding of broader implications. As a result, academics who bring nuanced or interconnected information may be presenting knowledge to the novice that is too complex at this foundational stage of their development. Thus, when presenting academic research, which is often nuanced and interconnected, academics must scaffold answers and "narrate the lines" so that novices can understand and apply the knowledge to broader educational contexts.

ADVANCED BEGINNER

In the second stage, advanced beginners have "gained prior experience in actual situations to recognize recurring meaningful components" (Benner 1982, 404). The advanced beginner

- begins to perceive meaningful patterns and to use guidelines to direct actions;
- cannot distinguish those concepts that are most meaningful, so all concepts are treated as if they are similarly important;
- needs help to set priorities.

Advanced beginners begin to stray from the rigidity of existing rules to making decisions from their own set of guidelines. Advanced beginners develop guidelines through experience where "experience is not the mere passage of time or longevity; it is the refinement of preconceived notions and theory by encountering many actual practical situations that add nuances or shades of differences" (Benner 1982, 407). Advanced beginners have acquired enough experience to recognize patterns and to predict how their actions create subsequent reactions in others. Advanced beginners also start to develop their own opinions and policy ideas. To them, however, everything is important. They are unable to prioritize information.

From my experience, the advanced beginner stage is when politicians begin to engage with academic research actively. Having heard policy ideas from all fronts (constituents, lobbyists, intermediaries, academics), the advanced beginner culls these ideas and selects those that they wish to champion in a policy context. They then turn to research, or to their staff to review the research, to support these policy ideas. Lacking context, however, advanced beginners do not understand that their policy ideas are not novel. Yet, they propose policy ideas as if the ideas are new.

Advanced beginners are also likely to regard a small set of research products, or even a single research product, as the complete body of knowledge to support their policy ideas. Similarly, the advanced beginner may be persuaded by the work of a specific academic, citing them as the single (or definitive) authority on a subject with no recognition of other academics working on the same subject. Advanced beginners often encounter ideas that are presented to them by others and; if their interest is piqued, they may turn to staff or outside experts for more information. It is not uncommon for the advanced beginner to return from a conference or speech and hand a report to staff as a guide to model future education policies. Lacking context, the advanced beginner has likely not conducted a review of the literature to understand the larger context for their policy ideas, to recognize potential pitfalls, or to consider possible alternatives that may be better suited to advancing their policy agenda.

Academics can be useful to politicians in the advanced beginner stage by acting as fortune tellers (in effect). First, academics can help the advanced beginner to recognize and, most importantly to prioritize, patterns, so that politicians can anticipate the potential outcomes of their policy ideas. While the policy issues may be new to the advanced beginner, academics understand the underlying educational and social dynamics that have influenced policies in the past and present and will likely affect future policies. For example, politicians often gravitate to "game-changing" ideas, seeking research on policies that position their state as leaders on an issue (Bogenschneider, Little, and Johnson 2013). Through

the foresight developed from expertise and experience, academics understand that while the policy ideas may be "new" to the politician, the ideas
must still operate in an environment where larger educational and societal forces will pull processes and outcomes into predictable directions.
Individual learning styles and attitudes, the level of familial investment
in education, neighborhood influences, peer effects, pedagogical practices, organizational dynamics, social inequities, racial inequalities, and
labor force conditions (to name a few), are powerful forces that influence
the implementation of education policy. Very, very few "game-changers"
(dare I say, none?) are broad enough or ambitious enough in scope to
change the balance of these forces. As such, game-changing policies are
more likely to be shaped by these broader forces rather than the other
way around.

Second, academics can help advanced beginners understand how
policy ideas may play out in different types of schools (e.g., rural, low-
income) or across student groups (e.g., special education, limited English
proficient) and thus identify potential pitfalls or red flags. These cautions
may lead the advanced beginner to modify or even abandon their policy
ideas once they come to understand that their ideas have been tried before,

As legislative staff, the political advanced beginner stage presents a delicate
challenge. Political advanced beginners have just enough information, coupled with abundant enthusiasm, to be dangerous. The politician who has
evolved from a novice to advanced beginner is full of policy ideas. For staff,
the challenge is to rein in the advanced beginner, helping them set priorities
and keeping questionable policy ideas from becoming reality. I marveled at
senior staff who could navigate this landmine field using a version of the "Jedi
Mind Trick," methodically questioning politicians until the politicians came
to the conclusion on their own that their policy idea was really not a good
one and should go no further. While the state of Arizona is commonly pointed
to as a sump of questionable policies in the eyes of some, it could have been
much, much worse without staff interjection to head off questionable policy
ideas on the spot. I credit the Jedi Mind Trick with preventing the implementation of "game-changing" policy ideas such as round schools (so students
could see each other at all times) and the curtailing of all school construction
(because the internet would render brick and mortar schools obsolete).

or they may not lead to the major outcomes they had hoped to accomplish. Third, advanced beginners likely have a singular vision of policy ideas and have not encountered or studied the various ways that their policy ideas, or a similar version of their policy ideas, have been implemented in practice. Academics are in a position to suggest modifications that build upon the advanced beginner's policy ideas and can fulfill the politician's policy agenda more expeditiously.

In addition, the "wide-eyed" nature of the advanced beginner is important to the academic in a couple of ways that are explored in detail later in the book. First, since the policy ideas are rarely novel, there is sufficient research available to inform the policy ideas brought forth by advanced beginners. Second, I push back on the idea that in an effort to make research more policy-relevant, academics should look to politicians to determine "use-inspired" research agendas. If the research enterprise is forward-thinking enough, policy ideas should be well-researched before the novice or advanced beginner "discovers" them.

COMPETENT PRACTITIONER

The next level of skill acquisition, competence, is characterized by

- more awareness of long-term plans or goals "based on considerable conscious, abstract, analytic contemplation of the problem" (Benner 1982, 404);
- broadened perspectives from planning their own actions which helps to achieve greater efficiency and organization;
- the ability to rely on standardization and routinization to manage problems.

The shift from advanced beginner to competent requires iterations in a specific field. Repeat experiences in a given field help the learner understand how their ideas play out and how to make adjustments to future plans to achieve desired outcomes. Competent politicians have experienced how their policy ideas are negotiated at the legislative level, implemented through regulatory bodies such as boards of education and governing boards, and administered at the district/school level. They have heard directly from constituents (administrators, teachers, parents, students) about how the policies they championed have led to desired outcomes (or not). They have come to understand how to strategize across multiple legislative sessions as a means to achieve their policy goals by passing initial legislation to implement their ideas in practice and following-up with bills that address any necessary adjustments in later legislative sessions. Competent politicians fall into a routine where they are able to understand, predict, and plan policy ideas. Furthermore, routinization is also helpful to other policy actors. Legislative staff, intermediaries, and lobbyists come to understand and predict the politicians' orientation and interests, taking some of the guesswork out of predicting which issues politicians are likely to champion—a useful management strategy for policy actors who work with several politicians across many different issues.

There is evidence that it is difficult to convince competent politicians to take a position that is counter to their established views. "The higher the politician's level of expertise, the more difficult it is for an interest group to change his opinion in its favor" (Felgenhauer 2013, 126). As a result, those who engage with legislators on a regular basis make strategic decisions about how much effort, in the form of time and quality of information, to expend on convincing competent legislators who are unlikely to favor their positions. By contrast, academics who have spent their time in an educational setting rather than tracking the legislature are not likely to be aware of the politician's tendencies. I am referring not just to where politicians may fall on issues; one can get a solid idea of that through publicly available information. I am referring to a more intimate understanding of which issues the politician is likely to champion or the extent to which other politicians may expend political capital to support an issue, setting the groundwork for potential collaborations. In essence, academics often enter the policy context with little to no understanding of where their issue fits with politicians may find it difficult to persuade them.

As academics engage directly with politicians who are content novices (or advanced beginners), it is instructive for academics to understand that knowledge at the more advanced stages, proficient practitioner and expert, is not just a matter of degree—where the former knows more than the latter. Rather, those with more advanced content knowledge access and apply knowledge (including research) very differently than novices.

Some idealistic constituents who become involved in legislature are heavily invested in a singular policy issue. These folks are often passionate and prepared. Many of them are also meeting their elected officials or working the legislature for the first time. They are unaware of which politicians are inclined to champion which issues and, most importantly, which politicians are inclined to expend political capital on the constituents' issues. They also have little to no idea of all the moving pieces at the legislature at that moment—of where their policy idea fits (or does not fit) in the current political climate, or what individual legislators are trying to accomplish at that point in the legislative session. These well-meaning constituents approach their issue on its merits alone. I was called into a lot of meetings with these types of constituents, and as I watched and listened and took notes, I knew that their policy idea was highly unlikely to go forward, not because the idea lacked merit, but because it didn't fit in with the current agenda. The politician may not have been able to move on the issue (or the cost was too high to move) because they were trying to get something done on another issue of greater importance to politician's policy agenda. It was not uncommon for these constituents to get frustrated and eventually abandon their legislative efforts dejected.

Table 3.1 Approaches to politicians at various stages of familiarity with education research and policy

Novice	Advanced Beginner	Competent Practitioner
Locate politicians' experiences in the research	Prioritize patterns so that politicians can anticipate the potential outcomes of their policy ideas	Recognize that it may be difficult to persuade politicians to change their policy positions
Scaffold answers and "narrate the lines"	Recognize red flags or potential pitfalls of politicians' policy ideas	Know which issues politicians are likely to "champion"
Introduce politicians to frameworks	Suggest modifications to fulfill politicians' policy agendas more expeditiously	

PROFICIENT PRACTITIONER

The proficient person

- perceives and understands situations holistically and is guided by maxims that provide "directions as to what is important to take into consideration" (Benner 1982, 405);
- learns from experience what to expect in certain situations and how to modify plans.

Those at the proficient level make decisions based on maxims, which are short, pithy statements that express a general truth or rule of conduct and are applicable to many situations. "Maxims are used to guide the proficient performer, but a deep understanding of the situation is required before a maxim can be used. Maxims reflect what would appear to the competent or novice performer as unintelligible nuances of the situation" (Benner 1982, 405).

For the academic, maxims are analogous to themes, common features of theories, frameworks, or concepts in education research or policy that the academic finds useful for understanding conditions across multiple

---

Themes derived from education research guided my decision-making process while serving as Arizona Superintendent of Public Instruction. One comes from Weick's (1976) concept of "loosely coupled systems," which I modified to describe the Arizona public education system as a "loosely coupled system (based on self-interest)." The modification arose from the fact that the Department of Education did not have direct control over local schools or school districts and that each administrative policy that the department of education put in place would be interpreted and modified at the district, school, and classroom levels in a manner that was most advantageous to the self-interest of those at the local level. Likewise, at the state level, the state interest would always lose out to local interests at the local level. It is the rare case where local officials made decisions based on the best interests of the state. So, I created explicit structures to "tighten" the connections between the state and local jurisdictions and at other times creating incentive structures, such as rewarding early adopters, to encourage local decision-making that facilitated consistency in decisions across school districts in spite of pockets of local opposition. Most importantly, I explained the theme to my team and politicians to shed light on the rationale for my decisions and to help them anticipate the likely outcomes of their ideas.

settings. Themes help the academic to apply education research without experiencing a phenomenon directly (generalization) or to anticipate outcomes before a policy has gone through a full iteration. Academics test policy ideas against these themes in an effort to predict outcomes. In a policy context, themes help the academic recognize that the next game-changing policy idea is in fact not new, and to consider the extent to which the policy is likely (or unlikely) to achieve the desired outcomes. For academics seeking to bring research to politicians, it is instructive to become aware of the themes that they find most predictive in education research and policy and use as them as the basis for frameworks, a preferred method for responding to politicians.

Insofar as academics are proficient in their content area, they possess a holistic view of education and thus understand how policies are interconnected. One challenge of working with novices is explaining how actions in one area affect other areas, especially in cases where the connections are either indirect or the reaction is delayed. The academic must be able to deconstruct themes in education research and policy to communicate frameworks to the novice politician so that the politician can recognize patterns across new educational experiences, helping them to predict future outcomes, and developing heuristics to guide the politician's actions based on research.

EXPERT

Expertise requires experience and formal education. The expert

- no longer relies exclusively on analytical principles (rules, guidelines, maxims) to connect situations and determine actions;
- "has an intuitive grasp of the situation and zeros in on the accurate region of the problem without wasteful consideration of a large range of unfruitful possible problem situations" (Benner 1982, 405);
- is fluid, flexible, and highly proficient in their field;
- understands systemic implications.

Experts make decisions based on "blueprints" held in their minds. They describe actively learning by merging concepts with real-world needs and improvising to develop new skills. Given the abstract and holistic manner in which they use knowledge, experts can be challenged to articulate what they know and how they know it to others. Pinker claims that academics are afflicted with the "curse of knowledge," caused by the "difficulty in imagining what it is like for someone else not to know something that you know" (Pinker 2014, 82). Experts organize their knowledge in "chunks" or mental units of increasing abstraction in ways that are fundamentally different from nonexperts.

In a policy content, experts must simplify what they know to communicate with novices, yet do so in a manner that is not condescending. "The key is to assume that your readers are as intelligent and sophisticated as you are, but that they happen not to know something you know" (Pinker 2014, 82). When educating novice politicians, experts must return to foundational principles (basic, not dumbed down). And experts cannot simply assert their expertise to make their case ("trust me, I'm an expert") (Weber and Word 2009). The second half of the book will provide concrete advice for experts to deconstruct what they know to translate research in a policy context in a way that helps the politician, an education research and policy novice, to predict outcomes and take action.

POLITICIANS FUNCTION WITH "HALF-KNOWLEDGE"

There is no shortage of theories of policymaking (Weible and Sabatier 2018) and the use of evidence in the process (Weible 2008). For this book, I chose the concept that best replicated a frequent occurrence I saw played out in a policy context. Politicians, in the demanding environment of policymaking, often appeal to staff and say, "Tell me what I need to know" in an effort to manage the deluge of information before them and to take action. From my experiences as a legislative staffer, trusted individual, and statewide candidate, "half-knowledge" is the most applicable description of how politicians approached knowledge acquisition and use.

What is half-knowledge? Faced with countless issues and many, many people vying for their attention, politicians must have a strategy to manage their time and allocate resources by determining which problems receive attention (or not) at any given time, and by extension, how they seek and use information, including research evidence. "The concept of half-knowledge basically refers to a process wherein authorities are vaguely aware of problems within their domain but manage to protect themselves from knowing—and thereby risking—too much" (Marin 1981, 44).

I was surprised by my own application of half-knowledge as a statewide candidate. My academic training and professional experiences prior to running for office involved gathering, synthesizing, and applying as much knowledge as possible. During the campaign, however, I learned that it was impossible to become well versed in every issue. But even if time permitted, I learned that extensive knowledge was not particularly helpful. It was not a sound use of time and energy to learn the details of a policy issue if during the campaign I would rarely (if ever) get the opportunity to discuss policies in detail.

As a professor, I am rewarded for researching widely and bringing together seemingly unconnected theoretical perspectives or concepts to create a new understanding of education issues (e.g., the application of the nursing literature to research utilization in a policy context). As a candidate, I found it extremely difficult and even counterproductive to communicate multifaceted ideas in the shortened format of campaign speeches and media soundbites. For example, prior to running for office I wrote an article framing public school parents, like me, as choosers in Arizona's education marketplace (Garcia 2012; 2013). The point was that the parental choice for their student(s) to attend public schools should demand the same policy attention from Arizona legislators as the choice to exit public schools. I presented the idea to public school audiences in Arizona with great success. Public school educators, after listening to my talk, sent me pictures of posters, billboards, or marquees proclaiming their public schools as schools of choice. But I was unable to translate this idea to my campaigns. My Democratic primary opponents labeled me as "pro–school choice," and I spent considerable time and energy countering the perception that I was soft on charter schools and even anti–public education. In fact, when I approached the Network for Public Education Action (NPEA), a group led by Diane Ravitch, I figured that based on my academic background and personal connections with the leadership, an endorsement would be a natural fit. Diane was skeptical of my pro–school choice position based on what she had heard. She wanted me to take a much stronger and oppositional stance against Arizona charter schools. NPEA eventually endorsed me, reluctantly.

Half-knowledge "may be seen as a set of rather subtle devices for focusing organized selective political attention and institutional neglect. Half-knowledge, then, is something like a collective defense mechanism, an equivalent within political organizations to processes like repression or perceptual denial in individual personalities" (Marin 1981, 47).

Politicians do not need "full" knowledge or complete information to run a campaign, develop a policy agenda, or to take action on policies.

Rather, they take a confined view of problems and restrict knowledge acquisition to facilitate their ability to take action. Too much information can be distracting and paralyzing. In fact, there are disincentives to politicians gaining too much knowledge and potential incentives to remaining uninformed (Cotton and Li 2018).

Half-knowledge does not mean knowing half the truth. Rather, it implies filtering out surplus knowledge to include information that appears to be "disturbing or unmanageable, i.e., knowledge which is beyond policymakers' control (but not cognitive capacity), and which they cannot face for this reason"; it can also mean filtering out useless knowledge, "i.e., knowledge that does not help the politician to keep up control, at least in the short run. Useless knowledge is rejected as being too 'esoteric,' 'overly abstract,' 'ideological' (critical), 'not in time' (too advanced, delayed), 'unsettled' (overly controversial) and so on" (Marin 1981, 49).

Half-knowledge is necessary for politicians to take action on particular issues where they can or intend to take action. Politicians are aware of larger problems but may ignore them because they perceive that "nothing can be

---

During my campaigns, some of my well-meaning academic colleagues and fellow educators brought me information that amounted to surplus knowledge from an electoral perspective. They had suggestions about the issues that I should talk about on the campaign, often directly related to their research or professional interests. To them, these issues are important. As a professor, I agree that these issues are important. My colleagues did not understand how heeding this advice would disrupt the campaign. You win elections by getting more votes than your opponent, so every campaign decision is run through the objective of getting votes. And one can only be in the position to influence policy if one gets the most votes. The education policy issues brought by my well-meaning colleagues would not yield more votes. Thus, one can understand why a politician would invest little time in gathering information on a policy issue or learning new knowledge if it would not help them with the principal objective of winning an election. For the colleagues I knew well enough, I was honest and said, "I need to win first. How do these issues turn into votes?" Begrudgingly, they would respond that the suggestions would not yield new votes but that I could take up the issue once in office. Other times, I listened and filtered out the information as knowledge that I didn't need in order to take action at the moment.

done about [them]" (Marin 1981, 52). As Marin (1981, 53) notes, "It is not the minor problems, but the more basic and structural ones like inequality, exploitation, unemployment, poverty, crime, and the like, the antagonizing aspects of which are removed this way [i.e., ignored]." Some problems are so chronic, persistent, and/or complex that they are come to be regarded as "unsolvable" (Edelman 1979). If politicians view problems as "unsolvable," they may be inclined to ignore the research associated with these problems, because they may have no intention to take action on the underlying problem itself.

For politicians, the balancing act involves understanding which problems and related information to recognize and which to ignore at any given time. "The politicians' problem is how to know what half-knowledge is sufficient at the moment, since this depends on factors as unpredictable as political or scientific developments themselves" (Marin 1981, 49). In other words, "Tell me what I need to know." Of the voluminous information in a policy context, that which tells politicians what they need to know to take action is considerably more likely to be used by them because it can be used to address practical problems. Other information runs the risk of being ignored by politicians as surplus knowledge (see figure 3.1).

It is precisely at this point that political and professional staff serve their essential role as gatekeepers, bringing the right information to the politician at the right time. As legislative staff, my job as a gatekeeper had three objectives: (1) to determine what information the politician needed

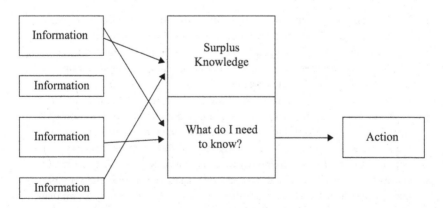

3.1 From information to surplus knowledge and action.

to know to take action; (2) to alert the politician to potentially harmful information so they could protect themselves; and (3) to tell the politician what information, and by extension which sources of information, they could ignore. As a candidate in the compressed schedule of a hectic statewide campaign, I counted on my staff to "tell me what I needed to know" and little more.

Half-knowledge has two major implications for learning the craft of engaging in education policy that will be taken up in more detail later in the book. First, half-knowledge further demonstrates the gulf between politicians and academics. While politicians can purposefully ignore information as a coping mechanism, experts are rewarded for delving deeper and deeper into evidence to advance their field. The "unsolvable" issues that politicians may be inclined to ignore are often the "big questions" that academics take up in their research. The second is strategic and involves the question "Do politicians need your research to take action?" When engaging with politicians, academics must be prepared to present a succinct, clear, and compelling argument for how their research can help politicians take action to address practical problems. In an effort to remain "neutral," some academics and organizations provide politicians with summaries of the "facts" on both sides of issues, but for busy politicians, who are preoccupied with narrowing the cacophony of voices and flood of information to what they "need to know" to take action, this may be surplus knowledge.

I was surprised by how little I "thought" during the campaign. Campaigns are not the place for deep thinking or new ideas. Sure, considerable thought went into developing a campaign plan, policy agenda, and related message. The bulk of this process was completed before the campaign launch, however, and was developed without academic research. For the rest of the campaign, nearly all my efforts went into executing the plan to "get the message out" to voters. My job as the candidate was painstakingly repetitive. For months, I sat in a small office for hours on end and made the same campaign fundraising call over and over again, routinely leaving five or more messages with potential donors before talking with them personally, if at all. I perfected a stump speech that I delivered over and over again. Over time, the speeches, questions, and answers became routine. There was little time or space for new ideas. By extension, there was little need for full knowledge on new issues.

SUMMARY

Politicians tend to be education research and policy novices. This does not mean that they are uneducated. Rather, it means that they rely heavily on their personal experiences and professional knowledge to learn about education research and policy to carry out their duties. Novices learn by applying existing rules to new phenomena. And, in an effort to manage the deluge of information presented to them, they use half-knowledge to filter information to allow them to take action. These insights can be incredibly useful for academics engaging in education policy. It sheds light on a window for academics to leverage their professional strengths to teach politicians with frameworks that help politicians understand the real-world impact of education policies, predict future trends, and develop heuristics to guide future actions. But academics must remember that to engage with politicians most effectively, they must go beyond providing research evidence for understanding and work toward providing evidence to help politicians take action to address practical problems.

4

PROBLEMS WITH RESEARCH

There is sufficient research available at any time to inform any policy idea brought forth by politicians. But, of the formal products used in a policy context (audits, analyses, evaluations, and research), research is the only product with no direct application in a local policy context.

Research can be defined as "empirical findings derived from systematic methods and analyses" (W. T. Grant Foundation 2019). Here, I examine research more closely beginning with a focus on the common criticisms of academic research. Next, I compare the four major types of formal products that are used in education policy (audits, analyses, evaluations, and research) from the perspective of how each product functions in a policy context. I argue that of the four, research is the only one that is not "shovel ready" for policy formation. Research is the least context specific and requires the most effort to translate to a policy context. On the other hand, research has the longest shelf-life by far of the other products, an advantageous trait that transforms individual research products into a cumulative, multi-year repository of evidence that can be applied to influence policy in many contexts. For this reason, sufficient research is available at any time to inform any policy idea. The research may be difficult to access, it may take time to sift through volumes of articles to find applicable studies, and the research certainly needs to be translated to a local policy context to be useful, but it is available, and applicable. I conclude that research does not need a major overhaul to be useful in a policy context, as long as it is translated for this purpose and academics maintain a forward-looking perspective and continue to build a repository *before* novice politicians put forth policy ideas. Finally, I detail the degree of specificity required for research to be useful in a policy context, making the case that what politicians ultimately covet is accounting to make policy decisions, not research.

WHAT IS RESEARCH?

What constitutes research is convoluted in practice and unclear in the academic literature. For example, Tseng (2012, 6) found that policymakers and practitioners "employed a broad conceptualization of research that included empirical findings, data, personal experiences and the experiences of others, and constituent feedback." School district staff defined research evidence to include social science research, but also student achievement data, expert testimony, practitioner knowledge, and input from parents and community members (Honig and Coburn 2008, 6). And practitioners do not "draw a distinction between research evidence and general evidence derived from these other sources" (Nelson, Leffler, and Hansen 2009, Executive Summary).

While these definitions reflect what practitioners consider as research, they are not helpful to elucidate the definition of research for engaging in policy because several qualitatively different types of information are combined into the same definition. For example, research, data, practitioner knowledge, and personal testimony are distinct types of information. Each one is produced differently, functions differently in a policy context, and they are not equally robust in the face of rigorous critique. I am not surprised, however, that practitioners, even politicians and professional staff, would conjoin multiple types of information into a broad, working definition of research because most practitioners are not trained in research methods and are not frequent research producers. From my perspective, these various types of information are commingled because they are all different "ways of knowing" that are used in a policy context, but they are distinct, particularly research.

The definitions may be convoluted because research is both a product and a process. Research as a process is often used to develop many types of products but the end the result is not necessarily research. For example, research methods, the techniques used to collect data, are applied to conduct evaluations and analyses but the products are distinct from research (chapter 4). To complicate matters further, politicians often request that staff conduct "research" on a policy proposal even if the staff are not qualified as researchers (Apollonio and Bero 2017) in which case they are essentially expecting the staff to conduct a review of the literature on the policy and return with a summary of findings, a process that is far different from the research process employed to conduct empirical studies.

The research and academic communities, however, are equally guilty of cluttering the definition of research with inconsistent terms. For example, in the academic literature, "researchers often employ the terms evidence and research interchangeably, defining them as empirical findings derived from scientific methods" (Tseng 2012, 6). The W. T. Grant Foundation's (2019) definition of "research evidence" tangles together different types of products such as "descriptive studies, intervention or evaluation studies, meta-analyses, and cost-effectiveness studies conducted within or outside research organizations" (W. T. Grant Foundation 2019). And in Weiss's influential work on research and evaluation one can find the terms "policy research," "evaluation research," "social research," "social science research," and "evaluation" being used almost interchangeably.

The academic definitions are problematic for a couple of reasons, First, they focus on a specific piece of information, in this case "evidence," while ignoring the larger product in which the evidence sits. In a policy context, however, the characteristics of evidence derived from an evaluation are qualitatively different from evidence from research (e.g., an academic article), such that the former may provide results from a politician's specific constituency and the latter does not include results from a politician's constituency, a key distinction that I elaborate on later in the chapter. Second, the definitions refer to "scientific" or "systematic" methods as necessary characteristics of research and research evidence. For politicians, however, that need not be the case.

For our purpose of engaging in education policy, I will employ a working definition of research that is specific to the politician's perspective and can be applied in multiple policy contexts. From the politician's perspective, research is effectively a product where the evidence is derived from people or organizations outside a politician's legislative jurisdiction. In other words, research includes evidence that must be applied or generalized to the politician's jurisdiction. This working definition defines all products that do not contain evidence from a politician's specific jurisdiction as research, including articles in academic journals, the papers and presentations at academic conferences, and reports from external organizations (such as think tanks, policy centers, university research centers, and so on).

The terms "data," "findings," "results," and "evidence" are often used interchangeably in a policy context. For our purpose, I organize them into levels where data are the most granular. Data are raw symbols (such as letters or numbers) that refer to or represent concepts or phenomena. Results, findings, and outcomes all function as organized representations of data (for example, descriptive statistics, regression coefficients, codes). The way evidence is used in this book includes one additional element, an interpretation or application of findings to an external context, such as a policy or program. Evidence can be found in many products, such as analyses and evaluations, to include research. These distinctions are similar to how Davies and Nutley (2008) define research, findings, and evidence:

Research is a process (explicit, systematic, and open to scrutiny), the outputs of which are research findings. Research findings do not speak for themselves—they must be collated, summarized, and synthesized, and then presented in ways that make them acceptable and informative. When these findings are used in support of an argument or position, they are being treated as evidence. Any particular set of research findings is simply that: outputs from research; these same set of findings might be accorded greater significance by a stakeholder and thus labeled evidence. (Davies and Nutley 2008, 2)

An example may be helpful here. If one were conducting research on a given program, one would collect data such as the number of people who completed the program successfully, as defined by the program goals. The count would then be organized into a finding (result or outcome) such as the percentage of participants who completed the program successfully. The finding would then be interpreted as evidence of program effectiveness by comparing the percentage to an external standard, such as the percentage of successful completers in similar programs or established benchmarks.

There are a number of assumptions that underlie our working definition of research that I will make clear. First, politicians are expected to make decisions based on the welfare of their constituents, the people and organizations in their political jurisdiction. To the politician, the welfare of the people and organizations in their district is paramount, while the welfare of those outside their district is of less interest. Politicians place the highest priority on evidence derived from their constituents because such evidence could impact the welfare of their constituents. Second, a defining characteristic of all research is that it must be applied (I would argue translated) to the people and organizations in a politician's legislative jurisdiction because the findings are not specific to their constituents, or any specific constituents for that matter. Last, the definition distinguishes evidence by the product in which it is contained because it is the product that defines the nature of the evidence. For example, the evidence in an evaluation is inherently more local, meaning applicable to specific political jurisdictions, than research evidence that is conducted in one setting and then generalized to other similar settings.

CRITIQUES OF RESEARCH

In this section, I review the common critiques of education research in the academic literature and then analyze the critiques from the perspective of using research to engage in policy per our working definition above. The most common critiques are that research is impractical, contradictory, inaccessible, untimely, voluminous, and lacks rigor. Examining the critiques from a politician's perspective reveals that research can be useful in policymaking if it translated for this purpose.

IMPRACTICAL

In a policy context, politicians believe that academics take on impractical topics that are simply not useful in a policy context (Flake 2016). This critique is particularly charged against heavily theoretical pieces, basic research, or studies intended to advance an academic discipline that are not targeted toward a specific policy. In these cases, politicians may not understand that not all research has a "take-home" message that makes it immediately useful in a policy context (Lavis et al. 2003).

To analyze the impracticality critique from the politician's perspective, I distinguish between research that is funded by public funds (e.g., government-funded contracts and grants) and research that is funded by resources other than public funds (e.g. researcher-generated, foundation-supported). This distinction is important for politicians, who, as stewards of public funds, have legitimate expectations about the relevance of government-funded research and a vested interest in how resources are expended to conduct it. In fact, the original problem posed by Carol Weiss in her seminal work on research utilization was related to political interest in government-funded research: "this is a time when more and more social scientists concerned are becoming about making their research useful for public policy makers, and policy makers are displaying spurts of well publicized concern about the usefulness of the social science research that government funds support" (Weiss 1979, 426).

For the purpose of engaging in policy, the lesson is that if you are bringing government-funded research into a policy context, you should expect politicians to question the practicality of your research (e.g., Flake 2016) and you should come prepared to defend government investment in research that may be viewed as impractical by some politicians.

If your work is not government-funded, politicians will hold little to no expectations about the practicality of your work nor will they be overly concerned about the resources expended to accomplish it. If you are bringing such research to politicians, you believe your research can be useful and the burden of demonstrating its practicality is on you.

The distinction between government-funded and research that is funded from non-public sources carves out a space for "blue-skies" research that is conducted with no expectations that it is useful in a policy context (Whitty 2006). In response to the criticism that all research should be practical, Whitty (2006, 162) contends that "while some of our work will be aligned in various ways to the Government's agenda, some of it will necessarily be regarded by government as irrelevant or useless. Furthermore, some of it may well be seen as oppositional. Such a range of orientations to government policy is entirely appropriate for education research in a free society."

There is more "research" from nongovernmental sources that is brought to politicians than readers may realize. In addition to academic studies, politicians receive proprietary research conducted by companies that are pitching a product or service, reports from various intermediary or advocacy organizations, information from lobbyists, and studies conducted by "average Joe" constituent groups to support their issues. I have never seen a politician question the practicality of a research product or the use of resources in cases where the research was funded by nongovernment sources. The prevailing mindset among politicians is that if others want to expend their resources, either time or money, on impractical research—that is their business. Similarly, academics who conduct work with nonpublic funds should not want politicians to have any interest in or expectations for the practicality of their work because interest and expectations can easily devolve into intrusion. Any good lobbyist would advise these academics to lay low. If politicians are not asking questions about the practicality of your research and the use of resources to conduct it, you should not give them a reason to start.

If the research is conducted with non-governmental sources, then there is little tension about conducting oppositional or critical research that rejects any "constructive" role in a policy context (Hammersley 2002).

I believe that few politicians would object to Whitty's argument, assuming that the government is not footing the bill.

CONTRADICTORY

The crux of this critique is that the results of academic research are inconsistent across different studies or reports. When different studies of the same policy come to different conclusions, conflicting findings can test politicians' confidence in research for the purpose of taking action based on evidence. Politicians are unable to rely on research for credibility or authority because their rivals can just as easily find another study with different findings, or a later study may be released that contradicts the evidence that politicians are communicating to colleagues and the public.

The quandary is that what politicians would regard as contradictory findings and wavering conclusions, academics would consider as essential steps in the advancement of knowledge, a process that ultimately broadens our collective understanding of education. Among academics there is no expectation that a single perspective or interpretation should dominate the intellectual discourse. Diverse viewpoints and alternative interpretations are welcomed and are regarded as healthy to the production and advancement of knowledge. What we know about the state of education changes over time as state-of-the-art research methods are developed, new data emerge, and populations and policies evolve, all of which lead to new findings, or the revision of historical findings that alter our perspective of what is happening in schools and communities.

Politicians can become frustrated with this process. Politicians who develop an interest in a specific policy and then inquire about research related to that policy at that moment, effectively enter an academic conversation largely unaware of the debate or research leading up to the point of entry, and without the appropriate expertise to understand that the academic conversation will continue to evolve once their interest dissipates. Politicians rely on professional staff to stay abreast of the literature. If professional staff are doing their work well, then they will reconcile potentially contradictory conclusions and present the most applicable research to politicians.

INACCESSIBLE

Academic research products may be inaccessible to politicians because the language may be dense or the study may be complex. Politicians are not alone in their criticism of academic research. Academics themselves believe that our prose can be a chore to read, even for experts, and have called for improvements in the quality of academic prose. They argue that research would be more readable if academics made improvements such as using simpler sentence structures, selecting more everyday words, and avoiding jargon (Rhode 2006). Certainly, these improvements would make academic research more readable, but they will not improve the applicability of research to policy. The content of research that politicians believe is not applicable to a policy context is not made more applicable through editing the prose.

The inaccessible critique also applies to the organization of academic articles. The traditional organizational structure of an academic article (introduction, literature review, methods, findings, and discussion) is impractical for communicating most effectively with busy politicians. The traditional article format is designed for academic audiences, where the author is expected to situate the particular study in the academic literature and to support the findings on methodological grounds before moving to the discussion of policy implications. Politicians are most interested in the last section of the article—the discussion of policy implications.

The major takeaway is not that the traditional formation of academic articles should change, but that when academics engage with politicians, they should resist the temptation to present research via the traditional organization of an academic article. The order should be flipped, with policy implications coming first. And, to the horror of all academics reading this book, research methods should be presented last or even eliminated all together because politicians pay little attention to research methods to meet their need to take action (Bogenschneider and Corbett 2010).

Academic research can also be inaccessible to the lay reader due to (overly) elaborate research designs and sophisticated data analysis techniques. The natural trajectory of academic research is to become more specialized and technical over time. For example, as large-scale data have become more common, data analysis techniques have become more advanced to take full advantage of the rich information available. And, journal editors are encouraging academics to use more and more sophisticated techniques by publishing more methodologically complex articles. The increasing sophistication of the academic literature presents formidable challenges for academics and politicians alike. As research becomes more technical and specialized, academics have to make a greater effort to translate it to a policy context that is occupied by education research and policy novices who need information fast. It requires specialized training to be an informed user of academic research who can understand, interpret, and criticize research methods, skills that are well beyond all but very few novice politicians.

Some have called for politicians to learn more about the research process as an effort bridge the two worlds of research and policy (Ball 2012). The idea is that if politicians knew more about research and had a better appreciation for the research process, then they would be more willing engage with the academic literature. It is an unrealistic expectation, however, to ask busy politicians to learn research methods well enough to gain the expertise necessary to stay abreast of a given field. Besides, politicians have many other shortcuts and resources for gathering and interpreting academic research, and they do not need to have knowledge of the research process is to fulfill their legislative or political duties.

Finally, most academic articles are published in academic journals that require paid subscriptions, so their contents are out of sight and out of mind for most politicians. There are efforts within academia to expedite knowledge mobilization to meet the time demands of the media and politicians, such as the National Education Policy Center (https://nepc.colorado.edu), but overall academic responses still center on traditional scholarly activities such as publishing in peer-reviewed journals and presenting at academic conferences (Zuiker et al. 2019). Also, although the growth of online platforms has facilitated efforts to "push out" research, it has done little to improve the connection between research producers and consumers (Goldhaber and Brewer 2008).

UNTIMELY

Politicians charge that academics fail to produce evidence quick enough to be used in a policy context. This critique is directed at the long and protracted research and publication cycle that operates too slowly to provide answers when politicians demand them. Commonly, several months and even years may pass from the time that data are gathered to the publication of findings in an academic article. There have been some efforts to shorten this cycle via online media and publishing working papers that are made available outside of peer review. These changes, however, have not been sufficient to meet the needs of politicians. The reality is that original, empirical research may never be produced on a fast-enough cycle after a politician requests it.

If one assumes the politician's request initiates the research process, then the untimely critique may very well be applicable. By the time that a politician requests a new, original research product to address a current policy issue, the multi-month (even multi-year) process would likely render the findings as effectively useless upon delivery. And, it is unrealistic politicians will wait on the research process to conclude before taking action.

The more likely scenario is that politicians have gained an interest in a specific policy idea and, understanding that policy windows open and close quickly, they cannot wait for the completion of original research to help them persuade their colleagues and others of the merits of their idea. In most cases, the politician, or professional staff, must rely on the existing literature to champion their policy issue. The research precedes the request. The good news is that there is sufficient research available at any time to inform any policy idea brought forth by politicians.

VOLUMINOUS

The production of academic materials doubles every nine years according to one estimate (Bornmann and Rüdiger 2015), the number of academic journals has increased steadily since 1900 (Gu and Blackmore 2016), and open-access and online publishing outlets continue to facilitate the dissemination of research content (Steele 2008). In education specifically, the Education Resources Information Center (ERIC), which is described as the "world's largest digital library of education literature," holds 1.6 million records, including journal articles, books, technical reports and conference papers (Institute of Education Sciences 2019). But then the reader can easily get a sense of the volume of education research that awaits the interested politician through a quick Google search on any policy topic, which is likely to yield hundreds to thousands of hits.

Given the volume of research available, it requires not only considerable effort but some training to find applicable studies to address specific policy questions of interest. Expertise is required to find the most fruitful search terms and sift through and assess the results. While academics are expected to possess these skills, politicians are not. One should not expect time-pressed politicians to have the ability or patience to wade through the volumes of research to find applicable studies. Politicians rely on staff or intermediaries to engage with the research literature directly and bring forth those items most applicable to politicians' inquiries.

LACKS RIGOR

The most damaging criticisms against the rigor of education research come primarily from academics themselves, not politicians. This is logical given that academics are trained in research methods and should be the standard bearer of research quality. As I addressed in chapter 3, politicians are education research and policy novices with little to no academic or professional training in research methods. As such, politicians are not in a position to assess the rigor of academic research. Politicians are not trained to filter out "weak" studies, and acquiring this skillset is not directly applicable to their responsibilities to set policy.

From politicians' perspectives, if a study is understandable, consistent with their everyday experiences, and provides support for their policy position, then what is there to gain in questioning its methodological rigor? For example, Goldhaber and Brewer (2008) describe how two colleagues discovered that a popular and widely distributed study included a sample of only sixteen respondents. Discovering this methodological limitation is not difficult and could be accomplished by anyone with even modest training in research methods. But politicians are education research and policy novices. I am not surprised that politicians would rely on methodologically questionable research that supports their position. In fact, I fully expect them to do so.

Academics have argued that the underutilization of research in the policy process is at least partly due to the lack of rigorous research methods (Seashore Louis 2005). The assumption of these critiques is that if academic research was more rigorous, politicians would make more or better use of it in the policy process. This critique is dubious because increased rigor does not make research more relevant or timely. In fact, one may argue that there is a balance between rigor and accessibility to the extent that increased rigor may yield more methodologically complex studies. In this case, increased rigor may widen the research and policy gap because it requires more effort and expertise to translate the results to a policy context.

In summary, politicians want practical research that is available at the moment when they are ready to make decisions. The findings should be consistent and should not stray too far from the politician's perception of what he or she considers the "real world." The research should be written in everyday language and should not be overly complex methodologically. And, politicians are busy and cannot digest too much information at one time, so research must be directed toward them or it may be ignored. As Nelson, Leffler, and Hansen (2009, 29) observed, "Politicians and practitioners indicated they want research evidence that can be directly applied to their situation and can inform decision making with little need for interpretation on their part—and that type of research evidence is in short supply." I would extend the observation further to say that there is *no* research that meets these criteria. Research is never directed to a specific local context, and all research requires translation to be used in a policy context.

WHAT DO POLITICIANS MEAN BY "RELEVANT" RESEARCH?

There is a common understanding in the academic literature that research should be relevant to the local policy context (Seashore Louis and Jones 2002). But what exactly is "relevant" from a politician's point of view? How localized must research be for it to be applicable? When politicians consider the relevance of research, they have two main considerations: context and timeliness. I argue that due to the fundamental structure and purpose of research, it is never context-specific (enough) for use in a local policy context. Research, even the most applied research, does not inform politicians about the impact of policies on their constituents. On the other hand, research is timely—meaning it's available to inform any policy idea at any time.

CONTEXT IS KING

The most important consideration among politicians with regard to the usefulness of research is context. Academics should expect politicians to ask, how does the evidence apply to *my* constituents? The Nelson, Leffler, and Hansen (2009, 19) study of research "identified research relevance to the user's context as the strongest issue across all groups and levels. Users judge all research evidence and other sources of information against their local context, pre-existing understandings, local needs, and expectations."

Politicians must answer to and advocate for those who get them elected. It is common sense for politicians to filter all evidence through the lens of how it applies to *their* constituents. Politicians do not evaluate the usefulness of research findings relative to hypothetical constituents, or even to those outside their jurisdiction; they evaluate the usefulness of research in reference to *their* constituents—the specific people and institutions that politicians know by name and will hold politicians accountable by name.

This reads like common sense, yet, I am not clear that academics have internalized the full implications of this point for the purpose of bringing research to politicians. While the relationship between educational policymakers and producers of educational research is not an adversarial one, a gulf of misunderstanding can separate them. "Researchers eschew the worlds of politics and administration as compromising the 'truths' revealed through research; policymakers are often skeptical of ideas that come from people who do not bear responsibility for their mistakes in the public arena" (Hetrick and van Horn 1988, 106).

For example, Gandara and Hearn (2019) described the implementation of higher education policy in Texas as the "Texas Way" because legislators preferred Texas-specific data made available by state agencies to make policy decisions. Politicians and professional staff cited Texas's unique size and demographics to support their position that cross-state comparisons were of little value. As a member of the Texas governor's office noted, "We look outside but I mean, a lot—but there's—there's just not a lot of states that are like us" (Gandara and Hearn, 17). The penchant for localized data, however, is not specific to Texas. Academics should expect politicians to seek data as context-specific as possible to make policy decisions with local implications.

Whenever possible, policy decisions are made according to an accounting model with findings on how resources and opportunities are distributed across every case (e.g., political jurisdictions, school districts, schools, and so on) that makes up a politician's constituency. Through accounting, politicians can understand (1) how resources and opportunities are distributed across the people and organizations in their political jurisdiction and (2) compare this distribution to other political jurisdictions. It would be negligent for a politician to make any policy decision without making every effort to acquire evidence that accounts for every case in his or her political jurisdiction. And, once acquired, accounting evidence is likely to take precedent over any other types of evidence, such as research, that may also be available at the time. As legislative staff, I interpreted my job as making accounting evidence available to facilitate decision-making, even if that meant gathering the evidence myself.

Here's the catch. Research, even the most applied research, is not directly applicable to specific contexts. Research must be generalized from the research context to other contexts because the subjects, and often the exact locations under study are anonymous. Academics mask the identities of the subjects and their locations for important reasons. The first is ethical. Academics abide by a code where they pledge not to harm their participants as a consequence of participating in the research. For example, in qualitative research, which is often rich in detail and personal narratives, academics use pseudonyms to disguise the identity of their subjects. Anonymity is also essential in order to elicit candid responses from participants. The second reason is practical. There is never enough time or money to study every location. Plus, it is not necessary to do so. With sound sampling techniques, one does not have to study each location to conduct sound research.

Thus, when one brings research to politicians for the purpose of informing policy decisions, there is never a one-to-one relationship between the context studied and the context that politicians consider when applying the evidence. For politicians, the lack of a one-to-one relationship between the contexts studied and the specific contexts in which research is applied means that research products are never localized enough to apply to their constituents directly.

For example, one of the most high-profile examples of sampling in education policy is the National Assessment of Education Progress (NAEP), which is the most reliable source of interstate academic achievement data. Due to sophisticated sampling techniques, estimates of student academic achievement are derived at the state level and for some very large districts based on sampling a subset of schools. NAEP is not administered to all students in every state, and the test results are not returned to individual schools or students. Thus, NAEP is not useful in local policy, such as school accountability decisions, because it does not include an accounting of findings for every school within and across political jurisdictions. Rather, politicians use the results of their state standardized tests for accountability purposes because results are available for all schools in their political jurisdictions.

TIME VERSUS TIMELINESS

Snow (1959) noted the vast difference between how social scientists and politicians perceive time: politicians have short timelines, and academics have long timelines. I distinguish the difference between the amount of time it takes to complete research and its timeliness in policy discussions. Timeliness refers to the availability of research at a given moment when it's needed to inform a particular policy debate. Timelines do not have to be shortened to make research timelier. In fact, it is not wise and likely not possible to put research on a political timeline. Shortened timelines to improve the timeliness of research in policy debates may jeopardize the quality of the knowledge produced and could lead to the release of spurious results, further tarnishing of the reputation of academic research (Henig 2008b).

Sound research takes time. But sound research also lasts a long time, too. Sound research has a long expiration date. The long time horizon of sound research means that it does not need to be accomplished on the timeline of any specific policy to be timely. Rather, I argue that, if academics remain forward-thinking in their work, then all the research necessary to inform a specific policy at any given moment should be available when it's needed by politicians.

Let me present the point another way, given what we have learned so far. Politicians are novices in education research and policy who apply their existing experiences to solve practical problems. They rarely, if ever, suggest brand new policy ideas that have never been put forth before. Academics, on the other hand, are experts in research, policy, or both. If politicians are novices and academics are experts, then it is the rare case where the novice comes up with an idea that the expert has not already contemplated. If research is forward-thinking enough, then there should be sufficient research evidence to bring to bear on the policy proposals brought forth by politicians. At any given moment, the professional staffer, designated by the politician to conduct research, or even

I found that newly elected politicians enter into office and put forward many of the same policy ideas as their newly elected predecessors. Remember, only months prior to being elected, politicians were involved members of the public so many of the policy ideas put forth by newly elected politicians derive from the ongoing public discourse on education. Also, once elected, they are bombarded by lobbyists, advocacy groups, and intermediary organizations that are peddling retreaded policy proposals in search of an open policy window. For professional staff, legislative sessions are like "Groundhogs Day," where many of the same policy issues are put forth from session to session, and the debates and outcomes often follow a predictable course. In the context of school choice, for example, "The issues on the table in today's debates about vouchers, charter schools, and school choice more generally are in many key respects the same issues that were presented—with urgency—10 and 15 and 20 years ago" (Henig 2009, 153). The predictability means that historical research conducted on a policy issue at one point in time remains largely applicable to similar policy issues at a later date.

the politician themselves can find sufficient research to inform any given policy proposal.

In the end, I disagree that research is not timely. The research may be hard to find. It may be difficult to understand. And it certainly requires translation to a localized policy context to be applicable—but it's available.

AUDITS, ANALYSES, EVALUATIONS, AND RESEARCH

There are four types of formal products used in a policy context: audits, analysis, evaluation, and research. Each one differs dramatically with respect to purpose and use. Of the four major types of products, research is the only one with no direct application in a local policy context. Research, and by extension research evidence, is not inherently useful in a policy context because it is not derived from the constituents of any individual politician and cannot be localized enough to be used in a local context directly. Audits, analyses, and evaluations, on the other hand, are localized enough to be useful in a policy context because they include evidence on specific people and organizations. The upside of research, however, is that of the four types of formal products, research has the

Table 4.1 Comparison of formal products used in policy contexts

	Purpose	Subjects	Stakes	References	Policy-Related Decisions	Life Span
Audits	— Ensure compliance	Identified	High	Laws and regulations	Personnel or agency sanctions	Annual
(Policy) Analysis	— Solve problems — Assess policy alternatives	Implied	High	Policy goals and legislative intent	Select among policy alternatives	Intermittent
(Program) Evaluation	— Assess operations and/or outcomes — Make judgements	Implied	High	Program goals	Program continuation or modification	Cyclical
Research	— Advance knowledge — Refine hypotheses	Anonymous	None	Other research, theory	None	Multiyear

longest lifespan by far, in that it produces a body of knowledge spanning multiple years that can be translated to any local policy context. To illustrate the differences between the four types of formal products, I compare them on six dimensions (purposes, subjects, stakes, references, policy-related decisions, and life span) with a specific focus on how each product compares with research (see table 4.1).

PURPOSE

The purpose of an audit is to ensure compliance with laws and regulations. For example, "Auditing is defined as the on-site verification activity, such as inspection or examination, of a process or quality system, to ensure compliance to requirements" (American Society for Quality n.d.). "Legislative auditors are the watchdogs of state government. They ensure state agencies and programs are carried out as they were intended, in an efficient way, and serving the public in the most effective way known" (Utah State Legislature 2019).

Analysis involves a detailed examination of problems to determine solutions. Wildavsky (1979, 17) defines policy analysis as "an activity creating problems that can be solved. Every policy is fashioned of tension between resources and objectives, planning and politics, skepticism and dogma. Solving problems involves temporarily resolving these tensions." Put another way, "policy analysis is concerned primarily with policy alternatives that are expected to produce novel solutions" ("Policy Analysis" n.d.).

An evaluation is intended to come to a judgment of a program (or policy) to improve its effectiveness. Weiss (1972) defines the purpose of evaluation as a process "to measure the effects of a program against the goals it set out to accomplish as a means of contributing to subsequent decision making about the program and improving future programming." The Centers for Disease Control (n.d., 1) define evaluation as "the activity through which we develop an understanding of the merit, worth, and utility of a policy."

The purpose of research is to advance knowledge and contribute to future research. Research validates, refutes, or refines existing knowledge to generate new knowledge (Naidoo 2011). According to the American Educational Research Association (n.d.), "Research embraces the full spectrum of rigorous methods appropriate to the questions being asked and also drives the development of new tools and methods." These purposes are detached from policymaking in any specific policy context.

SUBJECTS

In each product, the ability to identify the specific subjects (people and organizations) under study differs considerably. This dimension is consequential in a policy context because if politicians can identify the specific subjects under study then they can attribute the evidence to these subjects and take appropriate action. For example, in an audit, politicians know the exact people and organizations under consideration and can hold the subjects directly accountable. In an analysis and evaluation, the connection between the evidence and the subjects is also localized, a feature that facilitates their use in decision-making (Wye et al. 2015). The specific people or organizations may not be not identified by name, but politicians can isolate the universe of people and organizations to which the evidence is attributable to connect the evidence with policy actions. With research, however, both the people, and often the organizations under study are anonymous for ethical reasons. Politicians are unable to identify or even infer the people and organizations to which the evidence is attributable for the purpose of taking policy action.

STAKES

The stakes associated with each type of product vary dramatically. In an audit, the stakes are direct in that the findings could result in job terminations or legal actions in cases of noncompliance. In an analysis, the stakes are high for specific people and organizations. Depending on the outcomes, politicians could choose to create new investments or opportunities for specific people and organizations or to make fewer investments or opportunities. Similarly, the stakes are high as a result of an evaluation in that the evidence can influence whether or not a program is continued or modified. There are no stakes involved with research, however. No one loses their job. There is no change or shift in resource allocations or opportunities based on the outcomes of research evidence.

To maintain the integrity of research and to protect participants, no stakes should be associated with research evidence. But research, given the absence of stakes, can lack the political urgency that may be associated with the other products, making it more challenging to focus politicians' attention on research evidence.

REFERENCES

There is a clear contrast in the references necessary to complete each product. Auditors rely on local laws and regulations that politicians either enacted themselves or that politicians must be aware of to carry out their responsibilities. Analyses and evaluations are conducted using legislative language and program goals that are also familiar to politicians. Research, on the other hand, is conducted using other research, references that are foreign to the education research and policy novice and distant from the dynamics of any particular policy context.

The references are of note because they dictate the amount of background explanation that is needed for politicians to understand and use each product. If politicians are aware of the references used to develop the product, then less background explanation is necessary to prepare them to understand and use the product. Conversely, if the references are foreign to politicians, then more background explanation is necessary for politicians to understand and use the product. With respect to research, it is important to note that academics must not only communicate specific evidence, they may also need to explain the academic literature used to conduct the research, introducing concepts that are not only new to politicians but also those that politicians may never encounter again in fulfilling their duties to set policy.

POLICY-RELATED DECISIONS

Audits are used to make specific decisions with respect to personnel or agencies. Analyses are used to help politicians make decisions about policy effectiveness and alternatives. Evaluations are used to make decisions about the continuation or modification of specific programs. There are no policy decisions inherent to research. Research products, such as academic journal articles and conference proceedings, have no built-in policy-related decisions.

The key takeaway for academics is that their products (academic journal articles, conference papers, or reports conducted with people or organizations outside the politician's constituency) do not have a direct policy use because they do not include evidence on specific people or organizations specific political jurisdictions and are not tied to any specific policy-related decisions. At best, an individual research product can be "used" in a specific policy context by translating the results from the anonymous people and organizations under study to the specific people and organizations in a politician's jurisdiction.

LIFE SPAN

Lastly, what is the life span of each formal product? How long is the evidence of an individual formal product applicable to policy contexts?

Audits, analyses, and evaluations are applicable to a policy context until the next iteration of the product is produced. Audits are conducted on as-needed basis, sometimes annually, and may only be applicable for a year. The applicability of policy analyses is irregular because analyses are conducted as politicians gain an interest in a specific policy. Evaluations are cyclical, meaning that they are often conducted per defined intervals. For example, politicians may specify when a program is to be evaluated or an evaluation may be conducted in conjunction with sunset provisions that terminate a program after a certain date.

Research, on the other hand, has the longest life span by far. Research is not time- or place-specific, so it is applicable across multiple years and multiple policy contexts. In fact, its utility comes from the cumulative evidence derived from multiple individual research products, henceforth described as *the* research, that can be translated to multiple policy contexts. *The* research can predict future outcomes, which is extremely beneficial to politicians seeking control in their local context. But *the* research needs to be translated to a local policy context to maximize its predictive qualities.

For example, much of the background research used for this book was conducted in the 1970s and 1980s and was sparked by an intense interest in the question of how government-funded research was used in policymaking processes. To politicians, the press, and the public, the background material for this book may constitute nothing more than dusty articles and yesterday's news. Yet, many of the themes and findings of the background research material are still applicable today. For example, despite being developed over forty years ago and despite the introduction of new modes of communication and new actors in the policymaking space, Weiss' "enlightenment" theory (1977) is still used commonly in the academic literature to describe and understand the current state of research use in policy. Likewise, the list of current policies with a substantial body of applicable research is long. There is sufficient research to meet every politician's needs right now on pressing policy issues such as school accountability, teaching and learning practices, market models of education, teacher turnover, academic standards, and so on.

POLITICIANS WANT ACCOUNTING

Politicians must make specific decisions about specific policies that impact specific people and organizations. The decisions, policies, people, and institutions are not hypothetical or distant. They have names and faces. If politicians could waive a magic wand to satisfy their information needs, they would ask for the most context-specific type information possible. They would ask for an accounting of how resources and opportunities are distributed across every case (e.g., political jurisdictions, school districts, schools) in their political jurisdiction, as well as other jurisdictions. They are less interested in the generalization of research findings to their constituents because ultimately all information will be filtered through a political lens, meaning that before making a policy decision, politicians will consider how the information improves (or harms) the welfare of their constituents. What politicians covet before making a policy decision is an accounting of the impact or future impact of a policy for *every* relevant case possible.

Certainly, evaluation plays a role, particularly to make renewal decisions about programs. And analysis can be helpful to determine the best possible solutions, balancing the tensions between resources and policy objectives. Yet, even after receiving the evidence from an evaluation or analysis, politicians could still covet an accounting of every case before making a decision. Accounting is so persuasive that if the accounting results identified a potential negative impact on their constituents, and the result countered the research evidence, I would expect politicians to side with the accounting results. If so, academics should not be surprised to see politicians shelving reports that shed a negative light on an issue, discrediting the source, or making decisions on the basis of other information, such as anecdotes or locally generated findings.

For example, McDonnell and Weatherford (2013) studied research use in the adoption of the Common Core State Standards (CCSS). Despite the work of policy entrepreneurs who used research selectively to make the case to politicians for common standards and of the experts who turned to research to develop the policy options to implement the CCSS, when the CCSS was put forward for adoption at the state level, politicians still required an accounting of the impact on their constituents before making a final decision, regardless of the underlying research used to develop

Some of the most influential policy research that I conducted was successful precisely because the results accounted for all cases. In 2010, I converted
a mountain of hard-copy reports on the number of traditional, first-year students taking developmental classes at Arizona public universities and community colleges into the first statewide measure of "college readiness." The results
were a lead story in the media, and the methodology was repeated by others
for a number of years. I also presented the results to many community groups
and legislative committees. The college readiness report garnered considerable
attention because every high school in Arizona was accounted for in the results.
Every local paper could run the results for its schools, the schools could be listed
and ranked, and every legislator could see how their schools fared (and could
compare the results to other schools).

the CCSS: "Few state participants were concerned about the research supporting the CCSS. Rather, policy makers and groups whose members were
likely to be affected by the CCSS wanted detailed comparisons between
the Common Core and the state's status quo standards, and they sought
persuasive arguments that the benefits would outweigh the substantial
costs of such a major change" (McDonnell and Weatherford 2013, 18).

Accounting is not high-level research. In fact, it's not research. It is not
sufficiently rigorous to be published in academic or trade journals. Generally speaking, academics do not do accounting. Accounting is done by
government agencies via compliance reports, lobbyists who have access
to proprietary data by political jurisdiction, and some intermediary organizations with available data. Yet, to engage in education policy most
effectively, academics should appreciate the practical dynamics facing politicians who place high value on accounting results by legislative jurisdiction because they must ultimately answer to specific constituents by name.

SUMMARY

We arrive at a quandary. The characteristics of research are not consistent with politicians' informational needs. In fact, research evidence can
never be localized or detailed enough to meet the politician's purpose
of making policy decisions that impact the welfare of their constituents
(McDonnell 1988). So, where do we go from here? First, the academic

community needs to be more specific to distinguish research and research evidence from other formal products that are employed in a policy context. When the academic community is more precise, we free up research to serve its intended purpose to derive new knowledge and divorce it from academics' expectations that it apply to a policy context directly. Second, research must be translated into a completely different product designed to help politicians take action for their constituents in a pressure-filled and hectic environment. Shortened versions or summaries of academic articles are insufficient for engaging in education policy. Last, academics must leverage the most positive attribute of research, its long life-span, and use the cumulative knowledge derived from *the* research to provide timely information to politicians to take action on policy issues today and in the future.

5

RESEARCH USE IN POLICYMAKING

Research is one of many ways of knowing in policymaking. Academics are one of many actors in the policymaking process. And neither research nor academics hold a privileged position.

The academic literature on research utilization in policymaking goes through Carol Weiss, a prominent scholar who has conducted some of the most influential work in the field. In 1979, she categorized six models of research utilization that still serve as the most instructive guide to understanding the many ways that research is used in the policy-making process (Weiss 1979). The six models of research utilization include:

1. knowledge-driven
2. problem-solving
3. tactical
4. political
5. enlightenment
6. interactive.

In this chapter, I will review each model to highlight the implications of each model for academics engaging in policy, and in many cases, I quote Weiss's descriptions of the utilization models directly rather than paraphrase them because her words remain apt descriptors of research use and maintaining the original text illustrates the applicability of sound research over time. In addition, these six models, by and large, are sufficient to describe the current state of research utilization and thus suggest that little has changed in the conceptualization of research utilization despite the proliferation of new communication mediums (e.g., blogs, electronic messages, websites) and many new policy actors (e.g., think tanks, foundations, research organizations) (Lubienski, Scott, and DeBray 2014; Scott et al. 2014; Scott and Jabbar 2014).

Of Weiss's models, the interactive model is the most informative for the purpose of engaging with politicians because it recognizes that various actors and ways of knowing contribute to policymaking, but the model does not privilege academics or research in the process. I close the chapter with a detailed discussion of the eight ways of knowing that academics are likely to encounter when engaging in education policy along with practical examples of each in policymaking.

KNOWLEDGE-DRIVEN MODEL

The knowledge-driven model derives from the natural sciences and assumes a sequence from knowledge production to utilization, which begins with basic research and then leads to applied research, followed by development and application. The knowledge-driven model is regarded favorably by academics because it dedicates a specific place and purpose for basic research. Basic research produces fundamental knowledge, and in most cases, the outcomes of basic research are not expected to have immediate commercial or applicable uses. Basic research is unrelated to any particular policy context and is not motivated by a specific initiative or policy. Academics consider basic research to be the foundation for advancing knowledge (Task Force on American Innovation 2009). The arguments against investing in basic research are that it takes time, there no immediate payoffs to justify the expenditures, and there is no guarantee that there ever will be any returns at all. Also, the goals of basic research are inherently nebulous, which creates a challenge in policy contexts driven by accountability models that rely on measurable metrics (Hammersley 2002).

Thus, as Weiss and others have noted there are very few real-world examples of the knowledge-driven model of education research in policymaking.

For one, social science evidence is distinct from evidence in the natural sciences because social science research, such as education research, does not lend itself to technical applications. Also, the knowledge-driven model does not account for the political process. As Weiss (1979, 427) noted, "Unless a social condition has been consensually defined as a pressing social problem, and unless the condition has become fully politicized and debated, and the parameters of potential action agreed upon, there is little likelihood that policy-making bodies will be receptive to the results of social science research."

PROBLEM-SOLVING MODEL

The problem-solving model establishes a linear and rational relationship between policy questions or problems, research, and answers. The problem-solving model,

> involves the direct application of the results of a specific social science study to a pending decision. The expectation is that research provides empirical evidence and conclusions that help to solve a policy problem. . . . Here the decision drives the application of research. A problem exists and a decision has to be made, information or understanding is lacking either to generate a solution to the problem or to select among alternative solutions, research provides the missing knowledge. With the gap filled, a decision is reached. (Weiss 1979, 427)

The problem-solving model regards research as a necessary tool in the policymaking process. Such research use can be direct, like when a particular study or series of studies are referenced in making a policy decision. Or, research can shape how issues are framed in the policy discourse.

This rational view of decision-making is favored by academics because it shares many characteristics with the research process, such as logic, structure, and thoroughness (Albaek 1995). This approach also legitimizes the role of research in policymaking because research decisions are made after the evaluation of the best available research. Rational approaches are also convenient and advantageous for academics because, per these approaches, politicians are expected to come to them for answers on the academics' terms. Academics are left largely independent to conduct sound research and are not forced to compromise their values or tread into foreign waters and get sullied in the political process.

The problem-solving model has been criticized because it assumes an overly rational model of policymaking (Hammersley 2002; Lindblom and Cohen 1979) and fails to recognize the role that politics plays in policy formation (Gamoran 2018; McDonnell 2009). Yet, to argue against the problem-solving model because it relies on a rational perspective of the policy process does not mean that the policymaking process is irrational or unpredictable. Rather, those who are not familiar with policymaking may be surprised to learn that there is order and rationality in the incredibly complex policymaking process (Bogenschneider and Corbett 2010). In fact, there are many policy actors who understand this order to predict and influence policy decisions in concerted directions. For our purpose, lobbyists are policy actors who influence policy decisions and whose perspective is rarely included in the research utilization literature, maybe because the lobbyist's work is regarded as overly political. Anyone seeking to engage in policy should account for political dynamics, however (Wong 2008).

For academics, I contend that engaging in policy without political considerations is like being a "fish out of water" in the policymaking process. For an academic to provide information for its own sake in an effort to remain neutral or to avoid becoming "political" does not help politicians take action. In these cases, the evidence can be filtered out as surplus knowledge. In a policy context, academics can (and should) take informed policy positions based on evidence, actions that are well-within their bounds as experts. Once academics take a policy position, however, they compete with lobbyists and other policy actors, who also work to influence policy. For these reasons, the book is influenced by lessons that I learned from lobbyists on how to engage in policy effectively.

POLITICAL AND TACTICAL MODELS

In the eyes of many academics, the most cynical approaches to research utilization are the political and tactical models. Per the political model, politicians use research selectively—they pay attention only to research that supports their opinion. The political model is difficult for academics to accept and the easiest to criticize because it is antithetical to how academics view and use research. "Scholars have developed strong professional norms about the 'proper' uses of social science knowledge. They are repelled by policy makers who use them as hired guns or to make a case for a cause" (Wirt and Mitchell 1982, 4). Commenting on the political use of research, Weiss (1979, 429) writes:

Often the constellation of interests around a policy issue predetermines the positions that decision-makers take. Or debate has gone on over a period of years and opinions have hardened. At this point, decision-makers are not likely to be receptive to new evidence from social science research. For reasons of interest, ideology, or intellect, they have taken a stand that research is not likely to shake. In such cases, research can still be used. It becomes ammunition for the side that finds its conclusions congenial and supportive. Partisans flourish the evidence in an attempt to neutralize opponents, convince waverers, and bolster supporters. Even if conclusions have to be ripped out of context . . . research becomes grist to the mill.

Or, as a congressional staff member commented, "You often have the policy in mind . . . so, you look for only the research that will back up that policy" (Nelson, Leffler, and Hansen 2009, 27).

Weiss's observation about "hardened" opinions among policymakers is noteworthy, because such opinions create formidable obstacles to the consideration of new research by politicians, particularly if the research takes a position that is contrary to the current policy discourse or the prevailing policy position of the politician's political party. Hardened opinions heighten the "acceptability threshold" for research evidence in cases where politicians place themselves in a vulnerable public position by associating themselves with contrarian research (Hammersley 2002). Thus, as Seashore Louis (2005) has noted, more efforts are needed to connect with politicians on the front end before their policy positions have hardened—which, in turn, is a convincing argument for building relationships with politicians *before* they are politicians.

The tactical model is another technique that is used often in political circles but not considered widely in the academic literature. According to the tactical model,

Social science research is used for purposes that have little relation to the substance of the research. It is not the content of the findings that is invoked but the sheer fact that research is being done. For example, government agencies confronted with demands for action may respond by saying, "Yes, we know that's an important need. We're doing research on it right now." Research becomes proof of their responsiveness. Faced with unwelcome demands, they may use research as a tactic for delaying action. ("We are waiting until the research is completed.") (Weiss 1979, 429)

Study committees are a tactical use of research that amount to passive action. Politicians are inclined to create study committees on policy issues when they are unable to take legislative action. The formation of a study committee allows politicians to demonstrate that the issue is important and to maintain public attention on the issue. In forming them, politicians have some measure of control by selecting committee participants (including academics), shaping the committee's charge, and managing the manner in which documents are released publicly. The results of a study committee can lead to a public report or the creation of a bill to be introduced in a later legislative session. For academics, study committees are a productive venue for engaging in education policy because the committees often focus on a single issue, allowing for a deeper investigation into the research literature than in a legislative setting where time and attention are diverted in many directions at once.

"KNOWLEDGE CREEP" AND "ENLIGHTENMENT"

Academics have found that research is highly influential but via an indirect manner that eludes instrumental methods to measure its influence. In the more evolved theories of research utilization, research "creeps" into decision-making and can serve an "enlightenment" function in a policy context.

Weiss developed the concept of "knowledge creep" based on asking mental health professionals, and not politicians, about their active search for and conscious use of research evidence. In reply, an overwhelming majority of mental health professionals reported using research extensively to inform their work, a surprising finding because it contradicted a common perception among social scientists that research is largely ignored by decision-makers. Yet, only a small percentage of respondents could name an instrumental use of social science research and were able to provide examples of research only after considerable probing, "verging on nagging" in Weiss's words (Weiss 1980, 387). In most cases, the respondents struggled with identifying a conscious use of research in decision-making even though there was a common recognition that research was an important part of the decision-making process. As Weiss (1980, 384) observed, "The process by which they absorbed social science research was not focused around specific decisions or directed toward specific issues, and its impact on their behavior was difficult to pinpoint. But they had a sense that it made a difference." The content experts in Weiss's study used research to "keep up with the field," to legitimize a position, persuade others, or to make sense of the world. These contradictions led Weiss (1980, 381) to conclude that

knowledge that derives from systematic research and analysis, is not often "utilized" in direct and instrumental fashion in the formulation of policy. Only occasionally does it supply an answer that policy actors employ to solve a policy problem. Instead, research knowledge usually affects the development and modification of policy in diffuse ways. It provides a background of empirical generalizations and ideas that creep into policy deliberations.

Academics have largely settled on the idea that the highest aspiration for research is to serve an enlightenment function, whereby even though the direct application of research may be elusive to measure, there is an understanding that it transforms how politicians think about policy problems (Nutley, Walter, and Davies 2007; Weiss 1989).

Weiss (1979, 429) describes the enlightenment model as "the way in which social science research most frequently enters the policy arena. . . . Here it is not the findings of a single study nor even a body of related studies that directly affect policy. Rather it is the concepts and theoretical perspectives that social science research has engendered that permeate the policymaking process." In a practical sense, academics can witness when research has enlightened the collective understanding of policy actors "by noting the number of occasions on which a government official (or businessman, or interest group leader) was able to preface his remarks with the phrase, 'as everyone knows'" (Wilson 1981, 33).

There is no assumption in the knowledge creep or enlightenment models that politicians seek out social science research when faced with a policy issue or even that they are receptive to, or aware of, specific research findings. The imagery is that of research evidence percolating through the policymaking process and shaping the way in which people think about social issues. Social science research is diffused through many different channels such as professional conferences, mass media, advocacy organizations, and conversations between colleagues, and over time its substance provides politicians with new ways of making sense out of complex issues. Rarely will politicians be able to cite the findings of a specific study that influenced their decisions, but they have a sense that social science research has given them a backdrop of ideas and new orientations that help turn what were non-problems into policy problems (Weiss 1979).

For academics, one key finding in the enlightenment model is that government officials accepted research that challenged the status quo and welcomed research that "opens new avenues for perceiving and thinking and decision-making" (Weiss 1977, 543). It is important to point out that government officials are professional staff, experts who are inclined to stay abreast of the academic literature and whose perspectives on policy issues are fluid. These users value contradictory research because they:

see a role for research as social criticism. It finds a place for research based on variant theoretical premises. It implies that research need not necessarily be geared to the operating feasibility especially of today, but that research provides the intellectual background of concepts, orientations, and empirical generalizations that inform policy. As new concepts and data emerge, their gradual cumulative effect can be to change the conventions policy makers bide by and to reorder the goals and priorities of the practical policy world. (Weiss 1977, 544)

Given the diffuse nature of how research influences policy in the enlightenment model, academics are largely unable to explain or measure how our work has influence, an ironic state of affairs because academics are in the measurement business. From my perspective, the acceptance of the enlightenment model is a matter of convenience. Academics turn a collective blind eye to our inability to measure or operationalize the impact of research on policy because, like the problem-solving model, the enlightenment model privileges the role of research in a policy context. The enlightenment model gives academics permission to go about their work independently, and with the comfort that somehow, someway, their research will enlighten the policy discourse (hopefully for the better). Leading some to the misguided conclusion that they do not have to engage in policy for their research to have an impact. Yet, in our collective inertia and failing to question the enlightenment theory rigorously, academics act similar to the politicians whom we are prone to criticize—working from half-knowledge because full information about the discord between research and politicians may be too paralyzing. The reality is that Weiss's enlightenment model remains popular among academics, but it was created with professional staff and its generalizability to politicians is largely unknown.

INTERACTIVE MODEL

For the purpose of engaging in the policymaking process, I subscribe to Weiss's interactive model because it offers a "nuanced understanding of the ways in which research is taken up by politicians. The interactive model demonstrates how knowledge from research is shaped and reconstructed through the policy makers' pre-existing frameworks and understandings— which may be collectively, not just individually, held" (Nutley, Walter, and Davies 2007, 119). Weiss (1979, 428) described the interactive model as

another way that social science research can enter the decision arena is as part of an interactive search for knowledge. Those engaged in developing policy seek information not only from social scientists but from a variety of sources administrators, practitioners, politicians, planners, journalists, clients, interest groups, aides, friends, and social scientists, too. The process is not one of linear order from research to decision but a disorderly set of interconnections and back-and-forthness that defies neat diagrams. All kinds of people involved in an issue area pool their talents, beliefs, and understandings in an effort to make sense of a problem. Social scientists are one set of participants among many. Seldom do they have conclusions available that bear directly and explicitly on the issue at hand. More rarely still do they have a body of convergent evidence. Nevertheless, they can engage in mutual consultations that progressively move closer to potential policy responses.

The interactive model is illustrative because it recognizes several noteworthy characteristics of the policymaking process. First, academics are one of many voices in policymaking, but their voice is not privileged. There are many other actors whom politicians value equally in policymaking, including administrators, practitioners, other politicians, journalists, interest groups, aides, friends, and parents.

Second, it follows that if a diverse group of participants contribute evidence in the policymaking process, many of whom do not possess experience or knowledge about education research or policy, then many ways of knowing, in addition to research, contribute meaningfully to the policymaking process. The interactive model recognizes and validates the influence of these multiple ways of knowing in the policymaking process. For example, personal experiences are an influential way of knowing. Yet, when academics engage in the policy process they are often perplexed when a politician's singular personal experience outweighs the preponderance of research evidence. But in a policy context, personal experiences are a concrete way of knowing that may contradict abstract research evidence.

Third, policy formation emerges from a debate about the best possible action given the present circumstances. As Albaek (1995, 94) states, "To understand the linkage between research and the politico-administrative decision-making process, it is necessary to be aware that research is transferred to and becomes part of a discourse of action in a philosophical as well as a more everyday practical sense. In this discourse, self-reflecting participants deliberate on and debate norms and alternatives with a view to concrete action." It is important for academics to understand that in a policy context concrete action is "more a question of discussing and negotiating a practicable plan than the scientifically 'best' one" (Albaek 1995, 94); meaning that "good enough" may be the best possible result.

Fourth, the policymaking process is shaped by the individual participants involved with a specific issue at a given time. Policy outcomes are dependent upon the specific actors and circumstances at a given time and place. Personal contact and an understanding of the actors and circumstances of a specific policy context are vital sources of information for influencing policy.

WAYS OF KNOWING

Per the interactive model, research is one of many ways of knowing that contributes to policymaking. Academics engaging in policy should be aware of other ways of knowing and how they influence policymaking. "While we think that stakeholders should pay particular attention to research findings, we do not want to characterize findings as the only source of legitimate knowledge." Thus, academics should "view research

I often thought about the "4th grade problem" in my time as professional staff and during my political endeavors. The 4th grade problem posits that everyone considers themselves an education expert because they attended the 4th grade (Kaestle 1993). I found that unlike some other policy areas, everyone has a personal experience in education that either involves them or a family member directly, and these experiences are an extremely influential way of knowing. For example, politicians have spent countless hours in schools, but they may have visited hospitals infrequently or they have had only select experiences with the judicial system. Thus, every policy idea is filtered through these singular, personal experiences, and politicians may reject research evidence that contradicts their personal experience. Politicians may reject an evidence-based program because "it didn't work for my kids." Or, they may deny the urgency of a problem because they faced similar challenges "and look at me, I turned out just fine." The challenge when working with politicians is to validate these singular experiences, introduce them to new experiences so they can come to understand the extent to which their experiences may be (a)typical of the broader educational environment, and provide frameworks for politicians to develop heuristics to guide future actions.

findings in the context of other more situated and experiential ways of knowing" (Davies and Nutley 2008, 2).

Among the many ways of knowing, there are eight that are involved with policymaking (language, sense perception, emotion, imagination, faith, intuition, memory, and reason). For our purpose, it is not productive to debate which ways of knowing should count or should not count in a policy context or to debate the advantages and limitations of each one. Here, I point out how each way of knowing is evident in policymaking and the implications of each way of knowing for academics who are engaging in policy (see table 5.1).

LANGUAGE

Politicians prefer to gather evidence through conversations because learning through language (i.e., talking) is expedient for busy politicians (Nelson, Leffler, and Hansen 2009; Wye et al. 2015). They also tend to use speeches or media appearances, rather than written reports, to communicate to

Table 5.1 Ways of knowing, with policy examples

Way of Knowing	Description*	Policy Example
Language	The method of human communication, either spoken or written, consisting of the use of words in a structured and conventional way	Stories to "put a face" on policies and statistics
Sense Perception	Any of the faculties of sight, smell, hearing, taste, and touch, by which the body perceives an external stimulus	Visual displays (e.g. Mothers Against Drunk Driving wrecked car display, large orchestrated gatherings)
Emotion	A strong feeling, such as joy or anger; an instinctive feeling as distinguished from reasoning or knowledge	Passionate testimony
Imagination	The faculty or action of forming new ideas, images, or concepts of external objects not present to the senses	"Aspirational" policies
Faith	Complete trust or confidence in someone or something; a strong belief in the doctrines of a religion, based on spiritual conviction rather than proof	Religious teachings or beliefs
Intuition	The ability to understand something instinctively without the need for conscious reasoning	Affinity connections with *their* people
Memory	Something remembered from the past	Personal educational experiences
Reason	Finding a solution (to a problem) by considering possible options, or through a rational argument	Research evidence

*Source: Dombrowksi, Rotenberg, and Beck, 2013.

others. For academics, the importance of interpersonal communication for politicians translates to engaging with politicians directly. If politicians prefer to learn through conversation, then academics should be prepared to converse with politicians. Academics should also appreciate how politicians and policy actors use language to humanize issues—that is, to "put a face" on issues through stories that connect with others and reinforce the personal implications of policies and statistics. Academics should use the same narrative approach when communicating evidence to politicians. In the translation of research to policymaking, for example, I suggest that facts, figures, and statistics are accompanied with a story (or pictures) to humanize them. The persuasive influence of narratives presents an opportunity for the interjection of qualitative research in education policy. The deep descriptions and themes in qualitative research are an excellent resource for persuasive narratives that politicians could appropriate to put a face on issues to engage constituents.

SENSE PERCEPTION

Many groups and organizations have a "legislative day" when they encourage members to engage with their legislators directly to reinforce key policy positions. The groups and organizations often use visuals, such as having their members wear the same t-shirts, ribbons, or pins, to present a unified front. They may hold a rally. Or, they may bring a memento or trinket to legislators that both reinforces their message and serves as a tangible reminder of their policy issues after they leave. The events can be more dramatic, as in the case of Mothers Against Drunk Driving (MADD), an organization that places a demolished vehicle that was involved in a fatal accident involving a drunk driver at the steps of state capitals. The visual is powerful, captures attention, and provides a common starting point for MADD members to discuss the issue of stricter drunk driving laws with legislators.

The key lesson for academics is to consider how facts, figures, and statistics can be conveyed through visuals, or even audio, in a policy context. Images and sounds *are* worth a thousand words and they should accompany text so that politicians can experience the relationship between the research and real-world policy impact.

EMOTION

Passionate testimony can move politicians. The timely and persuasive testimony of a constituent who has suffered the brunt of a policy can make the case for a policy problem and solution better than research. While testifying before a legislative committee is often too late to influence the outcome because the votes are already counted, at times—albeit, rarely—the passionate testimony of a constituent can be enough for politicians to change course, either delaying the vote so that it does not occur with the affected constituents in the room or switching votes altogether. In these cases, I believe that academics, even those armed with "gold star" evidence acquired through excellent research methods, will have a nearly impossible time discounting or contradicting passionate testimony and the emotional response it can generate among politicians.

IMAGINATION

The purpose of imagination in policymaking is to expand the politicians' perspectives of what is possible. The ideas do not need to be realistic or backed by research evidence to shape the policy discourse. If a politician can sell an idea, it becomes possible, and, if carried out to its logical end, the idea can become policy. Imagination changes the policy discourse because it sets expectations that are difficult to argue against despite research evidence to the contrary or common-sense arguments that the policy outcomes are unlikely or even unattainable. The No Child Left Behind (NCLB) requirement that 100 percent of students demonstrate proficiency is an example of how imagination shaped education policy for a decade. NCLB passed with bipartisan support and included the aspirational provision that each state "shall ensure that not later than 12 years after the end of the 2001–2002 school year, all students . . . will meet or exceed the State's proficient level on academic achievement on the State assessments" (Public Law 107–110, 2002, 178). Academics roundly criticized the standard as unrealistic, yet states placed considerable effort into developing timelines and holding schools accountable (Forte 2010; Fuller et al. 2007). Twelve years after the passage of NCLB, student proficiency rates on National Assessment of Educational Progress (NAEP) remained

I was introduced to "aspirational" policies for the first time during my time at the Arizona state legislature. I noticed a strategy among outside actors to promote policy ideas that were borderline unattainable and/or policies that were prima facie unconstitutional. These outside actors called their ideas "aspirational policies" and the actors held extremely slim expectations (at times no expectations) that the aspirational policies would be enacted. Or, if enacted, there was a clear recognition among staff and experts that the outcomes were unattainable. Surprisingly, a few aspirational policies actually made it through the legislative process and became law. In some cases, legislators intentionally passed aspirational policies to challenge or influence judicial precedent. In other cases, the legislature passed policies that simply did not add up. For example, in an effort to increase instructional time, the legislature allowed school districts to provide 200 days of instructions, while maintaining the school funding allocation based on 180 school days, an untenable proposition that increased school days by 11 percent with a 0 percent increase in funding. The aspiration of increasing instructional time, despite an investment in the resources to carry out the policy, was powerful rhetoric that placed those educators who argued against the policy in the unfavorable position of coming across as complainers who were defending the status quo at the expense of student achievement.

below 50 percent, and were accompanied by criticisms that educators were "gaming the system" to boost test scores, consequences that academics predicted (Nichols and Berliner 2007). The 100 percent proficiency standard was an aspiration. Per one prominent academic, "I think it's safe to say, and we anticipated this early on, that policymakers erred. They turned an aspirational goal that inspires support, into a target for accountability, meant for consequences" (Kamenetz 2014).

FAITH

Religious beliefs are a powerful way of knowing that influence how politicians make policy decisions and the evidence they consider in making those decisions. The connection between a politician's religious beliefs and future policy decisions is foreshadowed early, when the candidate-politician chooses to showcase their religious beliefs (or not) during electoral campaigns.

For academics learning to engage in education policy, the key point is to understand that faith is a foundational way of knowing that involves trust, keeping promises, and accepting assumptions without further questioning. "Faith is acceptance without the justification that is demonstrable or convincing to someone who does not possess the belief. For many people who 'have faith,' little could be so self-evidently right as their own beliefs and the process of accepting them" (Dombrowksi, Rotenberg, and Beck 2013, 173). In policymaking, from my experience, it is impossible to override faith with research evidence. Academics should recognize when politicians base policy decisions on faith and remain flexible in providing evidence from other ways of knowing while refraining from negating the influence of faith-based claims.

The reading wars, a disagreement on whether the best way to teach students to read is through whole language or phonics, sparked contentious debate across the country (Lemann 1997). In Arizona, the debate hit particularly close to home because Ken and Yetta Goodman, two whole language pioneers, were faculty members at the University of Arizona. I was told by a fellow legislative staffer that phonics was preferred by some state senators for religious purposes, because it allowed for an explicit reading of the Bible. At the time, I did not validate this claim with further reading, but it appeared plausible because many of the elected officials whom I encountered were both staunch phonics supporters and religious conservatives. Based on a request from a legislative member, I met with whole-language proponents seeking a balanced approach to literacy where Arizona classrooms would be allowed to use many reading strategies, including whole language. I needed a diplomatic response because among some legislators, allowing options other than phonics could be viewed as "anti-phonics," a charge that would place me among the nonbelievers and damage my credibility. Delicately, I found a way to discuss pedagogical flexibility without negating the legislators' faith-based support for phonics. My approach was to use a toolbox analogy to demonstrate to politicians that students learn in many different ways (often referring to the members' own children as examples) and that teachers need all tools available to them so that each student could "achieve to their full potential" (which is a common pitch among those seeking support for policy decisions). In truth, I am not sure that I convinced any members to change their opinions. But I introduced another perspective, was not thrown out of the room, and members from both parties continued to confide in me.

INTUITION

One common example of intuition is when politicians establish a personal a connection with others that they consider *their* people based on affinity. The connection can be formed based on shared history or experiences, such as coming from the same place or living in similar places, attending the same or similar schools, or membership in the same organizations, as in the case of veterans' groups. This uncommunicated connection provides credibility to the constituents' account of events and lowers the politicians' threshold for evaluating evidence where the phrase "you know" or "you know how it is" becomes sufficient to support an argument.

I have witnessed this phenomenon with politicians from both political parties. I have also witnessed the opposite phenomenon, where politicians and constituent groups clash because they are unable to find commonalities, making communication more cumbersome and, at times, raising the threshold for credible evidence because the constituents were not able to present their case in a manner that was relatable to politicians. Politicians may not naturally count academics among *their* people, creating higher expectations for academics to influence politicians through research. Connecting with politicians *before* they are politicians and connecting with policy actors who are trusted by politicians are both effective methods for building productive affinity relationships.

MEMORY

Personal experiences are an enduring and highly influential way of knowing that shapes education policy at every level. The memories that politicians have about their personal education experiences, even if the experiences are years or even decades old, constitute their most intimate way of knowing about schools and schooling. Every person has personal educational experiences that for them are credible evidence of the state of education even if these experiences are dated. Or, the experiences may be specific to a unique set of circumstances or type of school or community environment. In either case, the experiences may not be reflective of the educational experiences of most students. But memory is a vivid and influential way of knowing that cannot be negated. Consequently, the politician's past educational experiences should be not be discounted.

Academics commonly argue that individual educational experiences are anecdotal and are unreliable as the basis of policy decisions that influence multiple students. Academics joke that when politicians make decisions based on personal experiences, they are making decisions based on an "n of 1" (insert laughter here). Yet, despite the faults and limitations of making decisions based on personal experiences, these experiences are valid ways of knowing. "We need to trust our own experiences because that's the best we have" (Epstein 2011, 17). Academics should expect that policy decisions, at some level, will always be made with some degrees of ordinary knowledge (Lindblom and Cohen 1979).

To understand how politicians' personal educational experiences may shape how they approach policy, one of the first questions I ask politicians is about their "education story." I probe until they have recounted their educational experiences in some detail. From this, I learn a great deal about them personally and the assumptions they may hold about education, schools, and schooling. I listen for experiences with teachers (good and bad), what type of schools they attended (public or private, urban or rural). Their stories often go beyond schools to include descriptions of their family, neighborhood, and personal experiences that shaped their educational path. This expansion beyond formal education as part of their education story is consistent with the holistic nature of education and can provide me with an opportunity to discuss the essential link between home and community factors and student achievement. For academics, it is enlightening to understand when politicians may have had no personal experiences with the types of schools or student populations that are the subjects of their research (e.g., politicians may have never attended an inner-city school or may have never experienced a special education classroom). In these cases, it will be necessary to provide politicians with new, concrete personal experiences to broaden their perspectives and make meaningful connections to your research.

REASON

Of the various ways of knowing, reason is the least experiential. Learning through reason requires an application of abstract information to real-world conditions, arguments as support, and logic to connect the evidence with potential policy solutions. There are two key points about research

My interest in the "education story" of others is what sparked my desire to attend graduate school in education. This interest carried over to my experiences in state policy, and I learned that talking about education stories was an effective way to connect with and learn about politicians. I am often intrigued by the depth and breadth of information politicians reveal when prompted to talk about their education story. They describe their family lives (e.g., parent's education and occupations), influential teachers (both positive and negative), supportive adults (e.g., coaches, neighbors, and so on), transformative experiences (e.g., books, chance encounters), along with information about the schools they attended. I found that these experiences influenced which issues that politicians chose to champion, the type of evidence they found either persuasive or ineffectual, and the groups that they considered to be *their* people.

as a way of knowing through reason that are important for academics to appreciate. First, much of what politicians learn through research they may never experience at all, or, in some cases, they may have had an experience that is counter to the research evidence. For example, there is considerable research evidence to document the achievement gap, defined as the persistent disparity in academic performance between groups of students as defined by race, gender and/or socioeconomic status (Anderson, Medrich, and Fowler 2007). When making a decision about potential policy recommendations, most politicians may have had little to no personal experience with the achievement gap, an understanding of the data used to document the gap, or familiarity with theories to explain it. In these cases, politicians rely on arguments, most often brought to them by others, to frame the real-world problem of the achievement gap and connect it with policy solutions. If politicians are introduced to real-world experiences that conflict the research evidence on the achievement gap, they will need reassurance that the research evidence is applicable, despite experiences to the contrary. I have worked with politicians who, after hearing the story of a low-income, minority student who earns admission to a prestigious university, are quick to discount the entire research evidence on the achievement gap based on the argument that "she made it, so that means all students can make it."

There is a second practical implication—learning through research evidence requires reading, actually reading the research, or at least a summary.

Reading to learn from research evidence requires a substantial commitment of time and energy, a precious commodity for busy politicians. For this reason, the long form of academic articles is not conducive to fast-paced policy contexts and politicians' preference for short and simple documents (Farmer 2010). Academics must be brutally realistic about the amount of time that politicians will dedicate to reading the materials you bring before them. And, in a face-to-face meeting, the amount of time that you can anticipate that politicians will dedicate to reading your research is surprisingly little. My estimate is twenty seconds. Yes, twenty seconds, which is why the research "one-pager," a translation of research to a policy context that is designed to communicate the key policy-relevant details of academic research at a glance (chapter 11), is essential.

SUMMARY

For academics, the interactive process of policymaking can be a messy, uncertain, and humbling experience. For these reasons academics may cling to the enlightenment model and focus on those things that we can control, mainly issues related to research production, such as methodological rigor, and hope that this is a productive path for our research to be useful in policy. As Seashore Louis (2005, 234) has noted, "There is still a prevailing assumption that if our research were sound, or our policy makers intelligent and honest, there would be a more significant relationship, and that the problem, therefore, is 'cleaning up our act' in both of our houses."

Yet, the interactive nature of research use in policymaking also provides the structure to introduce guidelines to make engaging in education policy predictable and manageable. For example, policymaking is local. You do not need to know how all actors engage in a global policy context, only those actors in your context. Also, the ability to recognize the evidence associated with the different ways of knowing will help you decode the types of evidence that politicians find persuasive, and, in later chapters, you will be equipped with strategies to present your research evidence in novel ways. Lastly, now that you recognize that engaging directly with politicians is necessary for facilitating research use and that research evidence is one way of knowing in a policy context, you can "leave your Ph.D. at the door, but not your expertise," to engage with politicians most effectively.

6

ASKED, BROUGHT, INSIDE, OUTSIDE

Politicians have the least control over and least inherent trust in unsolicited research that is brought to them by outsiders. Academics are outsiders who bring unsolicited research to politicians.

The asked/brought/inside/outside (ABIO) framework makes explicit the dynamics facing politicians when information is presented to them, including research from academics. The ABIO framework helps academics understand their position relative to politicians and other actors and enables them to predict how they (and their research) may be viewed by politicians before they walk in the door. Awareness of where you fit in a policy context can set the stage for the acceptance of your research by politicians, while ignorance of it can result in the rejection of your research before you start, regardless of its quality.

A key feature of the ABIO framework is that it is detached from the qualities of the research itself. The academic literature is replete with suggestions for improving the quality of research in an effort to improve the likelihood it will be used in a policy context (Oliver and Cairney 2019). But "good," or even excellent, research alone—that is, research that is methodologically sound or effectively summarized—is no more likely to garner attention in a policy context than research with methods that academics find questionable. Remember, politicians are novices in education research and policy.

In general, they are not trained to assess the methodological quality of research, nor do they have the time or incentives to learn.

When trying to explain why good things happen to bad research there is insufficient attention paid to the dynamics of the local context. Part of the answer to why some research captures politicians' attention and other research does not lies in who delivers the research to the politician, as well as when and how. Context is king. Local dynamics can help explain why research products that are regarded by academics as either low quality or even biased may gain an audience in a policy context. Likewise, local dynamics helps to explain why research that is considered to be "gold star" among academics may land in a policy context with a whimper, making no impact. My argument is that if the academic is an inept actor in a local policy context, then the research product alone, regardless of its quality, may not be persuasive enough to gain policymakers' attention.

The ABIO framework consists of two dimensions. The first is the origin of the inquiry: Did the politician ask for the information? Or was the information brought to the politician? The second is the source of the information: Did someone inside the politician's sphere generate the information? Or, did someone outside the politician's sphere generate the information? The two dimensions yield a quadrant (asked-inside, asked-outside, brought-inside, brought-outside). Within these quadrants, I look at two factors that politicians are likely to consider as they assess information; control and trust. Control refers to the ability of politicians to dictate both the research inquiry and the dissemination of the findings. Trust refers to the degree of inherent confidence that politicians hold in the person or organization presenting the information, including confidence that both the inquiry and the findings will remain private at the politician's request. Once articulated in this graphical manner, the ABIO framework helps academics make better sense of what is often perceived as the haphazard nature of bringing research to politicians.

ORIGIN OF THE INQUIRY

The first consideration is the origin of the inquiry. Did the politician ask for the information? Or, was the information brought to them? Whether the information was asked or brought impacts the degree of control that politicians have to shape the research question and their abilities to manage the nature of the inquiry along with the release of the findings to broader audiences.

ASKED

When politicians initiate the inquiry, they are able to dictate the question, which, in turn, shapes the nature of the answer. Contrary to academic inquiries, political inquiries are rarely open-ended. By dictating the question, politicians can put forth decidedly political questions with decidedly political answers. For example, when looking for policy ideas, politicians often ask for information on policies that "work." In a policy context, such inquiries make common sense. Why should a politician spend time understanding policies that don't work?

To the academic, an inquiry from a politician who seeks information on policies that work can come across as biased or one-sided. The one-sided nature of a research inquiry in a policy context is antithetical to the orientation of academics who are trained to conduct more thorough inquiries that include a treatment of both sides of an issue, a consideration of both intended and unintended outcomes, and policy recommendations that are accompanied by the background research to support them. While open-ended inquiries of this nature are helpful for a detailed understanding of an issue, they are superfluous to the main purpose of political inquires—to take action (Henig 2009). Politicians want information to help them know what actions they should take in their local context. To academics, the politicians' selective inquiries may seem disingenuous, even political, but these one-sided inquiries are a necessity in the time-pressed nature of policy discourse.

When politicians shape the inquiry, they have a profound impact on which research products, academics, and intermediary organizations are considered in the inquiry. In dictating the question, politicians may be biased toward some sources, organizations and people, as being relevant or credible from the outset. When politicians seek evidence and examples of what "works," for example, the inquiry will include those sources that hold a more positive orientation toward the policy in question. The focus on what works is a key reason why the research put forth by intermediary organizations or academics with a track record of supporting particular policies or providing concrete policy proposals may garner more attention from politicians than research that is reactionary, critical, or takes a narrow view of select provisions of a policy. When politicians ask for research through task forces, commissions, or governmental agencies, they still exert control by influencing the scope of the research questions, determining who leads the project or is involved in the research, and when and how the findings are released publicly.

Let's say that a politician is interested in pursuing a school choice policy. They are likely to ask about policies that have worked in other settings. As part of this inquiry, staff are unlikely to conduct a full review of the school choice research, which would be comparable to a literature review, nor will the written report include many examples where school choice resulted in unintended consequences (e.g., increased segregation). The nature of this one-sided inquiry would narrow the range of academics and intermediary organizations that are considered as relevant and credible sources. Pro–school choice organizations such as the Friedman Foundation (Edchoice.com), the National Alliance for Public Charter Schools (publiccharters.org), and the Center for Education Reform (edreform.com) are all likely candidates to be included in the inquiry. Academic journals, however, may be overlooked, not only because they could contain research that is critical of school choice policies but also because they do not usually provide easily accessible information on policies that work. Insofar as academics engage in debunking other research, pointing out the limitations of existing policies, advancing theoretical perspectives, or focusing on outcomes by disaggregated subgroups, their work does not provide a direct answer to which school policies may work in the politician's context.

When politicians initiate the inquiry, they have the most leverage to control what happens with the findings and when. At a practical level, control allows politicians to have influence over workflow. Informational inquiries are part of a larger policy agenda, meaning that politicians have a vested interest in which policy issues are discussed publicly or introduced into the policy sphere, as well as in the timing of the discussions. In cases where the findings are contrary to their publicly held positions, politicians may delay the release of the inquiry until public attention has moved on to other issues, or they or may never release the findings at all, if possible. Even in cases where politicians may agree with or favor research results, they may delay their public release in anticipation of the most opportune political moment to interject the findings into the public discourse. Then, too, when politicians initiate the inquiry, they can have confidence that both the inquiry and the findings will remain private at their request.

If politicians can control the inquiry, they are able to withhold or ignore research which contain findings that complicate the advancement of their policy agenda. A prime example is *A Nation at Risk*, one of the most influential policy reports in the history of US public education (National Commission on Excellence in Education 1983). The report, conducted by President Ronald Reagan's National Commission on Excellent in Education, a group comprised of political appointees, was an effective political and public relations tool. Memorably describing public education as a "rising tide of mediocrity," the report is credited with setting off over three decades of education reforms driven by academic standards and accountability policies. Despite its widespread policy influence, *A Nation at Risk* has been openly criticized by academics as inept and misleading (Besag 1986; Gardner 1984; Berliner and Biddle 1995).

Far fewer people are familiar with the *Sandia Report*, a follow-up to *A Nation at Risk*. The *Sandia Report* was commissioned by Admiral James Watkins, the US Secretary of Energy from 1989 to 1993, and conducted by the Sandia National Laboratories in Albuquerque, New Mexico (Carson, Huelskamp, and Woodall 1993). The report, completed in 1990, used much of the same national achievement data as *A Nation at Risk*, but employed different research methods and arrived at decidedly different conclusions. The *Sandia* findings are a classic example of Simpson's paradox, where trends across several different groups either disappear or are reversed when the groups are combined. For example, while both studies included longitudinal comparisons of Scholastic Assessment Test (SAT) scores, the *Sandia Report* disaggregated the results by race and ethnicity and found that the demographics of test takers had changed over time. From 1975 to 1990, more minority students, students from less affluent households, and students from lower socioeconomic classes took the SAT than in earlier time periods (Carson, Huelskamp, and Woodall 1993; Huelskamp 1993). Thus, the *Sandia Report* demonstrated that overall declines in SAT scores were not necessarily reflective of a decline in the quality of public education; rather, the decline was largely attributable to changes in the population of students taking the SAT (Stedman 1994).

The *Sandia Report* was not met with the same fanfare as *A Nation at Risk*. Upon completion, it was not released publicly, ultimately appearing in full text in a 1993 volume of the *Journal of Educational Research* only after more than 500 requests for the report. The authors themselves described their research as an "outsider" report, and it was suppressed by government officials for apparent political purposes because it presented a view of public education that was contrary to the public positions held by prevailing politicians at the time. In sum, the *Sandia Report* "went into peer review and there died a quiet death" (Ansary 2007). Its suppression has also been described as "a perfect lesson on censorship," and as late as 2015 Sandia Laboratory officials declined to comment publicly on the report (Huelskamp 2015).

BROUGHT

Brought information includes policy reports and academic research from many different external sources including governmental organizations, think tanks, university centers, and individual academics. Brought information consists of completed studies that are planted in front of politicians. Because politicians have little to no control over unsolicited information that is brought to them, they find themselves in a reactionary position. Where the politician did not shape the inquiry, the match between the information presented and the interests of the politician depends on the politician's policy agenda. In addition, it is not possible for politicians to control when and which findings are discussed publicly or whether they would remain private at their request.

Brought research creates practical, logistical challenges for the politician, ones that those who bring research to politicians should appreciate. To begin, the product is complete, meaning that the politician has to accept the full product as is—every last detail. Unlike inquiries in which the politician is able to direct the research question and the final product, brought inquiries are not immediately conducive to a selective reading or acceptance. There is no opportunity to edit the contents to avoid red-flag language or to make them more politically palpable or applicable to a specific local policy context.

More than likely, politicians, or more likely their staff, are reading brought information for the first time along with others, including members of the opposing party, the public, and the media. Politicians are then faced with both understanding the findings and developing a public response—with limited time to do both. In cases where politicians are made aware of negative or contradictory findings at the same time as the media, effective tactical responses include discrediting the source, disqualifying the data, questioning the methodology, or simply ignoring the research. These strategies can make it possible for politicians to withstand the news cycle without commenting on the substance of the findings. Conversely, politicians may laud research findings that support their policy interest without thorough vetting the quality of the underlying research methods.

As an associate professor at Arizona State University I created a data-sharing agreement with the State Board of Education, which included the provision that all research products would be provided to the state board before public release. The state board did not have editorial authority. It could not change any of the content. The privileged access to the contents before public release promoted buy-in among the members of the state board because it gave them some control over how to respond. They were given an opportunity to understand the findings and ask me questions before being approached by the media for comment. I butted heads with some of my university colleagues who objected to this arrangement because they wanted the "gotcha" moment of catching politicians off guard and compelling a response. They wanted to corner politicians or felt that providing the research in advance compromised the perception of it as objective. What my colleagues did not understand was that blindsiding politicians with brought research places them in reactionary mode. During my time as a staffer and associate superintendent, I did not appreciate being placed in such a position by the media. There was no time to understand and comment on the content of a given report. We were in spin mode. At times, our first response was to deflect, ignore, or discredit the report to get through the media cycle.

There are numerous minute details of brought research that could result in a potential disconnect between the findings and a politician's policy agenda and thus lead to the research being ignored or discredited in a policy context. Understanding these dynamics from a politician's perspective is a crucial lesson that is rarely taught to academics before they engage in education policy. If the potential points of disconnect between brought research and the likelihood that politicians will accept the research product seem haphazard, that's because at times, they are.

The most obvious mismatch is when the research findings are inconsistent with the politician's policy position or contradicts their political ideology. Academics are less aware, however, that any minor contradictory detail anywhere in the text could derail the use of research by politicians. For example, a single sentence could repeat a common phrase used by opponents on the other side of the aisle, the review of literature could be framed in a manner that is too critical of their political party discourse, or citing the research of a controversial figure may create conflicts by association for politicians. In cases where any detail in the text creates a troublesome political situation for politicians, impeccable research methods are not enough to provide cover for politicians to associate themselves with the research before their colleagues and the public.

I have experienced instances when politicians ignored a research product because a sentence or reference in the literature review could be taken out of context, and the politician was concerned with associating themselves with the content. I understand that the researchers had written sound literature reviews, which included a summary of both sides of an issue. But as part of a balanced literature review, the content included a critical perspective of policies that some politician favored; it placed these politicians in a conflicting position because they had to accept the full content of brought research as is. Some politicians disregarded the entire research product because sections of the literature reviews were critical of certain policies or quoted some academics with whom they disagreed. Similarly, some politicians promoted highly political research with one-sided literature reviews and questionable methods because the content and findings wholly supported their policy positions with little to no mention of potentially contradictory arguments or findings.

LOCATION OF THE RESEARCHER RELATIVE TO THE POLITICIAN

The second dimension of the ABIO framework refers to the position of the researcher relative to the politician. Is the researcher inside the politician's sphere of influence? Or, is the researcher outside the politician's sphere of influence?

INSIDE

When politicians initiate an inquiry, they tend to call upon trusted individuals within their sphere of influence. The most obvious insiders include legislative staff and agency employees. Politicians have direct control over insiders through hiring and firing, which assures their compliance and confidence. Trusted individuals not employed in a legislative setting also enjoy a special insider relationship with politicians (Hetrick and van Horn 1988). Trusted individuals "may operate within all three realms of the research process, acquiring, interpreting, and applying research" (Nelson, Leffler, and Hansen 2009, 49). Politicians hold indirect control over trusted individuals in the sense that trusted individuals have

> As professional staff, I was dubious of insiders, particularly political appointees, people who worked on campaigns and were then appointed to policy positions. My inexperienced opinion was that policy positions should be occupied by subject-matter experts. Through the course of running two campaigns, I came to better understand why politicians place campaign staff in policy positions. To begin, politicians build trusted relationships with those who campaign with them, and it stands to reason that they would look to these individuals once elected. Campaigns are grueling, filled with tense moments and decisions under pressure. Campaign staff are "fire-tested," meaning that politicians know what to expect from these individuals when times get tough. Also, many people work on campaigns expressly to be included on a politician's policy staff. It's a direct way to influence policy. What I did not realize until running for office myself is the loyalty I would feel to those individuals who invested in me as a candidate and engaged with me on the campaign through the grueling process of getting elected, not after. In good conscience, I would have to look out for those who battled with me on the campaign trail. Contrary to my instincts as an academic, I would have placed some political appointees in policy positions.

a vested interest in maintaining the politician's trust and confidentiality in exchange for access (Kingdon 2003).

OUTSIDE

Everyone not within the politician's sphere of influence is an outsider. This includes academics who are housed in universities or policy organizations.

Politicians do not control the creation or distribution of information generated by those outside their sphere of influence. Politicians must assume that information from outsiders either is or will become public per the outsider's discretion. Thus, politicians do not have the same inherent trust in the confidentiality of outsiders who bring information to them as they have for those insiders within their sphere of influence. Outsiders can communicate with whomever they want about their information, without informing politicians.

Outsiders should expect that the politicians or their staff will "check them out" before granting access (Ostrander 1993) and that they will focus specifically on "whether the researcher's politics are aligned with their own" (Monahan and Fisher 2015, 711). Moreover, given the ubiquity of the internet, profiling outsiders is not that challenging. "What is discovered online can determine whether access will be granted" (Marland and Esselment 2018, 6). This is particularly true for academics who see their role as activists or "movement intellectuals" who expressly "speak truth to power"—and, perchance, may hold contrary views to those of some politicians. Even in cases where an "enlightened" politician is interested in research evidence that challenges their world view or simply seeks a more comprehensive policy perspective than the political position of their party, how much trust can (or should) the politician place in academics who are on public record speaking out with an oppositional view? How should the politician treat research from "activist" academics, understanding that the lack of control over these academics means that neither the inquiry nor the findings may be held in confidence?

When I was appointed as Associate Superintendent of Standards, Assessment, and Accountability for the state of Arizona, I inherited a beleaguered state assessment system. Test scores routinely arrived late, were calculated incorrectly, and were rescinded from publication due to reporting errors. Educators were frustrated with the missteps, the public was losing confidence in the state assessment, and politicians were losing patience. I instituted a quality assurance policy where all assessment scores from the company responsible for calculating the scores would be verified by an outside expert before they were released publicly. I needed an assessment expert to serve as the outside expert. At the time, the Arizona State University College of Education housed two academics with the appropriate expertise, Gene Glass and David Berliner. I respected (and still do) the academic contributions of both and have had a personal relationship with Berliner dating back to his mentorship on my undergraduate honors thesis. Yet, I did not call on either of these outside academic experts to verify the results because both were publicly critical of the state assessment system (and rightfully so) and voiced their opposition in high-profile media outlets, including the local press. I was not confident that I could provide Glass or Berliner with (potentially) problematic assessment scores and be assured that they would not relay the problems to the press. Given that they were tenured academics, I also did not believe that I could secure their confidentiality through a contractual arrangement.

At the time, increased public attention to the problems with the assessment system was not helpful to fixing the issues—and could even hamper these efforts. I created a contractual agreement with a junior professor with psychometric training to verify the assessment results based on the condition that the results were reported back to the Department of Education, and only the Department of Education, with no interaction with the press on his part. In return, he was able to use the assessment data for publication in academic journals. I provided access to an outsider in exchange for control. For academics, this arrangement could raise another question: Why would I be comfortable with the results of a (potentially) problematic state assessment being published in an academic journal and not in other public outlets? I gambled that I would not have to deal with fallout from academic journal articles because the findings would not make their way to local politicians nor would the articles make headlines in the press. I gambled correctly. I was never approached about the findings from any academic articles based on the state assessment data.

PUTTING THE ABIO FRAMEWORK TOGETHER

Figure 6.1 displays four different scenarios based on the impetus of the research inquiry and the location of the person who conducted the work relative to the politician. The figure also includes the main considerations for politicians when using research evidence—control and trust. In addition, each quadrant lists the most common researchers, including academics, who carry out the work and the types of products produced.

	Asked	Brought
Inside	Politicians initiate an inquiry with someone within their sphere of influence (e.g., staff memos). Politicians have total control over the method of distribution and complete trust that the inquiry and the findings will remain confidential.	Politicians are brought information by someone within their sphere of influence (e.g., agency reports). Politicians control the method of distribution, and they can trust that the inquiry and the findings will remain confidential until made public.
Outside	Politicians initiate an inquiry from someone outside their sphere of influence (e.g., commissions, task forces). Politicians exert control by selecting the participants, providing input on the questions, and determining the method of distribution. Politicians have some trust that the inquiry and the findings will remain confidential until made public.	Politicians are brought information from someone outside their sphere of influence (e.g., academic research). Politicians have no control over the method of distribution and no trust that the inquiry and/or the findings will remain confidential.

6.1   Asked, brought, inside, outside (ABIO) framework.

ASKED-INSIDE

Asked-inside research includes the results of inquires that the politician requested from someone within their sphere of influence. These inquiries are the most intimate. Politicians have the most control and the highest level of trust in asked-inside information. The most common example of asked-inside information is when politicians charge professional staff to create policy briefs. The professional staff who are likely to conduct asked-inside inquiries include legislative analysts, assistants, and trusted individuals. Politicians have confidence in them and likely see them as "experts," even junior staffers who are themselves newcomers in the field but are often tasked with research assignments even though they are not qualified as researchers (Apollonio and Bero 2017). Asked-inside information will find an audience with politicians and is also more likely to be trusted by them than any other type of information.

Asked-inside inquiries are the most intimate because politicians are afforded the space to ask questions as they see fit. While asked-inside inquiries may be openly political, they are also one of the few opportunities for politicians to consider new ideas in a repercussion-free setting. If most politicians are novices who are learning the intricacies of education research and policy, asked-inside inquiries are one opportunity for them to ask "dumb" questions and be assured that their inquiry will not be made public There is no expectation that the results of asked-inside inquiries will be delivered to anyone besides the politician, and no expectation that politicians distribute the findings beyond their own network.

As a legislative staffer, I learned the value of asked-inside inquiries as confidential space. Once I earned the trust of legislators from both political parties, they often called me behind closed doors to ask a number of "dumb" questions about education, such as "Why do teachers have a problem with standardized tests?" and "Why don't low-income students learn as well?" While taken aback at first—after all, the same individuals asking these questions were responsible for setting education policy in my state—I came to realize that these politicians asked basic questions because they were not trained in education research or policy and had never been exposed to these issues. For these education research and policy novices, dumb questions were essentially developmental questions.

Asked-inside inquiries rarely involve original or empirical research, mainly because professional staff lack the expertise and resources to conduct such work. Most asked-inside inquiries consist of policy briefs or memos produced by staff who search the existing research to meet politicians' requests. Generally, professional staff are given the discretion to dictate the parameters of the search process, determining which academics and resources are included in the search and which are excluded. Professional staff may approach trusted individuals, think tanks, university centers, and lobbyists directly for assistance.

Outsiders, including academics, are aware of the trusting relationship between politicians and legislative staff and understand that staff are the conduit to politicians. That is, legislative staff are largely responsible for the "flow of social science information into the policy-making process" (Sundquist 1978, 131). Academics thus prepare short summaries of their research for legislative staff on the hope that the staff will take the document to politicians, taking advantage of the privileges of asked-inside research. This can be an effective strategy because legislative staff can hold more credibility with politicians than even the most accomplished academic expert and an endorsement of the academic's research by legislative staff will likely be received well by politicians.

ASKED-OUTSIDE

Asked-outside research includes inquiries that are carried out by someone outside the politician's sphere of influence at the politician's request. Asked-outside inquiries are often conducted by consultants, governmental agencies, or task forces and commissions. This quadrant is a potentially productive space for academics because asked-outside inquiries often involve original or empirical research. Politicians benefit from the public perception that research conducted by those outside their sphere is objective, rather than being politically motivated.

Politicians have some control over asked-outside inquiries because they can shape the question and select which experts are selected to conduct the research. For example, in the case of a commissioned task force, politicians can help establish the general parameters of the research questions, leaving the methodology to the content experts.

The initiation of the research inquiry and the release of the final report are likely to be public. Politicians may get a preview of the report in advance but most likely politicians do not have editorial authority over the content. Still, politicians may be able to control how and when the report is made public. For reports that politicians wish to highlight, they can hold a public forum or present the findings in an influential committee. In other cases where the findings are problematic, politicians may either delay or downplay the public release.

Invited testimony before a legislative committee is an example of an asked-outside inquiry. In these cases, politicians rely on outside experts to provide support, or "cover," for their policy positions. In some respects, invited testimony is as "political" as politically motivated research inquiries. Politicians invite experts with evidence to support their policy position to testify before committees.

What academics may not appreciate is that once an issue has been brought before committee, the time for deliberation is essentially over and invited testimony has a negligible impact on voting outcomes. The amendments are written before the hearing, the votes are counted, and the outcomes are effectively assured. Otherwise, the bill would not be presented in a public committee. In rare cases, such as when a constituent

In spring 2018, Arizona was the site of one of the largest teacher-led demonstrations in the country. Over 75,000 educators walked out of their classrooms, marched on the state capital to demand increased investment in public education, and packed legislative hearings until the budget was passed. For many educators, this was their first experience with politicians and the policymaking process and, judging by their social media posts, some were appalled to witness their elected officials playing online card games or surfing the web while teachers, parents, and even students testified before them. I witnessed such behavior during my time at the legislature often. What the educators did not realize is that the final committee votes were determined before the constituents testified before the committee. Not even the presence of thousands of educators clad in red t-shirts and chanting in the committee chambers would alter the final votes. At the end of the budget process, despite an impressive protest, Arizona educators received little more than what the governor committed to at the beginning of the budget process (Staff 2019).

unexpectedly provides emotional testimony that creates consternation among politicians, the vote may be delayed, or the outcome changed. I have never witnessed a situation where research evidence presented before committee was compelling enough to alter the outcome.

BROUGHT-INSIDE

The most common examples of brought-inside inquiries are reports conducted by state or federal agencies, often in the course of their required duties. Unlike asked-inside inquiries, these reports are commonly mandated by law or rule, conducted on a regular basis, and completed by agencies that are at least indirectly accountable to politicians. The researchers are likely public employees and may serve at the pleasure of an agency head who has been appointed by politicians. Thus, politicians can anticipate a certain level of control over brought-inside reports and can trust that the findings will remain confidential at the politician's request.

At the federal level, examples of brought-inside research include the reports and databases provided by the National Center for Education Statistics (NCES). The NCES "fulfills a Congressional mandate to collect, collate, analyze, and report complete statistics on the condition of American education; conduct and publish reports; and review and report on education activities internationally" (National Center for Education Statistics n.d.). At the state level, examples of brought-inside reports include annual dropout, graduation, and student count reports required by state law and carried out by state education agencies. There are few academics who operate in this quadrant because government agencies often conduct this research with in-house staff. The products are most often descriptive in nature, involving an accounting of services provided, programmatic outcomes, and descriptive statistics. The structure of brought-inside reports is generally void of the theoretical discussions and connections to the broader literature that are common in academic research.

Politicians can either mitigate or magnify the impact of brought-inside reports by controlling their distribution. Politicians can wait for a critical moment to pass before releasing a report or they can release the report during a dead period when they can anticipate less media coverage (e.g., Friday afternoons). Similarly, politicians can amplify the report by holding a press conference or issuing a press release for reports that they favor.

BROUGHT-OUTSIDE

When politicians do not initiate the inquiry and the product is brought to them anyway, it is brought-outside information. In this case, the politician does not shape the inquiry. Rather, the products are brought to them by someone from outside their sphere of influence. The politician has no control over the distribution of the information and no expectations of confidentiality. Politicians tend to trust brought-outside information and those who bring it the least. It is also the type of research most easily ignored by politicians because it is not necessarily part of their policy agenda. "Outside expertise that could challenge the power base of dominant actors is not welcome. It is easily discounted as irrelevant" (Marshall, Mitchell, and Wirt 1985, 107).

Academic research is brought-outside information. From a politician's perspective, research published in peer-reviewed academic journals and academic conference proceedings are brought-outside research. Likewise, nearly all of the research from policy centers and think tanks is brought-outside research.

Getting politicians' attention is the primarily challenge facing academics who conduct research and who aspire for their work to inform policymaking. Publishing in academic journals is not enough to garner political attention because few politicians read academic journals. Likewise, the presentation of results at an academic conference, almost always void of politicians, is too far removed from a policy context to garner political attention.

Commonly academics package their research in formats that they believe are more conducive to policymaking, most often summarizing their research in shortened formats or memos, with gatekeepers, such as legislative staff or school district administrators, as the intended audience bring the research before politicians. The content and effectiveness of research summaries have received some academic attention (Caird et al. 2015), but if such reviews follow the traditional structure of academic articles, they are not likely to be conducive to policymaking contexts. Shortened versions of academic research in the form of one-pagers or memos, while more accessible to lay readers, often suffer from the same barriers as academic articles. In other words, if politicians do not find the long form of academic research approachable and applicable to policymaking, then they are unlikely to find a shortened version any more approachable or applicable to policymaking. The research one-pager is the more policy-conducive format.

Connecting with outside research brokers, such as foundations, philanthropies, and intermediary organizations can be an effective strategy to for bringing research to politicians. The influence of this growing list of new policy actors at the state and national level is rising (Scott, Lubienski, and DeBray 2009; Ness and Gándara 2014). These organizations reach politicians by creating an "echo chamber" that promotes a select group of studies through repeated references and citations. While generally not conducting primary research themselves, intermediaries "sell" their preferred research evidence to politicians by positioning themselves "between research production and consumption in order to gather and then distribute evidence to support policymaking agendas" (Scott et al. 2014, 77).

Academics may also turn to the media as research brokers, but doing so is not likely to generate external pressure to compel politicians to respond to their findings. Even if the academic believes that they have an exceptional research product or what Henig (2009) refers to as a "killer" study, described as research with "strong data, such a strong design, such a clear and meaningful theoretical basis that it leads even a skeptical audience to conclude, 'well, now we've settled that" (Henig 2009, 145). Yet, such a study is highly unlikely to address the extent to which education policies "work" (Hess 2008). If the academic wants to make the media aware of their research, they will have to compete with the inundation of stories before the media at any time. Commonly, sophisticated communication apparatuses to conduct activities, such as social media campaigns and distributing press releases, are beneficial to garner the media's attention, a resource available in some larger intermediary organizations but rarely at the disposal of the lone academic. In short, generating external pressure on politicians through the media is a tall order for academics. There are strategies, however, that academics can employ themselves to capture the media's attention, such as enlisting the support of unexpected allies to advocate for their research (chapter 8).

TWO BROUGHT-OUTSIDE SCENARIOS

In this section, I examine brought-outside research in more detail because the preponderance of academic research occupies this space and because academics can benefit from learning more about how to maneuver from their position as outsiders. To this end, I analyze two brought-outside scenarios: when brought-outside research is used to critique brought-outside research and when brought-outside research is used to debunk asked-inside information.

BROUGHT-OUTSIDE RESEARCH TO CRITIQUE
BROUGHT-OUTSIDE RESEARCH

When academics criticize each other's research, these actions are brought-outside research critiquing other brought-outside research. To politicians, these critiques amount to academic squabbles, which may be important in academic circles and can yield prolific publication records that build academic careers, but they are too far removed from the policy context to influence policymaking in any meaningful way. From a political perspective, when brought-outside research is used to critique brought-outside research, those engaged in the controversy are essentially eating their own. The blow-by-blow academic points and counterpoints occur with little practical impact on policy. There is no need for politicians to get involved in academic squabbles, assuming that politicians are aware that the squabbles are happening in the first place. Academics are left to slug out methodological and theoretical differences in the confines of academic journals and conferences.

For example, the controversy over the academic achievement of charter schools compared to traditional public schools provided the context for a high-profile academic squabble. In August 2004, the American Federation of Teachers (AFT) released an analysis of National Assessment of Educational Progress (NAEP) results showing that the test scores of charter school students overall were lower than the test scores for students enrolled in traditional public schools. The AFT results were published in the *New York Times* under the headline, "Nation's Charter Schools Lagging Behind, U.S. Test Scores Reveal" (Schemo 2004). Charter school proponents took exception with the AFT report and what they perceived as uncritical reporting by the *New York Times*. In an unconventional response for academics, a group of social scientists representing themselves as "members of the research community" signed on to a full-page advertisement in the *New York Times* to condemn the AFT report and the *New York Times* itself stating that "the study in question does not meet current professional standards. As a result, it tells us nothing about whether charter schools are succeeding" (Howell, Peterson, and West 2004). The advertisement was sponsored by the Center for Education Reform, a pro–school choice organization.

The events surrounding the release of the AFT report and the subsequent response drew academics into the charter school debate in a manner that politicized research and elicited a public critique of those academics involved (Carnoy et al. 2005). In *Spin Cycle: How Research Is Used in Policy Debates: The Case of Charter Schools*, Jeffrey Henig (2008a) chronicles the unflattering history of the public academic squabbles leading up to the AFT/*Times* article to demonstrate how the lack of decorum in these debates threatens to tarnish the public perception of both research and academics. The feuds were replete with name calling and personal attacks as academics engaged in what was described as a "nerdy Celebrity Death Match." As Henig (2008b, 47) notes "If the face of educational policy research is one of personalization, polarization and partisanship, the loss of authority and fueling of skepticism toward social science research may be further fed and its potential contribution to democratic discourse diminished as a direct result." Ironically, while "the public face of charter school research [was] not a pretty one" (Henig 2008a, 90) at the time of the AFT/*Times* controversy, away from the public spotlight, the research community was forging a collective understanding about charter schools.

Some have suggested a "peak journal" similar to ones found in other fields, such as health and medicine, which provides nonacademics, such as journalists and politicians, with the highest quality peer-reviewed research available (Henig 2009). A peak journal would delegate the vetting process to academics, allowing them to determine which articles are ultimately identified as the "best of the best" or "gold star" research in education, understanding that some believe that peer reviews do not necessarily guarantee quality research (Jerrim and De Vries 2017).

From the perspective of politicians, the research in a peak journal is still brought-outside information. Once the most appropriate research methods or approaches are identified through the back channels of academic discourse, the connection between the prevailing gold star research and any specific local policy remains as tenuous as any other brought-outside information that did not go through the vetting process. Superlative methodology alone will not be enough to garner political attention. To influence policy, even the "best" research must get to politicians, who, assuming they are persuaded by the prestige of research vetted through a peak journal, may not champion research that could distract from their policy agenda. Given the localized and interpersonal nature of engaging in education policy, someone must still engage with politicians to translate gold star research into local policy contexts.

BROUGHT-OUTSIDE RESEARCH TO DEBUNK
ASKED-INSIDE INFORMATION

The bulk of this book is dedicated to the lack of research usage in policy, but on occasion the misuse of research can take hold and spread through policy contexts—an understandable frustration to academics. For example, Richard Ingersoll's (1995, 1996) research on out-of-field teaching, when teachers teach outside their subject areas, captured national media attention, was cited by President Bill Clinton, and was used to inform educational policies at the national and state levels, including No Child Left Behind. Some, however, including politicians have taken Ingersoll's research as demonstrating deficiencies in teacher preparation and problems with teacher shortages—interpretations that Ingersoll contends are inconsistent with the data. To correct the record, Ingersoll (2008, 118) has spent "much time over the past decade writing and speaking, trying to counter these misrepresentations and to develop, test, and disseminate alternative interpretations of the data."

In instances where research is misused, the most likely scenario is not that just politicians got it wrong, rather, staff also got it wrong. Astute academics who are using this book to guide their engagement in policy-making should know that the path to setting the record straight with politicians goes through direct engagement with politicians or with professional staff, not through engagement with other academics. One-sided modes of communication to set the record straight, such as publishing in academic journals, discussing the issue in academic settings, or posting on academic websites, are highly unlikely to reach politicians.

Moreover, when outsiders seek to debunk asked-inside information provided by staff, they are working against the trusted relationship between politicians and those inside their spheres of influence. In these cases, control and trust beat expertise and credibility. The trusted legislative staffer, even a junior staffer, likely has more influence with politicians than the most senior scholar in the field. In response, academics should leverage their expertise to get ahead of legislative insiders instead of attempting to correct or contradict them. They should predict the likely outcomes of misinterpreting their research and should alert politicians or others accordingly. If academics' predictions come to pass, then they have not only provided politicians with the tools to control undesirable outcomes, but also proven themselves as valuable assets for future policy deliberations.

In 1999, I marveled as an unassuming and affable agriculture professor from the University of Tennessee who charmed Arizona politicians with his description of the merits of the Tennessee Value-Added Assessment System (TVAAS) in school accountability systems (Sanders and Horn 1998). William Sanders got face-to-face with state politicians to explain his complex statistical methods in simple (but not dumbed-down) terms. While not one politician understood the statistical procedures of Sander's model, TVAAS provided them with a concrete policy response to educators' criticisms that the exclusive use of absolute test scores in school accountability systems failed to recognize student academic growth. While academics were expressing their skepticism of Sander's methodology in scholarly outlets (Bracey 2004), as brought-outside research, the academic critiques failed to resonate with or even reach politicians. Criticism lobbed from a distance was not enough to overcome Sander's in-person, persuasive arguments. At the time, I, was a graduate student serving as professional staff within politicians' spheres of influence. From this trusted position close to politicians, I was able to dissuade them from implementing TVAAS at the time.

SUMMARY

Academics are outside the policymaking process, and when they walk in the politician's door with brought-outside research, they should conduct themselves with a full understanding of their outsider position in a policy context. Politicians have no control over outsiders in a fast-paced, high-pressure environment where they seek some level of control to manage workflow. Politicians have little trust that the inquiry or findings will remain confidential. The outsider academic is competing with other actors, both insiders and outsiders, who are also seeking to influence policy and who may have done the groundwork to establish a trusted relationship with politicians. If you are unaware of these interpersonal dynamics, your research may well be dismissed, regardless of its quality. On the other hand, an appreciation of these dynamics points to two logical paths forward: academics should do the groundwork to create trusted relationships with politicians and learn to operate effectively as outsiders.

II

LEARNING THE CRAFT

7

BUILD RELATIONSHIPS WITH POLITICIANS *BEFORE* THEY ARE POLITICIANS

The most opportune time to build trusted relationships with politicians is before they get elected, not after.

Trusted individuals are important influencers in policymaking. Politicians lean on

trusted individuals as credible and objective sources of information to acquire, interpret, and apply research. In the acquisition stage, trusted individuals are the ones decision-makers go to first, when time is of the essence, or when they want to know the most important or most applicable research for their needs. In the interpretation stage, trusted individuals assist in processing, interpreting and translating the research into practical, understandable terms for consideration. In the application stage, trusted individuals often speak from experience, not in research settings, but in what are considered to be "real-life" situations and contexts. They help with the practical application of research into practice. (Nelson, Leffler, and Hansen 2009, 49)

In many instances, trusted individuals operate outside the formal policymaking process.

The most straightforward advice for an academic to become a trusted individual is to engage with politicians directly. Nearly all of the suggestions in the research literature are directed toward engaging with politicians *after* they have been elected to establish a relationship.

While connecting with politicians directly makes sense, there are many shortcomings with this approach. Academics are outsiders and must be aware of the fact when bringing research to politicians. Politicians are most skeptical of outsiders, particularly if the outsider is bringing them contrarian, complex, or controversial ideas. In addition, when approaching a politician, academics are working in a crowded space and competing with many other policy actors who are also bringing information to politicians, including lobbyists and intermediary organizations. Then, too, academics can expect politicians to operate with half-knowledge, sifting through excess information to cull what they need to know to take action.

I propose a different approach. To build trusted relationships, academics should connect with politicians *before* they become politicians. To accomplish this goal, academics must get out of the comfort of their educational settings and get selectively involved with the local, nonacademic community organizations where politicians come from.

THE IMPORTANCE OF INTERPERSONAL RELATIONSHIPS

One of the most consistent findings in the research utilization literature is that interpersonal connections are key to building relationships with politicians. There is widespread recognition that "policy and practice occur within social systems—webs of relationships and interactions with peers and intermediaries. It is not surprising, then, that relationships are important pathways by which policymakers and practitioners acquire, interpret, and use research. . . . Trust is key" (Tseng 2012, 7). This advice is so robust, that it should allay any academic's aversion to interacting with politicians.

Interacting with politicians may be new to many academics. As students, academics likely had few opportunities to interact with politicians directly as part of their training, particularly politicians who do not share their political views. There are few professional incentives and many unseen pitfalls associated with interacting with politicians. And if they choose to do so, many academics may simply not know how and where to get started.

Thus, academics are much more comfortable communicating from a distance, releasing policy briefs intended to reach politicians through research centers. Or, posting their thoughts on a blog with the hope that someone in a position of authority (i.e., a politician) will read the content and use it. These communication methods are not replacements for interpersonal connections. The advice to build relationships with politicians directly holds up even in the social media era. The explosion of social media platforms and their prevalent use among politicians have certainly opened up new venues for communication in policymaking, which can supplement but do not replace direct communication. Social media is most conducive to raising awareness, networking, and community building (Figenschou and Fredheim 2020; Online Publishers 2021), all of which amount to indirect lobbying efforts that may or may not reach the intended politicians. Social media is less effective in direct lobbying, which goes straight to politicians and/or their staffs (Arifon and Vanderbiest 2016; Pugliese Associates n.d.; Yorkshire Medical Marketing 2019). Social media cannot substitute for interpersonal interactions because it is conducted at arms-length and because it is often a one-way method of communication. These circumstances make social media insufficient for building trusted relationships. Lastly, social media does not lend itself to communicating the type of detailed information necessary for politicians and professional staff to create policy. This level of detail is best communicated directly (see figure 7.1).

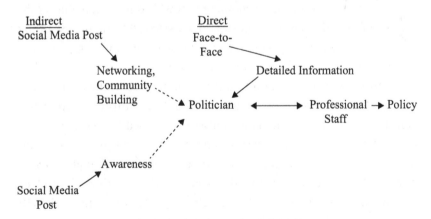

7.1 Social media in indirect lobbying and face-to-face interactions in direct lobbying.

WHY CONNECT WITH PROSPECTIVE POLITICIANS?

There is little to no focus on prospective politicians in the academic literature presumably because these individuals are not politicians (yet). Tomorrow's politicians, however, are members of the general public, laypersons who are involved in their local communities today, and whom, either politicians may appoint to serve in public roles, such as ad-hoc task forces, commissions, and boards, or who are interested in or are running for office themselves.

Prospective politicians are a productive group for academics to approach to influence policy agendas. If members of the local community are considering a run for office, then the time *before* they become politicians (preferably before they become candidates) is fruitful to influence the development of their policy agenda through research. "Academics can best influence policy in the quieter years *before* government, when politicians are formulating their broader policy visions, rather than *during* government when any academic contributions risk being seen as entirely expedient" (Evans 2013). Prior to becoming candidates, prospective politicians spend time, sometimes years, "gearing up" to run for office, during which time they are developing their policy agendas and, given that they are likely education research and policy novices, are inclined to engage with new ideas. Also, they are yet to enter the media spotlight that will come with political campaigns and elected office. They are not only free to meet with diverse people and listen to diverse perspectives, they may be inclined to engage in such activities to develop relationships of their own.

The time before someone announces a run for public office is the quiet time, and it is the most opportune for building a trusted relationship. During the campaign candidates can become closed to new ideas. Candidates have established a message and are in the business of reinforcing that message whenever possible. After getting elected, politicians are inundated with many new "friends" who are vying for access. If academics approach politicians after they are elected, they will compete directly with a host of others for politicians' time and attention.

When I first began considering a run for public office, I set up a meeting with a friend who was a locally elected official. One of his first questions to me was "What are you running for?" He knew that I was considering a run for office, even before I broached the topic with him. The same was true when I sat down with a lobbyist friend. Both friends assumed that I was considering a run for office because I had engaged in some activities that "people always do" when they are gearing up for office. The prior year, I participated in a leadership-training group that had the expressed purpose of preparing people for local and state office. I had begun to expand my public profile by writing op-eds and accepting more speaking engagements with community groups. I started to attend local political meetings to learn more about how the party structure worked. I began to connect my research to prescriptive policy solutions in public settings. The combination of these actions alerted my friends to my political ambitions. The suggestion to connect with politicians *before* they are politicians is intended to take advantage of the actions that "people always do" when gearing up to run for office.

WHERE TO FIND PROSPECTIVE POLITICIANS

Politicians routinely come from a variety of organizations that can be found in communities across the country. Academics should connect with these organizations in their community as part of a strategy to influence policy. On their face, these are not (necessarily) education organizations. But education is a universal policy issue of interest to many. All of these organizations will likely have an interest in some aspect of education. The organizations include

- chambers of commerce
- rotary clubs or other civic service groups
- neighborhood groups
- leadership training programs
- nonprofit organizations
- political groups
- candidate trainings
- professional or trade gatherings and associations
- legislative interim study groups.

Practically speaking, you should attend the meetings for these organizations to get acquainted with the attendees. Look out for attendees who you may recognize from other public settings, who may have written recent op-eds, or are particularly active on social media. These behaviors are indications that they may be raising their public profile, a common precursor to running for office. Pay attention to attendees who are attending meetings across multiple organizations, an indication that they may be building their networks.

Also, learn about which issues are of interest to the attendees. When you are ready, volunteer to speak on education policy issues of interest to the attendees. Or, if the attendees' interests are not related to your research directly, use your interactions with them to develop a connection to your research. In this sense, convincing these organizations to allow you to speak on your research will help you learn to create public interest in your work.

When your research has piqued the interest of an attendee, they are likely to approach you. Take this opportunity to exchange contact information. Or, take the initiative to introduce yourself and exchange contact information with those attendees who are particularly vocal, are in leadership positions, or who take a particular interest in education. Set up a meeting with everyone with whom you exchange contact information.

The goal is to get a one-on-one meeting with attendees. Often, in a one-on-one setting is when you learn of their political ambitions and their ideas about education policy. This a golden opportunity to build a trusted relationship with attendees and to influence the ideas that may constitute their policy agendas in the future.

At this point, you may be thinking, is this strategy worth my time? Connecting with politicians *before* they become politicians appears like a roundabout way to create relationships and influence policy. True. You will speak to many, many people, most of whom will not become politicians or appointees. There is no guarantee that this strategy, or any other strategy for that matter, will pay dividends. In this sense, academics are no different from other policy actors who are seeking to create connections with prospective politicians—connections that they hope prove fruitful someday. This strategy is targeted; however, your time is concentrated in those organizations where politicians are likely to come from.

Effectively, there are two major reasons to invest time in the strategy of engaging with politicians *before* they are politicians. First, the attendees

During the time when I was considering and preparing a run for office is when I looked to meet new people and was most welcome to new information to help me develop my policy agenda, particularly in the areas where I was a novice. In my run for governor, I had little to no policy experience in areas such as healthcare and energy. I arranged meetings with both old and new associates so that I could "learn what I needed to know" about these issues. Research methods were eliminated from these conversations. I assumed that, as experts in their field, the associates would bring forward credible research. I also had little patience for a literature review on these issues and I was not interested in historical perspectives that did not connect directly to addressing current-day practical problems. I wanted to know how the research applied to Arizona now and in the future. I was focused on what would happen next so that I could take action accordingly. I valued those who simplified the issues and not only taught me about policy but also helped me develop my ideas so that I could communicate with general audiences in the areas that were new to me.

may have connections with politicians and could serve as unexpected allies (chapter 8). If involved community members can get to know academics and learn from them, they may be inclined to pass along their research to others in their networks, including politicians. When the attendees bring your research to others in their networks, its potential influence is amplified.

Second, academics don't need relationships with many politicians to have an impact. A trusted relationship with a single influential politician can be sufficient to move their research forward and influence policy. For example, in 2006, my students and I organized an American Education Research Association session on bringing research to politicians and invited an influential lobbyist to speak. She was highly influential in Arizona education policy and she said that she worked through five relationships to make things happen. Five relationships. Her goal was to maintain these relationships and to predict who would be the future five whom she would need to know. She told the group that she agreed to participate in the seminar, without compensation, because one day her goodwill may pay dividends. She felt that I could be one of the five people in the future. At the time, I was a junior scholar with my head down writing for tenure; I had not considered a run for office. She obviously thought otherwise.

WHAT DO YOU DO AFTER YOU HAVE CONNECTED
WITH PROSPECTIVE POLITICIANS?

Teach. You have research to share that is of interest to the public—teach it. Begin with a practical problem that addresses real-world problems of consequence in peoples' lives as a segue to your research and eventually to the ask, even in group settings (chapter 10). Communicate frameworks that allow lay persons to understand policy problems for the purpose of narrowing the set of possible actions to address the problems. Showcase your expertise and value to policymaking by predicting likely policy outcomes. Through this process, you are building credibility as a policy expert. You are molding your public profile to put yourself in a position to be regarded as a knowledgeable and trusted individual.

8

THE INFLUENCE OF
UNEXPECTED ALLIES

Your research is likely to stand out if brought to politicians by unexpected allies.

Research dissemination is most effective when communicated through multiple sources. As Kirst (2000, 384) counsels, "Single channels, like single sources, prove ineffective for the dissemination of social science knowledge intended for policymakers, so the ideal dissemination strategy provides distinctive messages through multiple channels." Furthermore, Kirst (2000, 384) suggests that "the most effective formal and informal dissemination channels are the natural networks comprised of leaders and practitioners in the relevant social policy area." The networks Kirst refers to are also known as "issue networks" (Helco 1978), which in a policy setting are comprised of individuals, advocacy groups, and organizations that share interest in and are oriented toward a common policy issue. Sabatier (1988) extended the idea into a conceptual framework of policy change based on subsystems composed of issue networks, particularly advocacy organizations.

I agree with Kirst on both accounts. It is sound advice that politicians hear about your research from multiple channels. The more the better. And, issue networks are natural allies to disseminate your research. Issue networks will "get" your research and are inclined to bring it forward via their established channels. Academics should engage with issue networks because they are likely to find agreement with others about the importance of an issue, a shared appreciation for research, and an orientation toward policy solutions that are consistent with academics' recommendations.

Learning about your research through an affiliated issue network or advocacy organization, however, is also exactly what politicians expect.

While more communication channels are better, more of the same has limited utility over time. If your research is communicated to politicians solely through issue networks, it is likely to have marginal impact. This muted response is not based on the quality of the research nor the credibility of the issue network. It's due to repetition of message. Issue networks have likely communicated the same message through the same channels to the same politicians for some time. If brought into a policy context via an issue network, your research rings familiar in the chorus of information that issue networks communicate to politicians. Thus, it becomes more difficult for your research to stand out.

For example, issue networks that support teachers in policy settings pursue some common issues as part of their legislative agendas (e.g., class size, pay, professional autonomy). When members of these issue networks introduce research into a policy context, politicians can predict that the research addresses one of the issues on their legislative agenda. Politicians can also predict that the research puts the issue in a favorable light according to the networks' legislative interests. If your research is introduced via an issue network, this historical context influences how it is received. Your research may garner less attention than you hoped because politicians can generally predict the contents precisely because it was brought forward by issue networks that have brought forward similar research in the past to support their preferred policy issues.

Repetition of message makes it predictable. Issue networks advance similar policy positions from one legislative session to the next, touting the same types of studies (particularly those that put their policy issues in the best light) and making much the same arguments to support their policy positions. As a result of repetition, issue networks settle into predictable roles over time. An issue network of education-related organizations comes to be known as the "education community," and another network of business organizations comes to be known as the "business community." Similarly, their collective responses to policy come to be regarded by politicians as the positions of the education and business "communities," respectively. From one legislative session to the next, the policy positions of the respective communities remain generally consistent.

For academics seeking to influence policy through research, communicating via the usual suspects of affiliated issue networks may mute the impact of their research. It is safe to assume that your research is sufficiently aligned with the issue network's policy positions for them to bring it forward. Thus, your research becomes a refrain in a repetitive message, reinforcing the predictability of issue networks and their roles in a local policy context.

ACADEMICS SHOULD ENLIST UNEXPECTED ALLIES

When politicians learn about your research from unexpected allies, they are more likely to pay attention to your work. Unexpected allies are people or organizations outside the issue network for a particular issue that are willing to bring your research to others, especially politicians. For example, a real estate developer who is a member of the business community, who brings research on special education to politicians, is an unexpected ally because the research likely falls outside the developer's usual legislative interests. The more times that politicians hear about your research from unexpected allies, the more the findings are reinforced. The broader or more unexpected the allies, the more likely more your findings will stand out and garner political attention. For example, the developer bringing research on racial segregation in schools is certainly unexpected and would surely stand out.

There are two logistical advantages to connecting with unexpected allies. First, their contacts and networks are distinct from those involved in an issue network. Unexpected allies have connections with other unexpected allies, who together may provide new and unique channels to communicate research with politicians. Second, academics can learn to hone the presentation of their research when they explain it to unexpected allies. Unexpected allies are likely education research and policy novices, like politicians. How unexpected allies understand and interpret your research is an excellent test case for how politicians may approach your research.

Over multiple sessions, groups of policy actors bring the same message time after time. As a legislative staffer, when one of the usual suspects brought me new research, I glanced at it but rarely (if ever) read it because I had a strong indication of the contents. The research supported their policy positions; otherwise, they would not have brought it to me. I gave the same cursory treatment to reports from vendors who brought evidence to demonstrate the effectiveness of their products or members of think tanks who brought a new study to support their preferred policies. In a pressure-packed policy context, the documents were rarely new information, and I had little time to spend on repetitive messaging.

Every once in a while, though, unexpected allies would engage in a policy issue that was outside their usual legislative interests. For example, when someone from a housing organization took an interest in an education issue, it turned heads and opened doors. Politicians took notice. As a staffer, I took notice. The information delivered via an unexpected ally was given more careful consideration because the cadence of the legislative rhythm was interrupted.

Politicians also paid attention because unexpected allies signaled something of political interest: the potential formation of a new coalition. Why would a person from a housing organization take the time and expend the political capital to discuss an education issue that is outside their legislative interests? There are both threats and new possibilities in new coalitions. On the rare occasions when an unexpected ally engaged on an education issue, the politician followed up or I followed up to learn more.

UNEXPECTED ALLIES AS A TEST OF PUBLIC INTEREST

Academics believe that their research is of public interest. This belief is affirmed in academic echo chambers such as conferences and journals that are largely comprised of *our* people, other academics or those with an invested interest in similar research and policy issues where academics reassure each other that they are doing "important work." Collectively, academic echo chambers may have a lower, and even distorted, threshold of what topics are of interest to the public. I am not questioning the importance of the work. I am questioning its interest to the public, an important consideration because politicians are members of the public who won an election.

The enlistment of unexpected allies is a stringent test of whether there is public interest in your research. If your research is of public interest, then you should be able to convince someone outside of academia or outside a related issue network to bring it to their networks.

This is a stringent test because there is a cost to unexpected allies when they bring your research to their networks. To begin, unexpected allies must take the time and effort to learn your research well enough to bring it forward on their own. It can be a challenge for unexpected allies to learn new, and potentially complex, research. Also, unexpected allies expend relational capital as they leverage their contacts, relationships, and networks to discuss your research. And, for those who interact with politicians directly, they expend political capital when they approach politicians with an academic's research. Unexpected allies draw on their relationships with politicians to advance an issue that is outside the allies' usual legislative interests.

WHERE TO FIND UNEXPECTED ALLIES

In the beginning, it is more important to connect with any unexpected allies than to be concerned about connecting with the "best" unexpected allies. Start with low-hanging fruit and approach those unexpected allies with whom you have existing relationships or whom you are otherwise comfortable approaching. Then, let your networking success snowball from there as you extend farther away from issue networks or advocacy coalitions and closer to politicians. Here are several sources of unexpected allies:

1. Issue networks. The people and organizations that comprise issue networks can be divided into two groups: those who are directly involved with politicians and those who are not. Approach those people and organizations that are not involved with politicians directly or do not have a legislative presence and ask them for contacts in their networks who may also share an interest in your research and who are farther away from the issue network.

2. Personal contacts. Connect with those people outside of the issue network or academia with whom you have a personal relationship. Asking personal contacts to bring your research forward to others may be facilitated by your personal relationships with these unexpected allies. If these contacts are situated outside of the issue network, then

connecting with their networks is fertile ground for cultivating other unexpected allies.

3. Community contacts. Those involved with the welfare of either the communities associated with your research or involved with communities within politicians' jurisdictions are inclined to have a vested interest in the practical problems that your research addresses because it impacts the populations in whom they are vested. This list of potential contacts includes neighborhood groups, social service organizations, nonprofit organizations, and political clubs.

4. Those who share a concern about the importance of the practical problem that your research addresses. For example, if you argue that the practical problem is important because it contributes to the development of a highly skilled workforce, then business organizations, chambers of commerce, and professional trade groups are all potential unexpected allies. If you argue that the practical problem is important because it disadvantages some student groups disproportionately, then parental organizations and child welfare organizations become fruitful ground to connect with unexpected allies.

5. Politicians themselves. Find out who are the people whom the politician trusts. This group includes legislative staffers, lobbyists, or political allies who support the politician.

HOW TO ENLIST UNEXPECTED ALLIES

Start by connecting with unexpected allies in person. An email or social media hit is not likely to be enough to get their attention and to convince them to invest time and effort in your research. Once you are face to face, look for commonalities. Ask them to tell their education story. Listen carefully for connections to the practical problem that your research addresses and find a way to personalize your message for the unexpected ally. For example, in my class on translating research for educational change, I work with students to identify and approach unexpected allies. Although the students are generally hesitant, I encourage them to begin the conversation on a personal level, to learn more about the background and interests of prospective unexpected allies. In most cases, students are surprised to learn how much they have in common with someone associated with an organization outside the predictable issue networks or advocacy coalitions. Bolstered by this nascent personal connection, students become more comfortable with introducing their research to the unexpected ally.

The research one-pager is the perfect aide to connect your research with unexpected allies because it provides an understanding of your research, at a glance. Your research one-pager is designed to communicate with novices, including unexpected allies. You can find common ground with unexpected allies through a shared practical problem. The importance of your research can motivate unexpected allies to action.

Close with *the ask*. *The ask* must be direct so the unexpected allies know exactly what they can do to help. *The ask* should be framed as a yes/ no proposition and concrete enough so that you are able to determine if the unexpected allies have completed *the ask* and to follow up until *the ask* is completed (chapter 10). Networking and dissemination asks are appropriate for unexpected allies to start the snowballing effect that leads to direct contact with politicians. You can ask unexpected allies to bring the one-pager to their networks or to connect you with people or organizations in their networks (including politicians) that may have an interest in your research.

Lastly, if you want press coverage of your research, ask an unexpected ally to bring it to the media. The involvement of unexpected allies can help persuade the media to devote resources to reporting your research, especially if they are able to break through the routine messaging of issue networks and make a strong impression on a media contact, who, in turn, may publicize your work.

9

LEVERAGING *THE* RESEARCH TO PREDICT POLICY OUTCOMES

Academics can distinguish themselves from other lay voices in a policy context by leveraging *the* research to predict future policy outcomes.

The book opened with a promise to teach you how to bring *your* research to politicians. This individualistic orientation toward academics bringing *their* research to a policy context is typical of how the research and policy gap is framed in the academic literature. Academics, however, should distinguish between bringing their research into a policy context and bringing *the* research into a policy context. Your research is narrow. And, any single, narrow issue may not be a policy priority at the moment, given the interconnected nature of policymaking. Like single-issue constituents and policy entrepreneurs who are constantly inserting themselves into a policy context with specific policy proposals in hopes of timing an open policy window, academics entering a policy context armed with just their specific research may not find a welcoming environment due to a number of political or policy conditions that are unrelated to their research. Namely, the issues that your research addresses may not be a priority among the specific politicians in power at a given time.

To be available when a window opens to advance the issues associated with your research or to prompt such an opportunity, you should remain present and engaged in policy especially during those times when your issue is not a priority. Unlike single-issue constituents and policy entrepreneurs, academics have broad and coveted expertise to offer politicians beyond a singular policy issue. Long term, academics can be most relevant in policymaking by serving as intermediaries for *the* research, defined as, the cumulation of evidence available in the academic literature (Petes and Meyer 2018). With a mastery of *the* research, you can be available as an education policy expert who serves as a fortune teller of sorts to aide politicians and professional staff. This role allows you to contribute to policymaking in a constructive manner and potentially nudge open a policy window for your research.

To be relevant in a policy context, academics must orient themselves toward leveraging a unique skillset that they can offer to politicians—the ability to predict. Keep in mind that academics are one of many voices in policymaking, and research evidence is one of many ways of knowing. So, in thinking about their unique contribution to policymaking, academics should ask themselves the same insightful question as Marin (1981, 49) does: "Under what conditions do politicians need social science knowledge at all, instead of simply relying on everyday knowledge and accumulated experience, and where does this lead?" For policy purposes, academics can provide expertise to politicians beyond everyday knowledge by leveraging *the* research to predict future policy outcomes. If academics can help politicians anticipate what is coming next, they will become indispensable voices in a policy context.

I have approached academics who have reservations about the absolute nature of making a prediction because they are concerned with getting it wrong given that educational problems are highly complex, and many forces from various sources influence policy outcomes. Academics also have a tendency to focus on the exceptions, caveats, and special cases, failing to communicate the bulk of what they know in the process. Keep in mind that predictions can be as general or as specific as you can support. The point here is that academics should get into the practice of viewing their research and *the* research as predictive tools for policymaking.

Per the research utilization literature, academics commonly articulate their role in policy as helping politicians understand current policy issues through approaches such as problematization and critical inquiry. While research syntheses and literature reviews are useful for politicians to understand the present state of affairs (Davies 2000). Helping politicians understand current policy issues alone, even with sophisticated techniques, can place your expertise on par with other lay voices who can offer a similar perspective. Based on personal experiences and little else, lay voices can also provide a credible perspective of what is currently happening in the "real world" for politicians' edification.

How is it that politicians may side with the opinion of a lay constituent over an expert? This scenario may seem far-fetched but it's actually very common. Remember, politicians prefer to learn through language—talking and listening to others. After learning about new research, politicians are likely to assess its validity through their preferred way of knowing—language—particularly if the research makes an impression and is counter to their worldview. Politicians are likely to confer with people whom they trust. In fact, this response is a positive sign. It means that the politicians listened and that the research had an influence on them.

I have encountered many circumstances in which politicians looked to lay constituents to negate or confirm research evidence based on the constituents' personal experiences or opinions, despite the constituents having little to no expertise in the issue. Comments such as "My daughter was in those classes and never had a problem" or "I've never heard of that" will carry weight with politicians. As the politicians' "people," constituents have inherent credibility and thus a lower threshold of proof than academics and research evidence.

Academics can distinguish themselves from other lay voices in a policy context by leveraging *the* research to predict future policy outcomes. Prediction is invaluable in a policy context. If politicians can predict what is likely to happen next, they are in the desirable position to control events.

USING PAST RESEARCH TO PREDICT FUTURE POLICY OUTCOMES

When novice politicians become aware of an issue, it may be their first experience with that issue. With no prior experience or ability to contextualize the issue broadly, they are inclined to treat the issue as if it's unique. Novice politicians are prone to a context fallacy, assuming that because the context is new or current to them, the policy issue is new, as well.

They have little to no appreciation that the policy issue, or a variation of the policy issue, has likely occurred many times in the past. To politicians who thrive on the immediacy of the twenty-four-hour news cycle, what happened in the past, and by extension the research written in the past, is yesterday's news.

Academics understand that even though the policy issue is new to politicians, the policy issue itself is not new. Settings may change from one context to another, but the underlying dynamics of policy issues remain largely consistent. Overarching dynamics, such as the influence of socioeconomic factors and pedagogical practices, influence current policies in predictable ways and point toward their likely outcomes. For example, technology has changed content delivery in education and expanded access to information dramatically. Yet, socioeconomic influences that have had an impact on the outcomes of past policies portend that the digital divide, fundamentally an issue of disparate resources by socioeconomic differences, will disadvantage some students over others. Academics can then predict that policies, such as online learning, will be inequitable unless specifically structured to minimize disparities. Likewise, pedagogical fundamentals, such as time on task and student engagement, remain as relevant in an online environment as in a face-to-face classroom. Thus, *the* research on classroom management strategies, dating back decades, remains applicable to online environments.

The research is an informative resource to predict future policy outcomes. Remember, there is research available on nearly every present-day policy issue. To read *the* research for the purpose of predicting, academics should trace the academic literature as far back as possible using search engines, such as Web of Knowledge or Scopus. The academic should understand the origins of the issue and how it evolved. Academics may need to work through some antiquated language to appreciate that the underlying dynamics of policy issues remain largely the same, even though the settings change over time.

Let me give you a specific example that was useful to me when I was working as professional staff. During the past three decades, accountability polices, characterized by academic standards, assessments, and school labels, have become prominent features of k–12 education policy. These education reforms are new to many politicians. While the scope of accountability policies is unprecedented due to federal policies such as No Child Left Behind and the Every Student Succeeds Act, which mandated accountability policies in nearly every state, there is research on the application of accountability metrics in education dating back over a century. For example, in his 1962 book *Education and the Cult of Efficiency* Raymond Callahan examines how scientific management dominated business philosophy at the turn of the twentieth century, pressuring public educators to change the nature of their work to achieve operational efficiencies. Despite the antiquated language, academics will recognize that today's educational administrators have reacted in similar ways as their predecessors. Administrators applied business principles to educational activities, depended on "objective" metrics for accountability purposes, and struggled to integrate the humanistic elements of education into standardized processes. Understanding these historical responses allowed me to predict the challenges and responses of present-day administrators. I was able to influence policies, such as multiple measures and limiting the use of high stakes decisions based on test scores alone, to help present-day administrators address or avoid similar challenges.

If I had a dollar for every "game-changing" policy that politicians have touted to me . . . Politicians gravitate to the novel and provocative, and they are prone to the use of hyperbolic language in an effort to sell their policy ideas. They are apt to describe their ideas as "game-changers" in an effort to convince their colleagues and to spark public support. Likewise, policy entrepreneurs often pitch policy ideas the way that sales professionals do, filling politicians with exaggerated language and promises of unrealistic outcomes. Are there game-changers in education policy? Certainly. But game-changers are very, very few and far between. In addition, the game changes much more slowly than politicians appreciate and policy entrepreneurs divulge. Many interrelated events must transpire before game-changers have the anticipated impact, if they ever achieve the promised outcomes. The measured speed and sequence of interrelated events that eventually lead to major impact create ample opportunities for academics to predict how a game-changer will evolve and to provide guidance on how to maximize opportunities or mitigate unintended consequences.

GENERALIZING *THE* RESEARCH TO MAKE IT APPLICABLE
TO POLITICIANS' EXPERIENCES

Novice politicians often act as if a policy issue exists only in their jurisdictions because they are hyper-focused on their constituents. They are
likely unaware of the extent to which the policy issue is also present in
other settings outside their political jurisdictions. Here, generalization
from one setting to another becomes the tool of prediction. The main
goal of generalizing *the* research is to apply research findings to politicians' experiences to help them identify and anticipate policy outcomes
among the schools and communities in their jurisdictions. To achieve
this goal, academics should follow these suggestions when generalizing
the research for politicians:

1. Focus on research that addresses the same practical problems that concern politicians. As an expert, you are likely aware of both historical and
   cutting edge research on the practical problems that concern politicians
   that neither politicians nor professional staff have read. The findings
   from this research form the basis for predicting the outcomes of policies
   that address similar practical problems.

2. Apply the findings from studies conducted in educational settings that
   are consistent with those in politicians' jurisdictions. You should consider the types of schools or communities in which the research was
   conducted (e.g., urban or rural) and with which group(s) of people,
   and then apply the findings to the types of schools and groups(s) that
   are present in politicians' jurisdictions. In this way, you can predict
   the effects of different policies for schools and group(s) in politicians'
   jurisdictions. For example, in quantitative analyses, results such as the
   strength and direction of regression coefficients, can be extrapolated
   to predict which outcomes may be exacerbated or mitigated among
   the schools and group(s) in politicians' jurisdictions. The rich descriptions of qualitative analyses are particularly apt to express people's
   lived experiences. These descriptions can help politicians identify and
   anticipate the lived experiences of their constituents.

3. Think ahead to later stages of policies. Politicians are unlikely to understand how policies evolve and appreciate at which stage their policy
   stands. Academics should assess the stage of the policy and leverage

research that has been conducted at later stages of the policy to predict future outcomes and to identify strategies to maximize opportunities or mitigate unintended consequences.

4. Report strong and robust findings. In quantitative analysis, the reminder that "statistical significance is not meaningfulness" is sound advice to avoid the over-interpretation of small effects. In a policy context, if politicians are unable to detect real-world differences, then you should avoid reporting the results to politicians, even if the results are statistically significant. This is particularly relevant to studies with large sample sizes in which minimal real-world differences result in statistically significant results. But in a real-world context, the differences may be imperceptible, leading to an incongruence between your predictions and politicians' experiences. If politicians are unable to experience the outcomes directly, they may come to doubt the research. You should focus on the most robust results so that politicians are likely to experience the outcomes in multiple settings. The more often and in more places that politicians can experience the outcomes identified by research evidence, the more confidence they will have in *the* research and the more useful it becomes for predicting future policy outcomes.

5. Do not report minor limitations. Academics should think like professional staff and tell politicians "what they need to know." If the research limitations are minor, meaning that they are inconsequential to how politicians' are likely to experience phenomena, then it is unnecessary to communicate the limitations to politicians. While it may feel professionally irresponsible to omit limitations, the academic should remember that the goal of generalizing *the* research for a policy context is to reinforce the connection between research evidence and politicians' experiences. Communicating minor limitations in the name of thoroughness may detract from that goal. If politicians are unlikely to experience the limitations in a real-world setting, then what's the purpose of communicating the limitations to them? On the other hand, if it is likely that the limitations may influence how politicians experience policy outcomes, then it is important to alert them in advance.

10

FROM PRACTICAL PROBLEMS
TO *THE ASK*

To engage with politicians most effectively, academics must translate research to a local policy context by restructuring how they present their research to make the most compelling case for its applicability to policymaking.

The presentation of research to politicians should begin with a practical problem to capture the politician's attention and end with the ask, using rhetoric for inspiration, and citing research evidence as support along the way. This chapter will discuss the sequence from a practical problem to the ask in detail (see figure 10.1).

STEP 1: IDENTIFY THE PRACTICAL PROBLEM

A real-world condition is getting worse or could get better.

Making a policy case to politicians begins with connecting your research to a practical problem. Starting with the practical problem is important because, while the novice may not appreciate or understand your research, they can identify with a practical problem associated with your research. The practical problem makes it clear, up front, why politicians should listen to your research and how it applies to their constituents. Once the novice recognizes the practical problem, introducing research evidence follows readily.

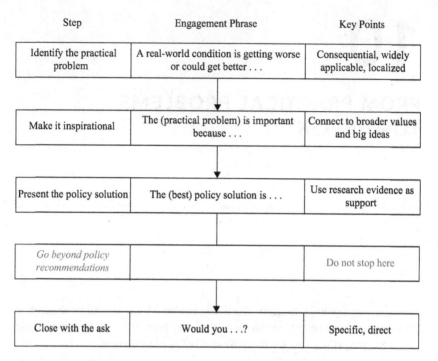

Step	Engagement Phrase	Key Points
Identify the practical problem	A real-world condition is getting worse or could get better . . .	Consequential, widely applicable, localized
Make it inspirational	The (practical problem) is important because . . .	Connect to broader values and big ideas
Present the policy solution	The (best) policy solution is . . .	Use research evidence as support
Go beyond policy recommendations		Do not stop here
Close with the ask	Would you . . .?	Specific, direct

10.1 The sequence from the practical problem to the ask.

The practical problem is a real-world condition that exacts a cost, such as time, money, or opportunity (Booth et al. 2016). To identify practical problems, consider the following questions from the politician's point of view. With respect to your research, what real-world conditions get, or could get, worse? What real-world conditions get, or could get, better? Be as specific as possible. The more specifically you define the practical problem, the better. Yet, think broadly as well. Brainstorm to identify as many practical problems associated with your research as possible and develop a robust list.

Once you have created the list of potential practical problems, the next step is to select the practical problem that may be most persuasive in a policy context. The most persuasive practical problem is consequential, widely applicable, and localized.

CONSEQUENTIAL

To identify the practical problem, Booth et al. (2016) suggest that academics repeatedly ask, "So what?" about their research to appreciate its significance from an outsider's point of view. "Practical problems . . . are easy to grasp because when people have it (the practical problem), we don't ask 'so what?'" (Booth et al. 2016). To identify a practical problem of consequence that others may also recognize as in need of a solution, you should ask "so what?" to the point that you reach a dead end. If after posing your practical problem to politicians, they ask (or think to themselves), "so what?" then they are probably not convinced that the costs associated with your practical problem is consequential enough to engage meaningfully with your research and take policy action.

For example, segregation, the separation of students by racial group, in and of itself, is not a practical problem. The answers to the "so what" question are the practical problems. What are the real-world conditions that get worse when students are separated by race/ethnicity? One "so what" is that segregated schools with high minority student populations often do not have the same educational opportunities as students in other schools. What real-world conditions get, or could get, better through desegregation? Another "so what" is that students who attend desegregated schools with students from other racial/ethnic backgrounds are exposed to and are likely to appreciate diverse viewpoints. The practical problems are inequitable opportunities that are associated with segregated schools (getting worse) and an appreciation for diverse viewpoints in desegregated schools (getting better).

For some academics, it may have been a long time since they have articulated their research in such applied terms. In professional settings among *our* people, academics are rarely required to identify the real-world conditions of their research so explicitly or they may refer to their research in shorthand, assuming a common level of appreciation. To answer the "so what" questions, academics may need to return to the fundamental motivations of their research, particularly when dealing with complex concepts. For example, what real-world conditions get worse under neoliberal education or get better with multicultural education? What real-world conditions get better if policies are subject to democratic deliberation or if they are based on market principles? Academics should consider their research at this applied level to make a persuasive case to the education research and policy novice that your research is addressing a practical problem that merits their attention.

WIDELY APPLICABLE

Building coalitions to support policy proposals is central to the political process. To facilitate coalition building, one should identify practical problems that can be applicable to as many different groups of people as possible. The more groups of people that can identify with a practical problem and acknowledge that it exacts a cost to them or communities they care about, the wider the net that politicians can cast to garner support. Academics should brainstorm about all the possible groups that are affected by the practical problem and how they are affected.

Wide applicability sets up an obvious contradiction with research that is carried out narrowly, particularly disaggregated analyses and intersectionality studies, because these studies involve subgroups by design. The common structure of many research articles involves the study of a subgroup x,y (where x is a group characteristic, such as race/ethnicity, and y is another group characteristic such as gender), in location k (where k is a setting other than the politician's jurisdiction). In a policy context, academics must make the case that the research conducted on subgroup x,y in location k is applicable to a politician's jurisdiction, location j. To argue the applicability of practical problems (p) from disaggregated research to a politician, academics can make two basic cases (see figure 10.2):

1. These are your constituents. The politician's constituents include the subgroup under study and are affected by the practical problem. (The subgroup x,y in location k is also present in location j and is affected by the practical problem p.)
2. The problem may be bigger than you think. Other constituent groups or institutions in the politician's jurisdiction, beyond those in the subgroup under study, may also be affected by the practical problem. (The practical problem p, identified in location k, is likely to affect others (z) in location j who are not members of subgroup x,y.)

The onus is on the academic to argue that their research about a given practical problem is widely applicable. The politician is very likely to turn

Study Context   Political Jurisdiction

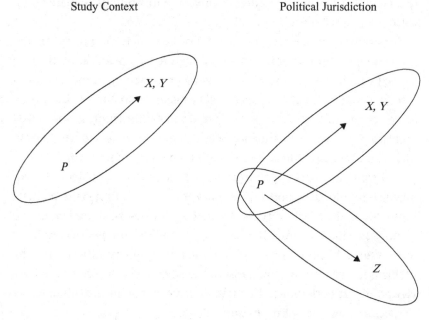

10.2 Applying research on disaggregated groups to specific political jurisdictions.

to staff to verify the academic's argument. Staff will tell the politician if the academic's claims are exaggerated, the extent to which the groups mentioned in the academic's research are present in the politician's jurisdiction, and what actions politicians should take (or not) going forward. Staff, however, are unlikely to make the case for the applicability of the research to a practical problem if the academic has not made a persuasive case in the first place.

LOCALIZED

One major advantage of articulating a practical problem as specifically as possible is the ability to localize it to individual political jurisdictions. Remember, politicians answer to constituents with names and faces. You do not need an accounting of all cases in a political jurisdiction that are potentially affected by the practical problem to make an effective localized argument. Your argument will be strengthened greatly, however, if you can identify some examples of the practical problem in a politician's jurisdiction to shift the practical problem from a hypothetical possibility to a tangible situation that affects people and institutions that are familiar to the politician (see figure 10.3).

For example, student academic achievement increasing or decreasing is measurable, but it is not localized enough to be a practical problem to a specific politician. Test scores improving or worsening in the schools in a politician's jurisdiction is a localized problem. Dropout rates increasing or decreasing in high schools in a politician's jurisdiction is a localized problem. Equal access to Advanced Placement (AP) courses for students in high schools in a politician's jurisdiction is a localized problem.

Returning to the segregation example, the practical problem of inequitable educational opportunities is easier to localize to specific political jurisdictions than lack of access to diverse viewpoints. If academics can identify specific inequities in segregated schools in the politician's jurisdiction (e.g., AP course offerings or enrichment opportunities), then the problem is localized. By comparison, the advantages of access to diverse viewpoints are both more difficult to measure and more difficult to tether to specific cases in a politician's jurisdiction.

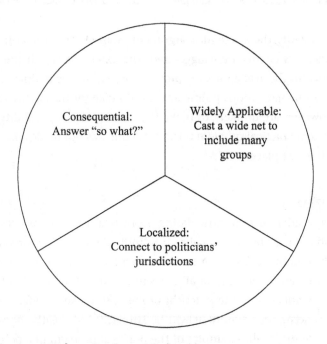

10.3 Components of a persuasive practical problem.

GETTING HELP WITH PRACTICAL PROBLEMS

Academics should help their colleagues to develop consequential, widely applicable, and localized practical problems. I understand that academics may find the inquiry uncomfortable because asking "so what?" could be interpreted as challenging the merit or worth of one's research or diminishing the populations it impacts. This is not the case. Through this process, we sharpen our arguments to be most effective in a policy context. Also, academics may find the process frustrating because it may seem overly simplistic to narrow a complex phenomenon to a single practical problem. Remember, however, that you will be working with research and policy novices who are not trained to appreciate how practical problems are interconnected. By identifying a single, persuasive problem, you are connecting your research to the lived experience of politicians and their constituents to help *them* (key word is *them*, not just you) build coalitions.

Also, narrowing the list of practical problems and bringing forward the most persuasive practical problem hones the ask. Think like a lobbyist. If you bring forward a laundry list of practical problems, politicians may address one of the many, at the politician's discretion, concluding that they took sufficient action. The practical problem that the politician chooses to address, however, may not be the one that you believe is the most important. A single practical problem keeps *the ask* focused on the most influential actions.

Lastly, keep in mind that you are working over multiple legislative sessions. Certainly, the totality of all the practical problems you identify may create an overwhelming sense of urgency. But if the practical problems are too scattered or are not well defined, it becomes a near impossibility to articulate an all-encompassing ask that addresses all the practical problems at once. Start by accomplishing one ask to address a practical problem and then move on to the next one. In this way, the interconnected nature of the practical problems can be scaffolded for the policy novice over time, the connection between the practical problem and *the ask* remains manageable, and *the asks* build on each other over time to address the totality of the practical problems.

STEP 2: MAKE IT INSPIRATIONAL

The practical problem is important because . . . (connect to broader values and big ideas).

This step is an opportunity for academics to frame the consequences of the practical problem as compelling and important enough to motivate politicians to invest time in your research. In completing the sentence above, the conclusion should appeal to big ideas and commonly held values, such as justice, fairness, equity, economic development, and so on (see table 10.1 for some ideas).

Remember, emotions are influential. Logic or analytical arguments alone are not enough to win the day in a policy context. Symbols and values are influential in policymaking and academics are wise to tap into them, which can be a fruitful space for research (Dumas and Anderson 2014). In problem definition, while "research results and indicator data play a role, other types of evidence may be equally important. These include appeals to values such as equality, liberty, and economic security. Metaphors may also be used to evoke strong political and cultural symbols" (McDonnell and Weatherford 2013, 4).

With respect to our discussion of segregation, the problem of ignoring the inequitable distribution of opportunities by race runs counter to the American belief in equality of opportunity—that all students should have

Table 10.1 Example inspirational words and phrases, by category

Civics	Economics	Policy	Social	Education
Freedom Opportunity	Future workforce Investment	Game-changer Efficiency	Progress Change	Critical-thinking Well-rounded
Democracy	Development	Effectiveness	Level playing field	Science, technology, engineering, math (STEM)
Equity Equality Constitutional	(Individual) prosperity Innovation Choice	Accountability Deregulation Privatization	Anti-racism Democratizing Access	College and career options Hands-on learning Creativity

the same shot at achieving the American dream regardless of zip code. Desegregating schools to expose students to different viewpoints appeals to broader values such as tolerance and diversity.

STEP 3: PRESENT THE POLICY SOLUTION

The (best) policy solution is . . . (use research evidence as support).

Next, connect the practical problem with a policy solution. The policy solution encapsulates the institutional responses that should occur to address the practical problem. The policy solution helps politicians to understand how they can take action to address the practical problem in terms that are relevant in a policy context.

To articulate the policy solution, complete the phrase: "The practical problem can be addressed by . . ." The responses that arises from completing this phrase should have a logical connection to the practical problem. In other words, academics should be prepared to argue that the practical problem can be ameliorated via the policy solution.

Step three is where academics are most likely to introduce the central themes and concepts of their research as they frame and study them. With respect to the practical problems of inequitable educational opportunities for students in high-minority schools or the merits of exposure to diverse viewpoints, this step is where academics would introduce desegregation as the policy solution that promotes equity and civil public discourse.

There are many ways to address a specific practical problem via policy, and there are many different policy solutions that are logically associated with addressing a specific practical problem. In a policy context, academics compete with a swarm of actors who are also working to convince politicians to address the practical problem through *their* preferred policy solution. Therefore, academics must be prepared to make a case, based on the research, that the policy solution that they have identified, is the most appropriate, most efficient, or the most effective to address the practical problem. For example, other policy actors may argue that inequitable educational opportunities can be ameliorated via competition among schools or, that intolerance can be addressed through character education programs in schools, rather than desegregation policies.

From my experience, academics often consider the lack of resources or failure to implement a specific program as a practical problem. The practical problem, however, concerns whatever local conditions that are getting worse as a result of a lack of resources. Or, the practical problem is what local conditions will get better as a result of implementing a specific program. Allocating resources or implementing a particular program are policy solutions: they are the institutional responses that can address the practical problem through policy. Allocating additional resources or implementing in a specific program, however, are likely two of many potential policy solutions to address the underlying practical problem. To make a strong argument to politicians for investment, academics must establish that the resources or programs are not only logically connected to addressing the practical problem but that these options are the most effective or efficient approach to address the practical problem.

Supporting policy solutions is where research can be most convincing compared to other ways of knowing that contribute to policymaking. Academics are able to make a precise case for their policy solutions based on an abundance of research evidence dating back decades, in some cases. Academics can call upon trials, experiments, and empirical studies to support their case. They may also articulate the relationship between particular inputs and outputs, suggest the level of investment necessary to achieve desired outcomes, and predict outcomes for particular subgroups or communities. The level of certainty and evidence that academics may interject into the policy discussion based on research establishes academics as experts. While many other policy actors may engage in the policy process with their own evidence to support their policy solutions, few have the expertise and evidence to make a predictive argument as cogently as academics.

Go beyond policy recommendations (do not stop here).

The sequence does not end with the kinds of policy recommendations that appear in academic journal articles to advise the reader of what needs to be done based on the findings. Often, policy recommendations are framed as general advice, rather than prescriptive actions that are localized to a specific political jurisdiction. In a policy context, academics need to take one additional step and articulate specifically what actions politicians can take. Academics must ask politicians to take action directly.

Specific and direct asks are the tangible appeals that move policy. For this reason, some policy entrepreneurs, in an effort to facilitate the execution of their policy solutions, take the astute step of directing politicians to action explicitly. For example, the American Legislative Exchange Council provides legislators with a model bill that contains specific policy language and asks them to give it to their staff for implementation.

STEP 4: CLOSE WITH THE ASK

Would you . . . ?

The rationale for this step is simple—to G-E-T, you have to A-S-K. The final step is to communicate the ask to politicians. The purpose of a specific and direct ask is to let politicians know exactly what they can do to address the practical problem. The ask should be framed as a yes/no proposition. The ask should be specific enough so that academics are able to determine if the politician has completed *the ask* or to follow up with the politician until *the ask* is completed. In the best-case scenario, academics deliver *the ask* to politicians in person. Academics can ask the politician to

- support/oppose policies or legislation
- amend policies or legislation
- connect academics with someone else in the politician's network
- take the research to someone else in the politician's network
- join a group or coalition suggested by academics
- attend a meeting or event identified by academics
- give the research to the politician's staff with instructions for implementation.

In my experience, academics are highly uncomfortable with the "ask." Academics have little to no professional experience with asking in person. Direct, face-to-face asks are not a customary requirement for academic jobs. Asking in person takes practice, but it gets easier with practice. Academics may believe that an "ask" is too political. Keep in mind, however, that *the ask* can take a number of forms, many of which are not related to taking a position on policy or legislation. Lastly, *the ask* does not need to be grand, but it needs to be direct.

Writing this book, I have come to understand why segregation was mentioned so infrequently on the campaign trail. Segregation, the separation of students by race, in and of itself, is not a practical problem of consequence to parents or community members. During the campaign, parents and community members often brought up practical problems, many of which had racial implications (e.g., dilapidated school buildings in high-minority communities, or restrictive language policies that disproportionately affect students of color). Segregation itself was not the practical problem for these citizens because the (best) policy solution, and related ask, was not to desegregate schools. If desegregation is framed as the policy solution, then addressing the practical problems (e.g., dilapidated school buildings or restrictive language policies) becomes a two-step process. Schools must be desegregated to then distribute educational opportunities equitably or to end restrictive language policies. Parents and community members were asking for direct action—the equitable distribution of educational opportunities or an end to discriminatory policies, not the redistribution of students by race/ethnicity as an intermediary step to addressing these practical problems.

Academics who are uncomfortable with the ask will be both relieved and empowered to learn that an "ask" is commonplace in a policy context. Candidates are conditioned to ask. Campaigns are won by asking a lot of people for a lot of support. Politicians routinely approach stakeholders, donors, and supporters with specific and direct asks. Likewise, politicians are accustomed to being asked, often.

There is an implied ask in nearly all interactions with politicians. For example, when an academic meets with a politician to present their research—that is an "ask." The academic asked the politician to take the meeting and listen. And, when the politician has listened, walking away without a specific and direct ask, the politician has taken action, as requested by the academic—to meet and listen. This is a softball-pitch ask, however. The academic has given the politician an easy action to take and missed an opportunity to direct the politician to a more impactful way to address the practical problem. The academic also missed a reason to follow up and maintain a connection to the politician. A specific and direct ask, on the other hand, means that the academic has taken full advantage of their opportunity to present their research to the politician and build an ongoing connection.

11

THE RESEARCH ONE-PAGER

Academics must translate research to a policy context in a manner that communicates the key policy-relevant details required for politicians to take action. All in 20 seconds.

Academics recognize that they should communicate with politicians differently than they would with academic audiences. Written communication to politicians should be in accessible language and abbreviated formats. Academics are further advised to consider what is politically feasible, take into account the policy context, and use real-life stories along with catchy phrases. The text should also be jargon-free, brief, and provide concrete illustrations (Lindblom and Cohen 1979; Kirst 2000; Hammersley 2002).

In practice, academics have interpreted this advice as writing at the eighth-grade level, using bullet points, and telling stories, but they often make only superficial changes when writing for a public audience, including politicians. These are some of my general impressions:

1. The findings are presented in bullet points. The bullet points, however, are often multiple, complex sentences, which are way too long for the political attention span.
2. The text reads like shortened or simplified versions of a research report or journal article. Complex or technical language, however, is a barrier for politicians to engage with research.

3. Readers are given little compelling reason to engage with the research. The document fails to make clear to politicians how the research can be used to address a practical problem. Common justifications for research in the literature, such as a lack of understanding of or research on a policy issue, are not compelling in and of themselves for politicians to invest their time to engage with the research.

4. The documents are not action-oriented. Policy recommendations, which are often listed at the end, are not specific enough to a local context to guide action.

5. The content is too careful. That is, the effort to present research unbiasedly, and thus include various perspectives, can hamstring politicians from using the documents as support for their ideas. The content can be so overmanipulated to maintain balance that it is not helpful to any one side.

6. There are very few stories. Academics often miss the opportunity to use the power of imagery and to tap into the politician's penchant for narratives to "put a face" on issues.

7. There is too much emphasis on research methods. Similar to the format of an academic publication, the methods often precede the findings in public documents. Research methods, however, are of little concern to politicians.

Unfortunately, the research utilization literature provides little guidance to the academic who is interested in learning how to write for a policy context. It is heavy with suggestions for what academics should do, but light on teaching academics how to do it (Oliver and Cairney 2019). In this section, I incorporate my training and experiences in writing for a policy context to detail how to communicate research to politicians in writing.

Let's start with what not to do. Don't cut and paste select sentences from an academic product, put them in a shortened version, and call it a public document for politicians. A shortened version of a research document is insufficient, because, as we discussed earlier, research does not have an explicit policy purpose. Thus, a shortened version of a research product does not have a policy purpose.

Rather, research must be translated to a policy context to give it an explicit policy purpose. As Hammersley (2002, 45) noted, "The fact that research can only produce factual conclusions limits considerably the contribution that it can make to their [practitioners] work. Certainly, it cannot solve their practical problems on its own." The term "translation" is descriptive because much like the translation of text from one language to another, the process requires one to consider the context of both sides to develop a modified product that is adapted to fit the situation (Hammersley 2002; 2014).

Translating research to a policy context involves developing an entirely new written product intended specifically for politicians. This product, the research one-pager, connects the politician to research through the practical problem, highlights those findings that are most applicable to specific policies, tells the politician exactly what they can do to take action, and does it all in twenty seconds. Yes, twenty seconds. The model for this type of communication is the legislative one-pager, a form of communication that is tailored to the fast pace of policymaking and is familiar to politicians.

THE LEGISLATIVE ONE-PAGER

One of the first skills that I learned as a legislative staffer was to write a one-pager to communicate all of the provisions of a bill and its full impact. The one-pager was a contested document. It was scrutinized by many policy actors who had competing legislative interests. Members of both parties, lobbyists, and policy entrepreneurs all read the one-pagers to assess if the content was thorough, accurate, and unbiased. These same policy actors also created their own one-pagers to communicate with politicians.

Initially, learning to write an articulate one-pager was difficult for me because it required a style of writing that I had not learned as a graduate student at the University of Chicago. Even now, I rarely see examples of this writing style in contemporary academic presentations from students and professors alike. Carrying out the seemingly impossible task to communicate the full provisions of a bill in one page requires a razor-sharp assessment of the policy issues at hand, the disciplined prioritization of the key findings, the economical use of words, and creative visual

Analyzing and summarizing bills, along with associated amendments, was a core activity of my position as a research analyst and a fundamental skill that we taught to legislative interns. To keep the content on one page, the background section was extremely short, so that the legislator could understand the issue and the affected parties in a few sentences. To facilitate reading in a hurry, the provisions (i.e., specific functions of the bill) were presented in bullet points with each bullet point dedicated to a single topic. No text was dedicated to speculative outcomes or conjecture. Even in cases where the bills were simply too big or complex to be summarized in one page, the same principle applied. The expectation was that even large and complex bills would be summarized as succinctly as possible. The research one-pager may seem impossibly short to many academics and graduate students. The restricted length, however, forces the writer to pare down the information to only the necessary details. You will be surprised with how much information can be communicated in one-page.

formatting. These are the skills that academics must hone to walk in the door with an impressive one-pager that can cut through the speed and noise of a policy context.

THE RESEARCH ONE-PAGER

In this section, I describe what should go into the research one-pager (content), outline how the content should be ordered (sequence), provide specific tactics for the physical layout of the document (format), and suggest a process for evaluating it.

CONTENT

The research one-pager should do the following:

1. Begin with specific examples of the practical problem from specific political jurisdictions. Politicians will take the most interest in research that helps them improve conditions for their constituents.
2. Describe what the results "mean" not just what they "are." For quantitative studies, you should tell the politician how the strength and direction of the statistics indicate that the practical problem is better or worse (or is getting better or worse) for their constituents.

For qualitative studies, you should indicate how the politician can learn about the lived experiences of their constituents from the findings.

3. Connect to a specific bill, policy, or policy agenda, with emphasis on the most consequential outcomes. This requires you to do your homework on which local policy issues or bills are in play at the moment. A policy actor who is actively working with the legislature is an excellent resource for this "up to the minute" insight. Also, party platforms and the stated policy positions of politicians themselves are other useful resources.

4. Focus on the most robust findings to show how academic research influences the practical problem. Unintended consequences should be presented sparingly, especially if they are speculative.

5. Accompany statistics with stories, especially those that the politician can retell themselves. Politicians are taught to use narratives to put a face on issues when communicating with the public and you should employ the same tactic. The rich description of qualitative studies is a fruitful resource for compelling stories (Sallee and Flood 2012). See Davidson (2017) and Crow and Jones (2018) for advice on how academics can incorporate storytelling to influence policy.

6. Use graphics or visuals, whenever possible. The old adage that a picture speaks a thousand words is fitting in a policy context.

7. Downplay or delete research methods from the main text. Most politicians do not have extensive training in research methods to assess the quality of research and will focus on its applicability to a local context instead.

8. Omit the literature review. While the academic literature is an important resource for conducting research, politicians are not particularly interested in the theories that undergird your research or how it contributes to the literature.

9. Include the ask. To facilitate action, link the research to the ask. Tell politicians exactly what they can do to improve the practical problem identified by the research.

10. Display all the content on one page, with white space and legible fonts, so that the content not only is legible, but also looks approachable. A block of text, corner to corner, is visually daunting. White

space on the page will force you to prepare a razor-sharp assessment of the policy issues, prioritize the research findings, employ words economically, and use visually appealing formats.

SEQUENCE

The research one-pager starts with the practical problem and ends with the ask. As a reminder, the sequence from practical problems to the ask is shown in figure 10.1. Given the fast-paced nature of policymaking and politicians as education research and policy novices, academics should not expect that politicians will read the research one-pager from start to finish. Rather, politicians are most likely to scan it, or read the document selectively at most. Thus, the research content should be presented in such a way as to ensure that politicians can locate the most important points quickly and easily.

The content of the research one-pager should be organized according to the "if the reader goes no further" principle. You should ask yourself, if the politician reads only one sentence of the research one-pager, what is that sentence? That sentence should come first in the document. You should then ask, what is the second most important sentence that politicians should read? That sentence should come second. And so on. Based on the "if the reader goes no further" principle, the research-pager should begin with the practical problem, displayed prominently. Politicians are much more likely to pay attention to the research one-pager if they understand clearly how it relates to a practical problem of consequence to their constituents.

The additional content, such as the importance of the research, major findings, stories, and visuals can be arranged in any logical order following the practical problem, provided that you follow the "if the reader goes no further" principle.

The research one-pager should close with *the ask* for several reasons. First, by the end of the document, you will have presented the research findings and made the case for its importance to the real-world conditions facing politicians' constituents. Second, the closing is where politicians themselves often include the "ask," so they are likely to expect it at the end. Third, *the ask* is a logical way for you to a follow-up with politicians. Like the practical problem, *the ask* should be displayed prominently so politicians can identify it easily.

Finally, while politicians may not read the research one-pager in detail, you should expect that the politician will hand the research one-pager to staff or to trusted individuals who have expertise in research or policy. The research one-pager should be written so that it can withstand the evaluation and critique of professional staff.

In the best-case scenario, you should expect legislative staff to follow up on the research one-pager. As professionals, legislative staff should be familiar with the references, be able to assess the quality of the research, and to understand the implications of *the ask* for politicians. If the research one-pager piques politicians' interests, legislative staff will seek out and synthesize the information that politicians need to know. Also, legislative staff may send it to other policy actors such as lobbyists or activists for comment.

FORMAT

The layout should create visual interest and facilitate the politician's navigation of the document. Some useful tips include:

- List content in (short) bullet points that are prioritized for the reader to take action.
- Use off-set text (other than left-justified) to facilitate flow and build in white space.
- Organize the text and graphics by sections on the page for visual interest.
- Use different fonts or font sizes to draw the eye to key points.
- Minimize in-text citations to maintain a conversational tone.
- Employ these tips sparingly to avoid a busy or amateurish appearance.

Lastly, place your contact information and date on the front of the page. Place any notes, references, or methodological details on the back of the research one-pager for professional staff to follow-up on the research content.

EVALUATING YOUR RESEARCH ONE-PAGER

To evaluative your research one-pager, conduct the following exercise:

1. Give the research one-pager to someone outside your field, preferably someone who is a novice or layperson.

In class, I ask students to estimate how long they believe that politicians will dedicate to reading the research one-pager. The most common answer is one minute. So, we conduct the following exercise. I ask students to sit across from a partner and stare at each other for one minute. They realize that a minute is a really, long time. The more realistic duration is twenty seconds. If you think twenty seconds is too short, sit across from someone and stare at them for twenty seconds. You'll see that that's a pretty lengthy stretch of time. In a well-written and formatted research one-pager, twenty seconds is sufficient for politicians to connect to the practical problem, get a general impression of the research findings, and understand *the ask*. At a later time, politicians or professional staff can read the details more closely.

2. Time the reader for twenty seconds, ask them to stop reading, and mark how far they got. In a well-written and formatted research one-pager, the reader should be able to connect to the practical problem, get a general impression of the research findings, and understand *the ask* in twenty seconds—the same amount of time that you can expect politicians to devote to reading the research one-pager.

3. Ask the reader to continue to the end of the document and time how long that takes.

4. Ask the reader about their impressions of the content and format. Was the research one-pager easy to read? Was it intimidating? Was the tone conversational? Was the research well-presented? Was the research compelling?

5. Ask the reader to identify and state the practical problem. Is the practical problem obvious to the reader? Does the reader agree that it is a real-world problem? Go through the "so what" sequence.

6. Ask the reader to find and state *the ask*. Is *the ask* specific and direct (yes/no)? What is a logical follow-up?

7. Based on this feedback, revise the research one-pager.

12

ANSWERS, ADVOCACY, ACTIVISM, AND FRAMEWORKS

When asked to contribute in a policymaking context, academics can answer questions, advocate for a policy change, engage in activism, or present a framework. Frameworks are best.

In this chapter I discuss the merits and limitations the different kinds of contributions that academics can make in a policy context and argue that academics should provide politicians with frameworks to guide future actions.

If academics engage in policy by answering questions from politicians as politicians frame the questions, they miss the opportunity to shape the questions. Advocates become marginalized sources of new information over time because advocates are predictable. Some academics choose to engage in policy through activism, which limits their entry into the full range of policy discussions because activists generally get to the table through political pressure, not expertise. The fourth response, providing politicians with frameworks, is particularly effective because frameworks help novice politicians to make sense of new experiences and to guide future actions based on research. Fortunately, academics are particularly experienced at developing and communicating frameworks.

ANSWERS

It is a win when politicians consult academics with a policy question. After all, a common assumption of the research utilization literature is that politicians ask academics about research in the policymaking process too infrequently. When asked, however, one can expect that politicians' questions will be narrow in scope, which makes sense given that novice politicians are focused on specific issues or settings and do not hold a broad view of education research or policy.

For academics, the logical response to a politicians' queries is to provide answers. Before answering, however, academics should keep a few things in mind. Politicians are action-oriented. They are not asking only to learn. They are asking to take action. Also, politicians are not likely to have the luxury of gathering full information before taking action, and so academics should tailor their interactions with politicians accordingly (Cairney and Kwiatkowski 2017). Therefore, politicians will find a literature review or a balanced treatment of both sides of an issue of limited utility.

When an academics answer questions, as posed by politicians, they limit the potential to fully display the varied ways that their expertise may help politicians. If academics answer questions as politicians asked them, they have missed the opportunity to frame the questions. Academics should keep in mind that novice politicians ask questions based on what they know. You are the expert, however, and you should scaffold the answer based on what you know in a manner that helps politicians take action.

In addition, resist the temptation to answer questions with other questions or a call for more research or information. While these are appropriate academic responses because one essential purpose of research is to generate new questions, it is not the most productive response in a policy context, even in cases where there is limited knowledge, because it does not help politicians to take action. As Shonkoff (2000, 182) succinctly observes, "Science is focused on what we do not know" while policymakers are interested in "what we should do." Therefore, academics should tell politicians what they know based on the available research and resist the temptation to answer questions by centering the answer on what they don't know. Keep in mind that if politicians do not get the information that they seek from academics, other policy actors will fill the void with information of their own because policy decisions await. In these cases, academics miss the opportunity to contribute to the policymaking process.

Furthermore, academics should discuss unintended consequences sparingly and the discussion should be limited to imminent outcomes—those that politicians are most likely to experience and, even better, those that are most likely to thwart politicians' policy agendas. Ambiguous, speculative, or long-range outcomes that either have a long horizon or may never materialize are likely to be ignored or filtered out by politicians or professional staff as surplus information.

I want to take a moment and connect the concept of "half-knowledge" with unintended policy consequences. Marin (1981) indicates that politicians filter out "disturbing or unmanageable knowledge" because it is beyond their control but not beyond their "cognitive capacity." From my experiences, this accurately describes how politicians treat potential unintended policy consequences. Politicians are peppered with the "sky is falling" scenarios of unintended consequences by policy actors looking to persuade (or dissuade) them. In many cases, politicians are aware of the potential unintended consequences of their policy decisions. They choose to ignore them. Sometimes, this is done for political reasons (e.g., politicians want to pressure or punish specific constituency groups). Or, legislative staff, after assessing the situation recommends that politicians can ignore some of the unintended consequences with little immediate ramifications. Other times, the unintended consequences are so ambiguous, speculative, or so far removed from the present that the evidence is ignored as purely hypothetical.

HOW TO SCAFFOLD YOUR ANSWERS FOR POLITICIANS

From my perspective, one fundamental fissure in the communication between the research and policy worlds comes from the difference between how politicians structure questions and how academics structure research. Politicians ask practical questions about real-world situations. For example, one common question that novice politicians often ask is, how to improve student achievement? On its face, it seems like an essential question for novice politicians to ask about education. Academics should remember that novice education and research policy politicians, while they may now be members of an influential legislative committee or commission, are essentially a member of the public who won an election. Thus, politicians are more than likely asking about how to raise test scores and they are looking for an answer at their level of understanding. It is highly unlikely that novice politicians have considered the type of critical perspectives that are prevalent in the academic literature, such as questioning the use of test scores as a measure of student achievement, and politicians are likely unprepared to champion the implementation of alternative measures.

The straightforward nature of the politicians' questions, however, is wholly more applied than how academics study education. Academics do not study how to raise test scores in isolation or for the sole purpose of raising test scores. The research literature is well beyond this type of pragmatic question. Academics are likely studying the relationship between policies, programs, or theories, and test scores. Thus, academics are inclined to talk about the policies, programs, and theories that they have studied. Furthermore, academics who are attuned to the unintended consequences of accountability policies may be critical of test scores as a measure of student achievement and they may feel obligated to take this opportunity to "speak truth to power" and question the very idea of using test scores as a measure of student achievement.

Miscommunication arises when academics answer from an abstract rather than a practical perspective. Novice politicians may not have an interest in or an awareness of the policies or programs that are important to academics. Theoretical responses are likely beyond politicians' understandings and do not help them take action. Novice politicians are neither prepared for this abstract response nor may they find the full information useful. With respect to critical responses that require one to understand and accept a critical perspective of policy, academics should not expect novice politicians to have a broad enough perspective of education policy to champion alternative policy options, yet.

When an academic supports an approach to addressing a practical problem based on a policy, program, or theory that is central to their research, they may not appreciate that the response is actually a two-step process for the politician. The politician must agree to (1) take action to address the problem and (2) take action via the policy, program, or theory supported by the academic. This creates a quandary for the academic: Is their goal to address the problem or is their goal to address the problem through the policy, program, or theory that is central to their research? At times, it may be difficult for the academic to divorce their preferred policy approach from addressing the problem itself. After all, the academic's research may be focused on addressing the problem through a specific policy, program, or theory. If the academic thinks like a lobbyist, they would not limit their involvement in policy to a specific approach toward addressing the problem because it may limit their participation in policymaking. Politicians may view the academic as a resource on a specific approach rather than as a general resource to address the practical problem more broadly. Thus, if the academic's preferred approach is off the table, then the academic could be as well.

Of course, academics should not provide a shallow answer; nor should academics forego the opportunity to question existing policies or paradigms entirely. My suggestion is that academics should scaffold the answers to eventually provide a framework. First, answer the question in its simple form. Second, anticipate the next question that the politician is most likely to pose and then answer that question. Third, identify consequences that are likely to thwart policy implementation or adversely impact outcomes in order to warn politicians. Lastly, provide a framework, the preferred response to politicians because frameworks empower them to assess future experiences, issues and policies on their own (see figure 12.1).

For example, on the question of how to improve student achievement (i.e., raise test scores), the scaffolded answer could be as follows:

- Answer the question: Practices such as test preparation activities using test score data to make instructional decisions, and setting high expectations school wide for test results are associated with raising test scores. Most likely, schools in your jurisdiction with high test scores use some combination of these practices.
- Anticipate the next question: When you interact with teachers, you are likely to find that they are not concerned with test scores as the sole measure of student achievement because it narrows the curriculum and lends itself to "drill and kill" instructional practices. (Similarly,

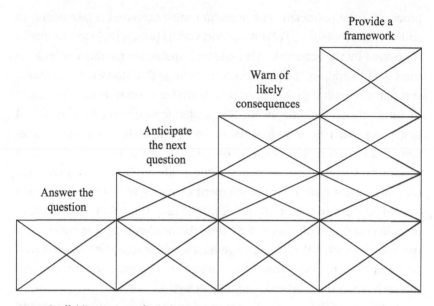

12.1   Scaffolding answers for politicians.

you could anticipate the next question by focusing on other issues, such as differences in test scores by socioeconomic status.)

- Warn the politician: An over-reliance on teaching practices that focus on raising test scores diminishes student engagement because students are unable to connect what they are learning in the classroom to their lives.
- Provide a framework: Authentic measures of academic achievement, such as projects and simulations, foster student engagement and promote student achievement because student learning is reinforced both within and outside the classroom.

The academic has covered a lot of ground in the scaffolded answer. They have addressed the politician's immediate needs and closed with an expanded response that is more consistent with the academic's research. The academic has demonstrated the value of their expertise and they have helped the politician anticipate unintended consequences that could derail their policy agenda. They also have aided the politician's advancement from a novice by providing a framework to help the politician recognize patterns in new experiences and to develop heuristics to guide future action.

After accomplishing all of this in the scaffolded answer, the academic has put themself in a position to be a trusted individual. The politician is likely to return with more questions. Then, the academic can take the opportunity to introduce more complex and critical approaches to education policy.

ADVOCACY

Public policy advocacy is "a structured and sequenced plan of action with the purpose to start, direct, or prevent a specific policy change" (International Centre for Policy Advocacy n.d.). Advocates are ubiquitous in legislative circles. Policy is moved by advocates who educate, collaborate, and motivate on issues of importance to the groups and individuals that they represent.

Advocates are also predictable. In fact, advocates are effective in policy precisely because they stay on message. It is clear to politicians, professional staff, stakeholders, and even the public where advocates stand on issues. There is rarely grey area in the type of research that advocates bring forth to support policy positions. For example, in my experience, when advocates testified in legislative hearings, their comments were exactly what politicians expected. Advocates rarely provided new or surprising perspectives in their testimony. As voices for the communities or causes that they represented, their goal was to get these perspectives on record, and the research they brought forward was consistent with the policy direction that supported advocates' preferred policy changes.

Once I understood where advocates stood on an issue and the research they were bringing forward, advocates were less useful as "new" sources of information. And, when advocates had new research, the findings were rarely new in the sense that they provided a unique perspective or were counter to the advocates' policy positions. Thus, academic advocates can expect to be included in those situations where politicians are interested in their specific policy position(s) and may be excluded from more general or exploratory inquiries.

There is a difference between advocating for a policy change and taking a stand on policy issues based on research. Advocates are constrained by their policy positions. Academics are not, and if they take a stand based on the preponderance of research, they are "honest brokers" (Eagly 2016; Pielke 2007), able to contribute to policy based on their expertise and without jeopardizing their objectivity.

ACTIVISM

Some academics see their role as activists for specific issues on behalf of communities that they care passionately about. Activism can yield emboldened academic writing and spirited student engagement. Activists, however, do not necessarily get to the policy table through research or expertise. They get there through political pressure. Activists, including academic activists, are rarely called upon to contribute research or information to policymaking. Because activists are not expected to be objective nor to maintain confidentiality, politicians have little control over how activists respond—what they do and with whom. Also, activism can include confrontational actions such as protests, demonstrations, and boycotts (Boehnke and Shani 2017). The "by any means necessary" methods of some activism to build political pressure means that politicians are understandably cautious in their interactions with activists and are likely to exclude them from participation in discussions of controversial or emerging issues. For these reasons, it is highly unlikely that activists would become trusted individuals to inform politicians through research (see figure 12.2).

FRAMEWORKS

In situations where there are various constraints—of time, knowledge, and the like—people use heuristics to guide their search for information and to make decisions (Gigerenzer 2001). "Heuristics are cues or 'mental shortcuts' people employ to solve problems or make decisions in situations where correct answers and effective courses of action may otherwise be difficult or impossible to discern" (Fagiano 2017, 354). Heuristics are developed through the synthesis and application of *past* experiences and information to new situations. As such, the ability to develop heuristics is limited to the breadth and scope of past experiences and information to which one has been exposed. In fact, there is evidence that when

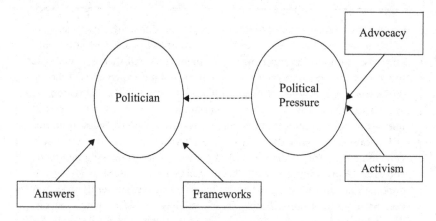

12.2 How answers, advocacy, activism, and frameworks influence politicians.

politicians are exposed to the interpretation and use of research evidence through explicit training, they call upon these experiences to generate heuristics and weigh policy alternatives (Apollonio and Bero 2017).

Candidates, and certainly politicians, are introduced to a number of new ideas, perspectives, and experiences. Pubic life means getting lots of new "friends," being exposed to new constituent stories from a diversity of perspectives, visiting new schools and communities, and receiving mountains of new information. So, when politicians visit schools that are unlike the ones' they know, experience a community that does not look like their neighborhood, or hear life stories beyond their own experiences, novice politicians are likely to use past experiences to make sense of these new experiences. Yet, as we have already discussed, these past experiences are likely not informed by academic research.

The fourth response to politicians, frameworks, is intended to help novices make sense of new experiences in ways that are informed by academic research. Frameworks can help them recognize meaningful patterns (and eventually predict future outcomes) in educational contexts to build new heuristics.

Frameworks are also in our professional wheelhouse as academics and educators. This is what we do. Academics develop and articulate frameworks to advance knowledge. We simplify complex phenomenon for our students so that they can understand and develop their own methods of inquiry.

Candidates, and especially politicians, are treated differently than members of the general public. From my experience, you meet people that you would otherwise not meet. Strangers introduce themselves, tell their stories, voice their concerns—often unsolicited. You have unique experiences. Schools, businesses, and social service organizations invite you to get a first-hand look at their work. You engage with new communities. You attend churches and festivals in communities that are not your own. You are the guest of honor at fundraisers in homes that you have never visited and with many people you are meeting for the first time. You get special access. Every group treats you as a VIP, providing you with direct connections to leadership, giving you a special tour, and allowing you to get hands on with whatever they do. You become more interesting. People are exceedingly moved by what you say. Your jokes are funnier. It's difficult to blend in. In fact, your campaign does not want you to blend in. To maximize your attendance, people must see you there. At every event, you are ushered to the front where people watch you, not the other way around. In many cases, these are all new experiences that were not afforded to you before you decided to run for office or get elected.

Frameworks influence how one views a phenomenon. What are its component parts? What are the relationships between the component parts? The novice or advanced beginner does not need to start over to determine which components of a problem are most important and how to prioritize information. Frameworks also manage the set of possible future actions by narrowing an infinite number of possible solutions to those consistent with how the problem is conceptualized per the framework. The novice politician is freed up to take action because they do not need to sift through all possible actions.

Frameworks function similarly in many fields—to understand and to guide action. In academic research, a framework "steers the whole research activity. The conceptual framework serves as a 'map' or 'rudder' that will guide you towards realizing the objectives or intent of your study" (Regoniel 2015). In business, a framework helps to crystallize a manageable problem in unstructured environments to focus organizations on applicable solutions. In social movements, frameworks "show how multiple factors interact to influence the problem or goal" and serve "to identify actions and interventions more likely to lead to the desired result" (Community Tool Box n.d.). In policy, frameworks are used to understand policy problems and to narrow the set of possible actions to address the problems.

Economics is an academic field with a long track record of interjecting applied frameworks for policymaking. Writing as an economist and former legislator, Brandl (1985, 344) notes that the economist's main contribution to public policy is to "construe a complex issue as a problem capable of solution." Economists provide "a number of simple techniques, aids to reasoning, which can be invoked by politicians and by their advisors" (Brandl 1985, 347). For example, understanding the administration of social services as "costs and benefits," viewing the responses and interactions of schools as a "market," drawing parallels between parental school choice and consumer behaviors, and extending the concept of capital beyond monetary wealth to include social constructs such as culture and family, are all examples of economic frameworks applied to public policy. Politicians from different backgrounds and different political parties use economic frameworks to understand policy issues and determine possible solutions. "It is when politicians come to understand public affairs by means of these constructs that . . . the 'ideas of economists' become more powerful than is commonly understood" (Brandl 1985, 348).

There are number of frameworks in education policy. For example, the achievement gap shifts our view of aggregate educational outcomes toward differences by student groups (e.g., race, gender, and socioeconomic status), narrowing policy solutions to those which involve the disaggregation of outcome data by student groups (e.g., No Child Left Behind) and minimizing differences in outcomes across student groups. The opportunity gap focuses on inequitable access to inputs, such as resources, across student groups to understand disparities in educational outcomes; accordingly, policy solutions center on equitable investments in quality educational experiences (Ladson-Billings 2006). Similarly, educational equity is a framework that concerns the distribution of resources, particularly for those students with the most need. Currently, "grit," which is an increasingly popular framework among politicians, explains educational outcomes as contingent on individual traits such as perseverance and persistence (Duckworth 2016). It thus diverts attention away from systemic policy solutions and toward promoting risk-taking and overcoming failures on an individual basis.

There are other frameworks that I have appropriated in my policy work. For example, many noneducators believe that schools and teachers are chiefly (sometimes wholly) responsible for student academic outcomes. To help lay audiences understand the strong influence of communities and families on academic outcomes, I present the "85/15" framework. First, I ask participants to estimate the amount of time that a student spends in school from birth to high school graduation (age 18). Participants estimate that students spend anywhere from 10 percent to 75 percent of their lives in school. The responses are telling. If an influential business CEO believes that students spend 75 percent of their lives in schools, they will have exaggerated expectations for what schools and teachers can realistically accomplish. The actual amount of time is 13.4 percent (Wherry 2004), a figure that I round up to 15 percent for presentation effect. Most participants are surprised by the low percentage of time that students spend in school.

Once the participants see student experiences through the "85/15" framework, I am provided the space to discuss a number of common themes in educational research. Participants come to appreciate that if students spend 85 percent of their lives outside of school, communities and families are tremendously influential. This also opens the door to thinking about realistic expectations for teachers in the 15 percent of time that students are in school. As noneducators come to recognize that outside school factors contribute to and exacerbate achievement and opportunity gaps, it becomes possible to discuss holistic policy solutions that connect neighborhood and familial conditions to educational outcomes.

HOW TO IDENTIFY AND DEVELOP FRAMEWORKS FOR POLICY

Working with conceptual approaches, such as frameworks, is familiar territory for academics. Academics develop frameworks to guide research. They develop models to explain complex phenomenon. They understand, apply, and develop theories about social and policy issues. This section is intended to help academics adapt the tools and skills that they use every day in their profession to identify and develop frameworks for policymaking.

THEORIES

Theories are tailor-made for creating frameworks. Theories describe behavior, formulate meaning, and predict future behaviors. In a policy context, theories can help novice politicians recognize patterns in the cacophony of incoming stimuli, like finding the hidden image in a stereogram. Theories provide a name for a phenomenon, which is critically important. "Giving something a name makes it real, as well as something that can be communicated about" (Rako 2018). If a phenomenon has a name, then politicians are not alone in recognizing it. Others have, and may also recognize it, too. A name helps politicians share the phenomenon with others. A word of caution here: the academic must remember that the goal is not to teach the theory. Rather, the goal is to demonstrate the manifestation of the theory to a layperson, so they can recognize an example of the theory in new experiences. Therefore, you do not need to refer to a "theory" explicitly. In fact, from my experiences some politicians would bristle at the word, "theory." Instead, simply name the phenomenon.

An unattributed theory sounds blasphemous. To the best of my knowledge, however, telling politicians a theory that is not yours is not plagiarism. Unfortunately, the academic who developed the theory will not get credit and one can expect novice politicians may inaccurately attribute the source of the theory to the messenger. But the academic whose work is either left unattributed or is incorrectly attributed to another can take some solace in the fact that their theory is being used in policy. And isn't the application of our work in policy the ultimate goal of research utilization, regardless of who gets credit?

THEMES

Academics identify themes from research articles that span multiple years and a multitude of studies. In fact, the purpose of a literature review is to organize and summarize the themes in the academic research. These themes are fertile ground for frameworks. For example, in review articles found in journals such as *Review of Educational Research* and *Research of Research in Education*, the academic literature is already organized into themes that act as guideposts to help readers understand patterns across different studies. If themes help academics to identify patterns in the academic literature, then they may also help politicians to recognize patterns in new experiences.

VARIABLES

Educational researchers, particularly quantitative researchers, often include common sets of explanatory variables in analyses. Some of these common variables include socio-economic characteristics (e.g., race, gender, education levels), attitudes toward education, and neighborhood or school characteristics. Across repeated trials, these variables can be found to function predictably. Insofar as they do, they can form the basis of frameworks that can help politicians to recognize similar patterns in new experiences. This is particularly helpful for politicians to recognize inequitable outcomes or disproportionate impacts for certain student groups.

HOW TO PUT A FRAMEWORK TOGETHER

As an exercise, write a statement to encapsulate what you have learned through your research, writing, and reading on an education topic. Academics communicate these types of summary statements frequently, often at the end of presentations. In a policy context, this summary statement is valuable material to develop a framework. But in a policy context, lead with the summary statement, don't end with it. Communicate this wisdom up front so politicians can benefit from the cumulation of your expertise and apply it themselves to recognize patterns in new experiences. For example, a colleague who studies writing summarized a lifetime of findings in the

---

I have received some pushback when I use variables as frameworks. Politicians who are uncomfortable with issues such as race and gender have questioned why "those" variables are included in analyses. My answer is that the variables are included because there are real-world differences across these groups. If there were no differences across these groups, then academics would not include these variables in analyses. For example, academics do not include characteristics such as shoe size as variables because there are no meaningful differences in academic achievement by shoe size. Politicians also charge that these patterns are deterministic. They interpret my point as declaring that there will differences by select groups in advance, before a policy is implemented. This, of course, is not the case. What I am saying is that the inclusion of these variables in study after study has come out in some consistent directions. Unless the policy in question includes some explicit provisions to the contrary, then one should expect to see similar outcomes when a new policy is implemented.

sentence: "If teachers don't teach it, students won't learn it." This simple summary statement could be the basis for a useful framework for novice education research and policy politicians to recognize patterns when they visit new classrooms (which they will inevitably do as elected officials) where explicit writing instruction is lacking. The framework helps politicians to understand the perplexing policy problem of low writing achievement as one that can be solved by explicit instruction.

When we are engaged in informal conversations with *our* people (i.e., other academics), I have witnessed the tendency for academics to introduce a well-accepted point with a phrase such as, "We know that . . ." What follows the phrase is a potential framework. If "we"—meaning the academic community in this case—collectively know something or if something is so obvious to us that we can simply state it, without further explication, then we should let politicians in on our shared knowledge. Tell them what we know in the same conversational, approachable way that we communicate with each other.

13

TEACH TO CHAMPION

Teaching to champion entails enabling and empowering politicians to bring research forward to the people and networks that they choose—without the academic in the room.

One underlying assumption of the research utilization literature is that academics should take an educational approach to communicating their research to politicians (Bogenschneider and Corbett 2010). But, as we have discussed already, politicians do not gather information to understand, they gather information to act.

In this section, I put academics' policy communication efforts in focus. Academics teach. Teaching is central to our professional responsibilities and identities as educators. I build on our strengths as teachers in order to apply our teaching skills most adroitly in policymaking.

I introduce the crucial role of politicians as "champions" of policy change. When politicians champion a policy issue, they take action and expend political capital to achieve desired policy outcomes, on their own. Academics' role in the policymaking process then is to teach to champion—to teach so that politicians are armed with research and can *bring research forward themselves to the people and networks that they choose—without the academic in the room.*

WHAT IS A POLICY CHAMPION?

Originally studied in the management literature and applied to fields such as technology and business (Greenhalgh et al. 2003), champions are important drivers of policy change (Gallagher 2009). A champion is someone who is "persuasive and willing to take calculated risks"; thus, "champions adopt programs, ideas or projects as their own and relentlessly promote them" (Thompson, Estabrooks, and Degner 2006, 695). As enthusiastic promoters of new ideas, champions counter the organizational inertia to resist change. Schon (1963, 84) found champions to be essential to the adoption of new ideas and claimed that "the new idea either finds a champion or dies." Champions choose the initiatives that they support, volunteer to see them come to fruition, take personal ownership of the outcomes, and exert influence by persuading others (Thompson, Estabrooks, and Degner 2006).

When politicians champion a policy issue, they expend political capital to accomplish desired policy outcomes. The policy outcomes take priority over other issues or ideas and politicians may compromise to achieve their goals. In this process, politicians bring research forward to share with colleagues and influential external networks to generate support for their preferred policy outcomes (Bogenschneider, Day, and Parrott 2019). In this role, politicians are the ultimate intermediaries as they appropriate research for their purposes.

PREPARING TO TEACH TO CHAMPION

There are three points that academics must consider as they prepare to teach to champion. First, teaching to champion is not about you. You are not preparing research to present yourself. In fact, when the process goes well, the academic will not be in room when politicians present research. Also, you are not preparing research evidence for others like you to present. You are enabling and empowering education research and policy novices to bring research to other laypersons.

Second, the audience consists of laypersons, not experts. Therefore, academics should prepare politicians to communicate to laypersons on education policy issues at the layperson's level of understanding. Laypersons hold a much more basic understanding of research than academics or even students, meaning that academics should assume that the audience does not share common background knowledge on education research or policy.

Third, the end goal of teaching to champion is for politicians to appropriate research for their own use. Politicians choose the audiences to whom they present the research and in so doing take some ownership over the content. Therefore, the materials provided to politicians, to include presentations, speeches, support documents, should avoid politically charged language, strike a conversation tone, and incorporate concepts or frameworks that politicians can communicate on their own.

Teaching to champion requires academics to put themselves in the shoes of others, in this case the novice presenter and lay audience members who do not know what academics know about research or policy (Pinker 2014). Teaching to champion requires a shift in how academics think about communicating with politicians. The goal is not to show what you know. Rather, the goal is for politicians to take what you know and show it to others themselves.

Academics should communicate in ways and with materials so that the end goal is is to reach beyond politicians' desks or professional staff. Politicians should feel comfortable enough with the materials that you provide them to bring the materials forward themselves. When I engage with politicians, I create materials with the intent that they may make it to the governor's office by way of politicians and other policy actors, without my intervention. To teach to champion, academics should create approachable materials, stay action-oriented, narrate the lines, and make it motivational.

CREATE APPROACHABLE MATERIALS

Approachable materials are light in appearance and tone, but not content. The research one-pager is an example of an approachable document. The research one-pager is a highly informative document that covers a lot of ground from a practical problem to the ask in twenty seconds. But the rich content is organized to allow the reader to work through the document easily.

In other communications, the text should avoid jargon. This is not novel advice. Rather, it is probably the most common advice in the literature on how to communicate in a policy context (e.g., Cramm et al. 2017; Lintle 2009; Oliver and Cairney 2019). The advice is so ubiquitous that it begs the question, why have academics failed to heed it? One reason for the continued use of jargon may be that as academics prepare to present research in policy contexts, they are still the ones doing the presenting. As presenters, academics are comfortable with jargon and technical language. When academics write text for others to present on their own, it re-centers the education research and policy novice as the presenter, giving academics an added incentive to avoid jargon because they are required to consider the presentation from the novice's point of view. The novice can't appropriate jargon as their own, so they are unlikely to use it.

Lighten the cognitive load for politicians through visuals, creative formatting, drawings, cartoons, and even humor. Block text is visually dense. Materials that break up the text with other mediums will likely fit politicians' presentation styles better than a dense academic document (for an expanded treatment on how to create approachable materials see Rankin [2019; 2020]).

As an academic, creating approachable materials for novices to present to laypersons may seem beneath your level of education and expertise. Frankly, it probably is. But remember, the materials are not for you. They are for politicians to present without you.

Some years ago, a legislator who connected with an argument that I made about the relationship between socioeconomic status and standardized test scores asked me to create a poster to illustrate the idea. At first, I was discouraged by the request. This was an elementary request that, frankly, I thought was beneath me as a university academic because my job was not to create posters. But given that my students and I were heavily engaged in informing politicians about assessment policies, we pulled out the markers and glue and made a poster. The poster got a lot of mileage. The legislator took it to several gatherings as a visual aide to solicit support for a change in assessment policies. We were victims of our own success. While I was too embarrassed to put my name on the poster and take credit, word got around and other legislators contacted me to create them an individualized poster. We didn't make any more posters because there was no end in sight.

STAY ACTION-ORIENTED

Political champions take action. Your suggestions to them should be equally action-oriented. To that end, academics should think of recommendations not as suggestions, but as courses of action. When academics are presenting a course of action, the list should be

- parsimonious and include only the most important actions;
- prioritized in a clear way;
- organized so that the sequence of the actions—which one comes first, second, and so on—is explicit.

NARRATE THE LINES

When presenting complex concepts, academics should "narrate the lines." The idea comes from visual models and diagrams, but it is applicable to any explanation of complex concepts. Visual models and diagrams include two general parts: (1) the components that comprise the concept and (2) connectors (often displayed as lines) to explain the interactions between the components. While it is obvious that a thorough explanation of complex concepts should include a description of its components, academics should take equal time to explain the connection between the components so that politicians have a clear understanding of how the components work and work together. For example, does one component cause another? Which components precede the others? Do the components coexist in the same setting with no meaningful interaction? When politicians understand how complex concepts work, not just what they are, it demonstrates a deeper level of understanding so politicians can explain the concepts on their own.

MAKE IT MOTIVATIONAL

Champions influence others through motivation, inspiration, and vision (Howell and Higgins 1990). To aide politicians' efforts, academics should present research in a motivational way. The goal is to generate secondary excitement. Novice politicians should show a sense of enthusiasm and interest when they talk about research.

Academics can inspire politicians by tapping into their own motivations. Why do you study what you study? Why is the research important?

Also, in the progression from practical problems to the ask, you identified a practical problem and an argument for its importance. The practical
problem is another motivator. Based on the research, remind politicians
of what real-world conditions can get better and how the research is a
vital part of addressing the practical problem. Also, in making the case
for the importance of the practical problem, you appealed to emotions
and widely held values and goals (e.g., justice, fairness, equity, economic
development, etc.), all of which can be persuasive and, in the hands of
politicians, can motivate others to take action as well.

14

A RENEWED ROLE FOR ACADEMICS

First, academics are optimally positioned to influence education policy. Second, a well-rounded faculty of education should include a professor of impact whose job requirements include translating research to influence policy.

The *Teach Truth to Power* approach to engaging in education policy culminates in two sweeping implications that bookend the research utilization process. First, the point at which research is used in policymaking is where academics are optimally positioned to influence education policy. Second, since academia is where research is created, a well-rounded faculty in a school of education should include a professor of impact whose job requirements include translating research to influence policy because *engaging* in education policy should be a critical requirement of *studying* education policy. To frame these recommendations, I start the chapter with an overview of the lessons learned for engaging in education policy derived from the action-oriented approach of *Teach Truth to Power*. I end the chapter with words of encouragement for those who are inspired to use this book to engage in education policy.

TAKE AN ACTION-ORIENTED APPROACH TO THE POLICYMAKING PROCESS

Politicians set policy, while professional staff engage in the technical details involved in implementing it. Academics should be aware that the preponderance of research has been conducted with professional staff who likely have some expertise in education, research, or policy. Politicians, by contrast, are education research and policy novices.

Novices assimilate information by connecting it to past experiences and make decisions based on the "best-fit" even if they know such a fit is not the most appropriate or correct. They rely on existing rules to perform tasks, turning to convenient sources such as political party platforms, ideological think tanks, and trusted individuals for guidance. Novices lack an understanding of how their ideas fit in a holistic context. By contrast, academic experts have an intuitive grasp of education research and policy. Academics must translate what they know to communicate with novices most effectively.

Politicians are extremely busy. They function with half-knowledge as a deliberate strategy to manage their time and allocate resources by determining which information receives attention (or not) at any given time, and by extension, how they seek and use knowledge, including research evidence. Half-knowledge does not mean knowing "half the truth." Rather, it implies filtering out surplus knowledge that is "beyond policymakers' control (but not cognitive capacity)" (Marin 1981, 49). This, in turn, means that politicians are more likely to focus on information in cases where they can take action. Thus, academics should expect politicians to engage with research not solely to gain a greater understanding of a particular issue, but to take action.

Academic research is not "shovel ready" for policy formation because it is not detailed enough to apply to a specific policy context. Politicians want information on the specific people and institutions in their political jurisdiction because these constituents will hold politicians accountable. Ultimately, what politicians covet is an accounting of cases in a local context. Politicians are inclined to rely on localized information to take action, even if the localized information counters the prevailing research evidence. On the positive side, research has a long shelf-life, meaning that there is sufficient research available at any time to inform any policy idea put forth by politicians. The research may be difficult to access, it may take time to sift through volumes of articles to find applicable studies, and the research certainly needs to be translated to a local policy context to be useful, but it is available, and applicable.

Policymaking is an interactive process in which academics are one of many voices. Moreover, many ways of knowing, in addition to research, contribute meaningfully to the policymaking process. Policy formation involves debate over the best possible action given the present circumstances, and it is shaped by the individual participants involved with a specific issue at a given time. To be most useful to novice politicians in a policy context, academics should leverage *the* research, defined as the cumulation of evidence available in the academic literature (Petes and Meyer 2018), to predict policy outcomes.

From politicians' perspectives, all academic research is brought-outside information. Politicians do not initiate the inquiry; academics do, and academics are outside the politicians' spheres of influence. Politicians have no control over the distribution of brought-outside information and little trust that outsiders will maintain confidentiality. They are also most likely to ignore brought-outside research. Getting political attention is the primarily challenge facing academics who aspire to have their work inform policymaking.

USE YOUR ACADEMIC POSITION TO INFLUENCE EDUCATION POLICY

Prediction is an invaluable asset in a policymaking, and academics possess a tailor-made skillset to predict policy outcomes in an education landscape that is constantly changing, whether this be because of new technologies, shifting demographics, breakthroughs in learning sciences, political shifts, social and community challenges, or any combination thereof. Academics are at the forefront of understanding these constant changes. We observe them first. We measure them first. We name them first. We put them in context first. Thus, we should be the first to predict how these changes will impact education.

By contrast, politicians are novices with respect to recognizing, understanding, and predicting how these nonstop changes impact education. There are four ways that politicians embody this:

1. Their academic or professional backgrounds are not in education research and/or policy.
2. They must make sense of new experiences in new environments (e.g., schools and communities unlike their own).
3. They are challenged to keep up with multiple legislative responsibilities, including education.
4. They benefit from assistance to understand the ever-changing educational landscape.

Furthermore, it is highly unlikely that politicians will recognize and understand changes in education on their own. Rather, the more likely scenario is that these educational changes will be brought to the politician's attention by outside policy actors who interpret these changes according to their preferred policy orientation and propose policy solutions accordingly. Academics are well-positioned to inform politicians.

Similarly, academics should not to wait for politicians to set research agendas. The limited perspective of education research and policy novices means that such agendas will likely be too practical, too reactionary, and too present-oriented to predict future policy outcomes. Rather, academic experts should continue to research ahead—well, well ahead—of novice politicians.

INCLUDE SCHOLARS WHO INFLUENCE EDUCATION POLICY IN ACADEMIC SETTINGS

University-based efforts to train scholars to engage in education policy are intermittent and uneven. The same holds for the research utilization literature and academic efforts to influence policy through research. Presently, think tanks and activist foundations have the most sustained direct engagement with politicians. Universities engage in policy through research centers that publishing politically neutral documents that are of limited utility to the action-oriented politician. But at times, the lone academic, with little to no institutional support and facing many disincentives, leaves the

friendly confines of academia to engage politicians directly in the unfamiliar and treacherous world of education policy.

To persist on the present course is to continue this fragmented progress. Busy novice politicians will continue to shape policy based on their
previous experiences, which are largely void of research influences, and
will gravitate to those organizations that tailor their message to action,
leaving out those academics who do not engage in policy with an action

Entering academia from an applied policy background, I have always viewed
my work and the profession through an impact lens. As a junior scholar, while
I sequestered myself to write for other scholars who make publication decisions, I asked many of these same scholars how their research made an impact
in policy. Their examples were surprisingly few and generally superficial. They
could think of an instance or two, but the bulk of their work had been read
and discussed in academic settings with no politicians in the room.

My belief that academic research has much to contribute to education
policy prompted my journey to the "dark side"—namely, politics. During my
academic career, I had been contacted by many politicians to contribute my
expertise to policymaking, but due to the churning of new politicians entering
the arena, I found myself covering much of the same topics while Arizona public education was treading in place. Furthermore, when I turned to the academic
literature to learn about how to engage in education policy, I became impatient
with overly theorized explanations of Arizona politics. The descriptions of most
Arizona politicians in the academic literature gave them much more credit for
innovative and intentional policymaking decisions than what they deserved,
in my opinion. I knew many of these people. They were members of the public
who won an election and were now in a position to make consequential education policy decisions. They relied heavily on direction from others to form
their policy decisions. To remain focused on action, they shielded themselves
from contradictory information and contrarians who challenged their policy
positions.

To bring research evidence to bear directly, I realized that more educators,
and academics specially, needed to run for office. Inclined to action myself,
I ran for office. In full disclosure, I hope more academics follow a similar course
and that they are inspired by this book to engage in educational policy,
which is likely to demystify the policymaking process and the politicians who
govern it. When academics realize that the only difference between them and
politicians is an election, they may be prompted to run for office to make
policy decisions themselves.

orientation. Academics will continue to study research utilization using professional staff with whom they share much in common and who are more likely to agree to participate in research, but whose ability to influence policy is constrained by the politicians who hire and fire them. Academics will also continue to put faith in "enlightenment" as the means by which their work has impact, while lamenting that too many education policy decisions are made without considering research.

Academia is both the primary obstacle to advancing research utilization and the locus for changing these dynamics. Currently, academic career expectations are almost exclusively based on publication requirements. These traditional measures produce copious volumes of research but little to no formalized mechanisms to bridge the research and policy gap. Coincidentally, academia is at a crucial juncture where bridging gaps is more important than ever as the value of academic contributions are under increased scrutiny (Hess 2017; Garcia 2017).

In response, academic education programs should be reimagined to value influencing education policy as a meaningful contribution to the field worthy of monetary compensation and professional recognition for advancement. For the benefit of the multitude of academics doing research in schools and colleges of education across the country, a well-rounded education faculty should include a scholar, a professor of impact, dedicated to influencing policy through research. The tenure and promotion requirements of a professor impact should be split between conducting research, either to advance the research utilization literature or in a separate field of their choice, and engaging in a policy context as part of their academic duties.

In addition, while education policy is a common subfield in every college of education, there are very few institutions where students are taught to engage in education policy. Too often, education policy programs end at the point of research production, leaving students largely unprepared to take what they have learned to influence their local context. I contend that *engaging* in education policy is a critical requirement of *studying* education policy. Most education policy students will work in an applied setting rather than academia. The professor of impact can be charged with teaching students how to take bring they know to make a difference in local policy contexts. This will make for a well-rounded educational experience for students who aspire to "do something" with their research.

USE *TEACH TRUTH TO POWER* AS A GUIDE FOR ACADEMICS WHO ARE INSPIRED TO ENGAGE IN POLICY

You're ready to engage with politicians in a policy context. You start with a practical problem as a way to introduce your research. The practical problem is consequential, widely applicable, and localized to capture the political attention. You are disciplined and end all your interactions with a specific and direct ask. To beat the swarm of information and policy actors that bombard politicians and their appointees, you are thinking beyond present-day politicians and building trusted relationships with prospective politicians. You have the courage to enlist unexpected allies so that your research does not get drowned out by others who have propagated the same message legislative session after session and so your research disrupts the local political dynamics to stand out.

When engaging with politicians directly, you leverage *the* research to predict policy outcomes and become indispensable to politicians. The ability to predict distinguishes your contributions as an academic expert from the cacophony of lay voices in a policy context. You present your research to politicians via a research one-pager so politicians can understand the key features in twenty seconds. You scaffold answers to bridge from the politician's practical questions to more complex concepts. You have reflected on your own knowledge to develop frameworks that help novice politicians put their past experiences, and new experiences, in context to create guidelines for future action. And your policy engagement is targeted toward teaching to champion, empowering and enabling politicians to appropriate research to achieve their policy goals.

For the sake of creating quality and equitable educational outcomes for all students, I look forward to your policy success. My aspiration is that you can turn to this book as an inspiration and a concrete guide for engaging in education policy to "teach truth to power."

REFERENCES

Albaek, Erik. 1995. "Between Knowledge and Power: Utilization of Social Science in Public Policy Making." *Policy Sciences* 28 (1): 79–100. https://www.jstor.org/stable/4532339?origin=JSTOR-pdf&seq=1.

American Educational Research Association. N.d. "What Is Education Research?" Accessed August 21, 2019. http://www.aera.net/About-AERA/What-is-Education-Research.

American Society for Quality. N.d. "What Is Auditing?" Accessed July 9, 2019. https://asq.org/quality-resources/auditing.

Anderson, Sharon, Elliott Medrich, and Donna Fowler. 2007. "Which Achievement Gap?" *Phi Delta Kappan* 88 (7): 547–550. https://doi.org/10.1177/003172170708800716.

Ansary, Tamim. 2007. "Education at Risk: Fallout from a Flawed Report." *Edutopia*. Accessed March 9. https://www.edutopia.org/landmark-education-report-nation-risk.

Apollonio, Dorie E., and Lisa A. Bero. 2017. "Interpretation and Use of Evidence in State Policymaking: A Qualitative Analysis." *BMJ Open* 7 (2). https://doi.org/10.1136/bmjopen-2016-012738.

Arifon, Olivier, and Nicolas Vanderbiest. 2016. "Integrating Social Networks in a Lobbying Campaign: The Case Study of Intermarché, a Supermarket Chain." *Telematics and Informatics* 33 (4): 1105–1118. https://doi.org/10.1016/j.tele.2016.03.007.

Ball, Arnetha F. 2012. "To Know Is Not Enough." *Educational Researcher* 41 (8): 283–293. https://doi.org/10.3102/0013189X12465334.

Barnes, Carol A., Margaret E. Goertz, and Diane Massell. 2014. "How State Education Agencies Acquire and Use Research Knowledge for School Improvement." In *Using*

Research Evidence in Education: From the Schoolhouse Door to Capitol Hill, edited by Kara S. Finnigan and Alan J. Daly, 99–116. Cham, Switzerland: Springer International.

Benner, Patricia. 1982. "From Novice to Expert." *American Journal of Nursing* 82 (3): 402–407. https://doi.org/10.2307/3462928.

Berliner, David C., and Bruce J. Biddle. 1995. *The Manufactured Crisis: Myths, Fraud, and the Attack on America's Public Schools*. Cambridge, MA: Perseus Books.

Besag, Frank. 1986. "Reality and Research: Problem Statement and Philosophy." *American Behavioral Scientist* 30 (1): 6–14. https://doi.org/10.1177/000276486030001002.

Boehnke, Klaus, and Maor Shani. 2017. "Activism." In *The SAGE Encyclopedia of Political Behavior*, edited by Fathali M. Moghaddam, 1–52. Thousand Oaks, CA: SAGE Publications, Inc. https://sk.sagepub.com/reference/the-sage-encyclopedia-of-political-behavior.

Bogenschneider, Karen. 2006. *Family Policy Matters: How Policymaking Affects Families and What Professionals Can Do*, 2nd ed. Mahwah, NJ: Lawrence Erlbaum.

Bogenschneider, Karen, and Thomas J. Corbett. 2010. *Evidence-Based Policymaking: Insights from Policy-Minded Researchers and Research-Minded Policymakers*. New York: Taylor & Francis Group.

Bogenschneider, Karen, Elizabeth Day, and Emily Parrott. 2019. "Revisiting Theory on Research Use: Turning to Policymakers for Fresh Insights." *American Psychologist* 74 (7): 778–793. https://doi.org/10.1037/amp0000460.

Bogenschneider, Karen, Olivia M. Little, and Kristen Johnson. 2013. "Policymakers' Use of Social Science Research: Looking within and across Policy Actors." *Journal of Marriage and Family* 75 (2): 263–275. https://doi.org/10.1111/jomf.12009.

Booth, Wayne C., Gregory G. Colomb, Joseph M. Williams, Joseph Bizup, and William T. Fitzgerald. 2016. *The Craft of Research*, 4th ed. Chicago: University of Chicago Press.

Bornmann, Lutz, and Mutz Rüdiger. 2015. "Growth Rates of Modern Science: A Bibliometric Analysis Based on the Number of Publications and Cited References." *Journal of the Association for Information Science and Technology* 66 (11): 2215–2222. https://doi.org/10.1002/asi.23329.

Bracey, G. W. 2004. "Serious Questions about the TVAAS." *Phi Delta Kappan* 85 (9): 716–17.

Brandl, John E. 1985. "Distilling Frenzy from Academic Scribbling: How Economics Influences Politicians." *Journal of Policy Analysis and Management* 4 (3): 344–353. https://doi.org/10.2307/3324189.

Caird, Jenny, Katy Sutcliffe, Irene Kwan, Kelly Dickson, and James Thomas. 2015. "Mediating Policy-Relevant Evidence at Speed: Are Systematic Reviews of Systematic Reviews a Useful Approach?" *Evidence and Policy* 11 (1): 81–97. https://doi.org/10.1332/174426514X13988609036850.

Cairney, Paul, and Richard Kwiatkowski. 2017. "How to Communicate Effectively with Policymakers: Combine Insights from Psychology and Policy Studies." *Palgrave Communications* 3 (1). https://doi.org/10.1057/s41599-017-0046-8.

Cairney, Paul, and Kathryn Oliver. 2017. "Evidence-Based Policymaking is Not Like Evidence-Based Medicine, So How Far Should You Go to Bridge the Divide between Evidence and Policy?" *Health Research Policy and Systems* 15 (35): 1–11. https://doi .org/10.1186/s12961-017-0192-x.

Cairney, Paul, and Kathryn Oliver. 2020. "How Should Academics Engage in Policy-making to Achieve Impact?" *Political Studies Review* 18 (2): 228–244. https://doi.org /10.1177/1478929918807714.

Callahan, Raymond E. 1962. *Education and the Cult of Efficiency*. Chicago: University of Chicago Press.

Caplan, Nathan. 1979. "The Two-Communities Theory and Knowledge Utilization." *American Behavioral Scientist* 22 (3): 459–470.

Carnoy, Martin, Rebecca Jacobsen, Lawrence Mishel, and Richard Rothstein. 2005. *The Charter School Dust-Up: Examining the Evidence on Enrollment and Achievement*. New York, NY: Teachers College Press & Economic Policy Institute.

Carson, C. C., R. M. Huelskamp, and T. D. Woodall. 1993. "Perspectives on Education in America: An Annotated Briefing." *Journal of Educational Research* 86 (5): 259–265, 267–291, 293–297, 299–307, 309–310. https://doi.org/10.1080/00220671 .1993.9941211.

Centers for Disease Control. N.d. "Overview of Policy Evaluation." Atlanta, GA. Accessed July 9, 2019. https://www.cdc.gov/injury/pdfs/policy/brief%201-a.pdf.

Coburn, Cynthia E., Meredith I. Honig, and Mary K. Stein. 2009. "What's the Evidence on Districts' Use of Evidence?" In *The Role of Research in Educational Improvement*, edited by John D. Bransford, Deborah J. Stipek, Nancy J. Vye, Louis M. Gomez, and Diana Lam, 67–87. Cambridge, MA: Harvard Education Press.

Coburn, Cynthia E., and Joan E. Talbert. 2006. "Conceptions of Evidence Use in School Districts: Mapping the Terrain." *American Journal of Education* 112 (4): 469–495. https://doi.org/10.1086/505056.

Community Tool Box. N.d. "Developing a Framework or Model of Change." Accessed July 21, 2020. https://ctb.ku.edu/en/4-developing-framework-or-model-change.

Cotton, Christopher S., and Cheng Li. 2018. "Clueless Politicians: On Policymaker Incentives for Information Acquisition in a Model of Lobbying." *Journal of Law, Economics, and Organization* 34 (3): 425–456. https://doi.org/10.1093/jleo/ewy009.

Cramm, Heidi, Janet Breimer, Lydia Lee, Julie Burch, Valerie Ashford, and Mike Schaub. 2017. "Best Practices for Writing Effective Lay Summaries." *Journal of Military, Veteran and Family Health* 3 (1): 7–20. https://doi.org/10.3138/jmvfh.3.1.004.

Crow, Deserai, and Michael Jones. 2018. "Narratives as Tools for Influencing Policy Change." *Policy and Politics* 46 (2): 217–234. https://doi.org/10.1332/030557318X152 30061022899.

Daley, Barbara J. 1999. "Novice to Expert: An Exploration of How Professionals Learn." *Adult Education Quarterly* 49 (4): 133–147. https://doi.org/10.1177/07417 1369904900401.

Davidson, Brett. 2017. "Storytelling and Evidence-Based Policy: Lessons from the Grey Literature." *Palgrave Communications* 3 (1). https://doi.org/10.1057/palcomms .2017.93.

Davies, Huw T. O., and Sandra M. Nutley. 2008. "Learning More about How Research-Based Knowledge Gets Used: Guidance in the Development of New Empirical Research." New York: William T. Grant Foundation. https://wtgrantfoundation.org /library/uploads/2015/10/Guidance-in-the-Development-of-New-Empirical-Research .pdf.

Davies, Philip. 2000. "The Relevance of Systematic Reviews to Educational Policy and Practice." *Oxford Review of Education* 26 (3): 365–378. https://doi.org/10.1080 /3054980020001882.

Dombrowksi, Eileen, Lena Rotenberg, and Mimi Beck. 2013. *Theory of Knowledge*, 2nd ed. Oxford: Oxford University Press.

Dreyfus, Stuart E., and Hubert L. Dreyfus. 1980. "A Five-Stage Model of the Mental Activities Involved in Directed Skill Acquisition Operations & Research." Berkeley, CA: University of California, Berkeley. https://apps.dtic.mil/dtic/tr/fulltext/u2/a084551.pdf.

Duckworth, Angela. 2016. *Grit: The Power of Passion and Perseverance*. New York: Scribner.

Dumas, Michael J., and Gary Anderson. 2014. "Qualitative Research as Policy Knowledge: Framing Policy Problems and Transforming Education from the Ground Up." *Education Policy Archives*, special issue, "Qualitative Inquiry" 22 (11). https://doi .org/10.14507/epaa.v22n11.2014.

Dunn, William N. 1980. "The Two-Communities Metaphor and Models of Knowledge Use: An Exploratory Case Survey." *Science Communication* 1 (4): 515–536. https:// doi.org/10.1177/107554708000100403.

Eagly, Alice H. 2016. "When Passionate Advocates Meet Research on Diversity, Does the Honest Broker Stand a Chance?" *Journal of Social Issues* 72 (1): 199–222. https:// doi.org/10.1111/josi.12163.

Edelman, Murray. 1979. *Political Language: Words That Succeed and Policies That Fail*. New York: Academic Press.

Edelstein, Hilary. 2016. "Collaborative Research Partnerships for Knowledge Mobilisation." *Evidence & Policy: A Journal of Research, Debate and Practice* 12 (2): 199–216. http://dx.doi.org/10.1332/174426415X14399903490979

Epstein, Richard L. 2011. *The Pocket Guide to Critical Thinking*, 4th ed. Socorro, NM: Advanced Reasoning Forum.

Evans, Julie. 2013. "How Arts and Humanities Can Influence Public Policy." *Huffpost*, April 20. https://www.huffingtonpost.co.uk/jules-evans/arts-humanities-influence-public-policy_b_2709614.html.

Farmer, Rick. 2010. "How to Influence Government Policy with Your Research: Tips from Practicing Political Scientists in Government." *PS—Political Science and Politics* 43 (4): 717–19. https://doi.org/10.1017/S1049096510001368.

Felgenhauer, Mike. 2013. "Informational and Monetary Lobbying: Expert Politicians, Good Decisions?" *Journal of Public Economic Theory* 15 (1): 125–155.

Figenschou, Tine Ustad, and Nanna Alida Fredheim. 2020. "Interest Groups on Social Media: Four Forms of Networked Advocacy." *Journal of Public Affairs* 20 (2): 1–8. https://doi.org/10.1002/pa.2012.

Fischman, Gustavo E., Kate T. Anderson, Adai A. Tefera, and Steven J. Zuiker. 2018. "If Mobilizing Educational Research Is the Answer, Who Can Afford to Ask the Question? An Analysis of Faculty Perspectives on Knowledge Mobilization for Scholarship in Education." *AERA Open* 4 (1): 1–17.

Flake, Jeff. 2016. "Twenty Questions: Government Studies That Will Leave You Scratching Your Head." Washington, DC.

Forte, Ellen. 2010. "Examining the Assumptions Underlying the NCLB Federal Accountability Policy on School Improvement." *Educational Psychologist* 45 (2): 76–88. https://doi.org/10.1080/00461521003704738.

Fuller, Bruce, Joseph Wright, Kathryn Gesicki, and Erin Kang. 2007. "Gauging Growth: How to Judge No Child Left Behind?" *Educational Researcher* 36 (5): 268–278. https://doi.org/10.3102/0013189x07306556.

Gallagher, Deborah Rigling. 2009. "Advocates for Environmental Justice: The Role of the Champion in Public Participation Implementation." *Local Environment* 14 (10): 905–916. https://doi.org/10.1080/13549830903244417.

Gamoran, Adam. 2018. "Evidence-Based Policy in the Real World: A Cautionary View." *Annals of the American Academy of Political and Social Science* 678 (1): 180–191. https://doi.org/10.1177/0002716218770138.

Gandara, Denisa, and James C Hearn. 2019. "College Completion, the Texas Way: An Examination of the Development of College Completion Policy in a Distinctive Political Culture." *Teachers College Record* 121 (1): 1–40.

Garcia, David R. 2012. "Protecting the Choice to Stay: 'Education Savings Accounts' and Legislative Priorities." *Teachers College Record*, December 7. ID Number: 16962.

Garcia, David R. 2013. "Traditional Public School Is a Legitimate Choice, Too." *Arizona Republic*, January 28.

Garcia, David R. 2017. "Ed. Scholars Are Talking Past the Public." *Education Week*, January 11.

Garcia, David R. 2018a. "An Engaged Approach to Public Scholarship: Shaping the Policy Agenda through Research Evidence." In *Moving Forward: Policies, Planning and Promoting Access of Hispanic College Students*, edited by Alfredo G. De los Santos Jr., Laura I. Rendon, Gary Francisco Keller, Alberto Acereda, Estela Mara Bensimon, and Richard J. Tannenbaum, 37–54. Tempe, AZ: Bilingual Press.

Garcia, David R. 2018b. "Bridging the Research and Policy Gap to Set the Policy Agenda." In *Wiley-Blackwell Handbook on Education Policy*, edited by Rosemary Papa and Shadow W.J. Armfield, 73–96. Medford, MA: Wiley & Sons.

Gardner, William E. 1984. "A Nation at Risk: Some Critical Comments." *Journal of Teacher Education* 35 (1): 13–15. https://doi.org/10.1177/002248718403500104.

Gigerenzer, Gerd. 2001. "The Adaptive Toolbox." In *Bounded Rationality: The Adaptive Toolbox*, edited by Gerd Gigerenzer and Reinhard Seltan, 37–50. Cambridge, MA: MIT Press.

Gluckman, P. 2014. "Policy: The Art of Science Advice to Government." *Nature*, 2014. https://www.nature.com/news/policy-the-art-of-science-advice-to-government-1.14838.

Gobet, Fernand, and Philippe Chassy. 2009. "Expertise and Intuition: A Tale of Three Theories." *Minds and Machines* 19 (2): 151–180. https://doi.org/10.1007/s11023-008-9131-5.

Goldhaber, Dan D., and Dominic J. Brewer. 2008. "What Gets Studied and Why: Examining the Incentives That Drive Education Research." In *When Research Matters: How Scholarship Influences Education Policy*, edited by Frederick M. Hess, 197–208. Cambridge, MA: Harvard Education Press.

Goodwin, M. 2013. "How Academics Can Engage with Policy: 10 Tips for a Better Conversation." *The Guardian*, March 25. https://www.theguardian.com/higher-education-network/blog/2013/mar/25/academics-policy-engagement-ten-tips.

Greenhalgh, Trisha, Robert Glenn, Paul Bate, Olympia Kyriakidou, Fraser Macfarlane, and Richard Peacock. 2003. "A Systematic Review of the Literature on Diffusion, Dissemination and Sustainability of Innovations in Health Service Delivery and Organisation." London: National Co-ordinating Center for NHS Service Delivery and Organisation R & D. https://doi.org/10.1111/j.0887-378X.2004.00325.x.

Gu, Xin, and Karen L. Blackmore. 2016. "Recent Trends in Academic Journal Growth." *Scientometrics* 108: 693–716. https://doi.org/10.1007/s11192-016-1985-3.

Hammersley, Martyn. 2002. *Educational Research and Policymaking in Practice*. London: Paul Chapman Publishing.

Hammersley, Martyn. 2005. "The Myth of Research-Based Practice: The Critical Case of Educational Inquiry." *International Journal of Social Science Research Methodology* 8 (4): 317–330.

Hammersley, Martyn. 2014. "Translating Research Findings into Educational Policy and Practice: The Virtues and Vices of a Metaphor." *Nouveaux Cahiers de la Recherche en Éducation* 17 (1): 54–74. https://doi.org/10.7202/1027321ar.

Hart-Tervalon, Donna, and David R. Garcia. 2014. "Educational Systems Change at the State Level." In *Ability, Equity, and Culture: Sustaining Inclusive Urban Education Reform*, edited by Elizabeth B. Kozleski and Kathleen K. Thorius, 199–216. New York: Teachers College Press.

Helco, Hugh. 1978. "Issue Networks and the Executive Establishment." In *The New American Political System*, edited by Anthony King, 87–124. Washington, DC: American Enterprise Institute for Public Policy Research.

Henig, Jeffrey R. 2008a. *Spin Cycle: How Research Is Used in Policy Debates: The Case of Charter Schools*. New York: Russell Sage Foundation.

Henig, Jeffrey R. 2008b. "The Evolving Relationship Between Researchers and Public Policy." In *When Research Matters: How Scholarship Influences Education Policy*, edited by Frederick M. Hess, 41–62. Cambridge, MA: Harvard Education Press.

Henig, Jeffrey R. 2009. "Politicization of Evidence: Lessons for an Informed Democracy." *Educational Policy* 23 (1): 137–160. https://doi.org/10.1177/0895904808328525.

Hess, Frederick M. 2008. "When Research Matters: How Scholarship Influences Education Policy." *Society* 45: 534–539. https://doi.org/10.1007/s12115-008-9142-0.

Hess, Frederick M. 2017. "Why Ed. Scholarship Could Soon Be Sidelined." *Education Week*, January 11, 2017.

Hess, Frederick M., and Olivia Meeks. 2010. "Governance in the Accountability Era." Washington, DC: National School Boards Association, The Thomas B. Fordham Institute, and the Iowa School Boards Association.

Hetrick, Beverly, and Carl E. van Horn. 1988. "Educational Research Information: Meeting the Needs of State Policymakers." *Theory into Practice* 27 (2): 106–110. http://www.jstor.org/stable/1476465.

Hill, Paul T. 1996. "Education." In *Reality and Research: Social Science and U.S. Urban Policy Since 1960*, edited by George C. Galster, 131–156. Washington, DC: Urban Institute Press.

Hird, John A. 2009. "The Study and Use of Policy Research in State Legislatures." *International Regional Science Review* 32 (4): 523–535. https://doi.org/10.1177/016001 7609341401.

Honig, Meredith I., and Cynthia Coburn. 2008. "Evidence-Based Decision Making in School District Central Offices." *Educational Policy* 22 (4): 578–608. https://doi.org /10.1177/0895904807307067.

Howell, Jane M., and Christopher A. Higgins. 1990. "Champions of Change: Identifying, Understanding, and Supporting Champions of Technological Innovations." *Organizational Dynamics* 19 (1): 40–55. https://doi.org/10.1016/0090-2616(90)90047-S.

Howell, William G., Paul E. Peterson, and Martin R. West. 2004. "Dog Eats AFT Homework." *Wall Street Journal*, August 18, 2004.

Howell, William G. 2008. "Education Policy, Academic Research and Public Opinion." In *When Research Matters: How Scholarship Influences Education Policy*, edited by Frederick M. Hess, 135–144. Cambridge, MA: Harvard Education Press.

Huang, Gary, Mindy Reiser, Albert Parker, Judith Muniec, and Sameena Salvucci. 2003. "Institute of Education Sciences Findings from Interviews with Education Policymakers." Arlington, VA: Synetics.

Huelskamp, Robert M. 1993. "Perspectives on Education in America: An Annotated Briefing." *Phi Delta Kappan* 74 (9): 718–721. https://doi.org/10.1080/00220671.1993.9941211.

Huelskamp, Robert M. 2015. "The Sandia Report on Education: A Perfect Lesson in Censorship." Project Censored, July 7. https://www.projectcensored.org/3-the-sandia-report-on-education-a-perfect-lesson-in-censorship/.

Ingersoll, Richard M. 1995. "Teacher Supply, Teacher Qualifications and Teacher Turnover." Washington, DC: National Center for Education Statistics.

Ingersoll, Richard M. 1996. "Out-of-Field Teaching and Educational Equality." Washington, D.C: National Center for Education Statistics.

Ingersoll, Richard M. 2008. "Researcher Meets the Policy Realm: A Personal Account." In *When Research Matters: How Scholarship Influences Education Policy*, edited by Frederick M. Hess, 113–34. Cambridge, MA: Harvard Education Press.

Institute of Education Sciences. 2019. "Welcome to the What Works Clearinghouse." https://ies.ed.gov/ncee/wwc/FWW.

International Centre for Policy Advocacy. N.d. "Defining Policy Advocacy: Making Research Evidence Matter: A Guide to Policy Advocacy in Transition Countries." Accessed July 22, 2020. https://advocacyguide.icpolicyadvocacy.org/21-defining-policy-advocacy.

Jerrim, John, and Robert De Vries. 2017. "The Limitations of Quantitative Social Science for Informing Public Policy." *Evidence and Policy* 13 (1): 117–133. https://doi.org/10.1332/174426415X14431000856662.

Kaestle, Carl F. 1993. "Research News and Comment: The Awful Reputation of Education Research." *Educational Researcher* 22 (1): 23–31. https://doi.org/10.3102/0013189X022001023.

Kamenetz, Anya. 2014. "It's 2014. All Children Are Supposed to Be Proficient. What Happened?" National Public Radio, October 11. https://www.npr.org/sections/ed/2014/10/11/354931351/it-s-2014-all-children-are-supposed-to-be-proficient-under-federal-law.

Kingdon, John. 2003. *Agendas, Alternatives and Public Policies*, 2nd ed. Boston, MA: Addison-Wesley Educational Publishers.

Kirst, Michael W. 2000. "Bridging Education Research and Education Policymaking." *Oxford Review of Education* 26 (3/4): 379–391. https://doi.org/10.1080/30549800 20001891.

Ladson-Billings, Gloria. 2006. "From the Achievement Gap to the Education Debt: Understanding Achievement in U.S. Schools." *Educational Researcher* 35 (7): 3–12. https://doi.org/10.3102/0013189x035007003.

Landry, Rejean, Nabil Amara, and Moktar Lamari. 2001. "Climbing the Ladder of Research Utilization: Evidence from Social Science Research." *Science Communication* 22 (4): 396–422. https://doi.org/10.1177/1075547001022004003.

Lavis, John N., Dave Robertson, Jennifer M. Woodside, Christopher B. McLeod, and Julia Abelson. 2003. "How Can Research Organizations More Effectively Transfer Research Knowledge to Decision-Makers?" *Milbank Quarterly* 81 (2): 221–48. https://doi.org/10.1111/1468-0009.t01-1-00052.

Lemann, Nicholas. "The Reading Wars." *The Atlantic*, November 1997. https://www .theatlantic.com/magazine/archive/1997/11/the-reading-wars/376990/.

Lindblom, Charles E, and David K Cohen. 1979. *Usable Knowledge: Social Science and Social Problem Solving.* New Haven, CT: Yale University Press.

Lintle, Christian A. 2009. "Student's Corner: Communicating Your Language in Lay Language." *IEEE Engineering in Medicine and Biology Magazine*, May 2009.

Lubienski, Christopher L, Janelle Scott, and Elizabeth DeBray. 2014. "The Politics of Research Production, Promotion, and Utilization in Educational Policy." *Educational Policy* 28 (1): 131–144. https://doi.org/10.1177/0895904813515329.

Manna, Paul, and Michael J. Petrilli. 2008. "Double Standard? 'Scientifically Based Research' and the No Child Left Behind Act." In *When Research Matters: How Scholarship Influences Education Policy*, edited by Frederick M. Hess, 63–88. Cambridge, MA: Harvard Education Press.

Maranto, Robert, Scott Milliman, Frederick M. Hess, and April Gresham, eds. 1999. *School Choice in the Real World: Lessons from Arizona Charter Schools.* New York: Routledge.

Marin, Bernd. 1981. "What Is 'Half-Knowledge' Sufficient for and When?: Theoretical Comment on Policymakers' Uses of Social Science." *Science Communication* 3 (1): 43–60. https://doi.org/10.1177/107554708100300103.

Marland, Alex, and Anna Lennox Esselment. 2018. "Negotiating with Gatekeepers to Get Interviews with Politicians: Qualitative Research Recruitment in a Digital Media Environment." *Qualitative Research* 19 (6): 685–702. https://doi.org/10.1177 /1468794118803022.

Marshall, Catherine, Douglas E Mitchell, and Frederick Wirt. 1985. "Assumptive Worlds of Education Policymakers." *Peabody Journal of Education* 62 (4): 90–115. https:// www.jstor.org/stable/1492672?origin=JSTOR-pdf&seq=1.

Mattozzi, Andrea, and Antonio Merlo. 2015. "Mediocracy." *Journal of Public Economics* 130: 32–44. https://doi.org/10.1016/j.jpubeco.2015.07.001.

McDonnell, Lorraine M. 1988. "Can Education Research Speak to State Policy?" *Theory into Practice* 27 (2): 91–97. https://www.jstor.org/stable/1476463?origin=JSTOR-pdf &seq=1.

McDonnell, Lorraine M. 2009. "Repositioning Politics in Education's Circle of Knowledge." *Educational Researcher* 38 (6): 417–427. https://doi.org/10.3102/00131 89x09342584.

McDonnell, Lorraine M., and Stephen M. Weatherford. 2013. "Evidence Use and the Common Core State Standards Movement: From Problem Definition to Policy Adoption." *American Journal of Education* 120 (1): 1–25. https://doi.org/10.4324/9781 315408545-3.

McGann, James G. 2016. *The Fifth Estate: Think Tanks, Public Policy, and Governance.* Washington, DC: The Brookings Institution.

McGrady, Michael. 2017. "Arizona Approves Minor Changes to Common Core Standards." The Heartland Institute. https://www.heartland.org/news-opinion/news /arizona-approves-minor-changes-to-common-core-standards?source=policybot.

Miller, Steven I., and Marcel Fredericks. 2000. "Social Science Research Findings and Educational Policy Dilemmas: Some Additional Distinctions." *Education Policy Analysis Archives* 8 (3). https://epaa.asu.edu/ojs/article/view/394.

Monahan, Torin, and Jill A. Fisher. 2015. "Strategies for Obtaining Access to Secretive or Guarded Organizations." *Journal of Contemporary Ethnography* 44 (6): 709–736. https://doi.org/10.1177/0891241614549834.

Naidoo, Navindhra. 2011. "What Is Research? A Conceptual Understanding." *African Journal of Emergency Medicine* 1 (1). https://www.researchgate.net/publication /265704878_What_is_research_A_conceptual_understanding.

Nathan, Richard P. 1985. "Research Lessons from the Great Society." *Journal of Policy Analysis and Management* 4 (3): 422–426. https://doi.org/10.2307/3324196.

National Center for Education Statistics. N.d. "About Us." Accessed May 15, 2019. https://nces.ed.gov/about/.

National Commission on Excellence in Education. 1983. "A Nation at Risk: The Imperative for Educational Reform." Washington, DC: The National Commission on Excellence in Education.

National Conference of State Legislatures. 2020. "How States Define Lobbying and Lobbyist." September 8. https://www.ncsl.org/research/ethics/50-state-chart-lobby -definitions.aspx.

National Council of State Legislatures. 2017. "Full- and Part-Time Legislatures." Washington, DC, June 4. http://www.ncsl.org/research/about-state-legislatures/full-and -part-time-legislatures.aspx.

Nelson, Stephen R., James C. Leffler, and Barbara A. Hansen. 2009. "Toward a Research Agenda for Understanding and Improving the Use of Research Evidence." Portland, OR: Northwest Regional Educational Laboratory. http://educationnorthwest.org/sites /default/files/toward-a-research-agenda.pdf.

Ness, Erik C, and Denisa Gándara. 2014. "Ideological Think Tanks in the States: An Inventory of Their Prevalence, Networks, and Higher Education Policy Activity." *Educational Policy* 28 (2): 258–280. https://doi.org/10.1177/0895904813515328.

Newman, Joshua, Adrian Cherney, and Brian W. Head. 2016. "Do Policy Makers Use Academic Research? Reexamining the 'Two Communities' Theory of Research Utilization." *Public Administration Review* 76 (1): 24–32. https://doi.org/10.1111/puar .12464.

Nichols, Sharon L., and David C. Berliner. 2007. *Collateral Damage: How High-Stakes Testing Corrupts America's Schools*. Cambridge, MA: Harvard Education Press.

Nutley, Sandra M., Isabel Walter, and Huw T. O. Davies. 2007. *Using Evidence: How Research Can Inform Public Services*. Bristol, UK: Policy Press.

Oliver, Kathryn, and Paul Cairney. 2019. "The Dos and Don'ts of Influencing Policy: A Systematic Review of Advice to Academics." *Palgrave Communications* 5 (1): 1–11. https://doi.org/10.1057/s41599-019-0232-y.

Oliver, Kathryn, Simon Innvar, Theo Lorenc, Jenny Woodman, and James Thomas. 2014. "A Systematic Review of Barriers to and Facilitators of the Use of Evidence by Policymakers." *BMC Health Services Research* 14 (2). https://doi.org/10.1186/1472 -6963-14-2.

Online Publishers. 2021. "The Role of Social Media in Online Lobbying." 2021. https://www.theonlinepublishers.com/blog/the-role-of-social-media-in-online -lobbying#:~:text=But%2C.

Ostrander, Susan A. 1993. "'Surely You're Not in This Just to Be Helpful': Access, Rapport, and Interviews in Three Studies of Elites." *Journal of Contemporary Ethnography* 22 (1): 7–27.

Parkhurst, Justin. 2017. *The Politics of Evidence: From Evidence-Based Policy to the Good Governance of Evidence*. New York: Routledge.

Petes, Laura E., and Marc D. Meyer. 2018. "An Ecologist's Guide to Careers in Science Policy Advising." *Frontiers in Ecology and the Environment* 16 (1): 53–54. https:// doi.org/10.1002/fee.1761.

Petkovic, Jennifer, Vivian Welch, and Peter Tugwell. 2015. "Do Evidence Summaries Increase Policy-Makers' Use of Evidence from Systematic Reviews: A Systematic Review Protocol." *Systematic Reviews*, September 28. https://systematicreviewsjournal .biomedcentral.com/articles/10.1186/s13643-015-0116-1.

Pielke, Roger A. Jr. 2007. *The Honest Broker: Making Sense of Science in Policy and Politics*. Cambridge: Cambridge University Press.

Pinker, Steven. 2014. *The Sense of Style: The Thinking Person's Guide to Writing in the 21st Century*. New York, NY: Penguin Books.

"Policy Analysis." N.d. Britannica Academic. Accessed August 8, 2019.

Public Law 107–110. 2002. *No Child Left Behind Act of 2001*.

Pugliese Associates. N.d. "Social Media Killed the Lobbying Star?" Accessed January 12, 2021. https://puglieseassociates.com/social-media-killed-the-lobbying-star/.

Rako, Susan. 2018. "The Power of Naming: Ethnic Cleansing; Chain Immigration: Numbing Phrases." *Psychology Today*, February 23. https://www.psychologytoday.com /us/blog/more-light/201802/the-power-naming?amp=.

Rankin, Jenny G. 2019. *Sharing Your Education Expertise with the World: Make Research Resonate and Widen Your Impact*. New York: Routledge.

Rankin, Jenny G. 2020. *Increasing the Impact of Your Research: A Practical Guide to Sharing Your Findings and Widening Your Reach*. New York: Routledge.

Regoniel, Patrick. 2015. "Conceptual Framework: A Step by Step Guide on How to Make One." January 5. https://simplyeducate.me/2015/01/05/conceptual-framework-guide.

Rhode, Deborah L. 2006. *In Pursuit of Knowledge: Scholars, Status, and Academic Culture*. Stanford, CA: Stanford University Press.

Rich, Andrew. 2005. "War of Ideas." *Stanford Social Innovation Review* 3 (1): 18–25.

Sabatier, Paul A. 1988. "An Advocacy Coalition Framework of Policy Change and the Role of Policy-Oriented Learning." *Policy Sciences* 21 (2/3): 129–168. https://www .jstor.org/stable/4532139?seq=1.

Sallee, Margaret W., and Julee T. Flood. 2012. "Using Qualitative Research to Bridge Research, Policy, and Practice." *Theory into Practice* 51 (2): 137–144. https://doi.org /http://dx.doi.org/10.1080/00405841.2012.662873.

Sanders, William L., and Sandra P. Horn. 1998. "Research Findings from the Tennessee Value-Added Assessment System (TVAAS) Database: Implications for Educational Evaluation and Research." *Journal of Personnel Evaluation in Education* 12 (3): 247– 256. https://doi.org/10.1023/A:1008067210518.

Schemo, Diana J. 2004. "Nation's Charter Schools Lagging Behind, U.S. Test Scores Reveal." *New York Times*, August 17.

Schon, Donald. 1963. "Champions for Radical New Inventions." *Harvard Business Review* 41 (2): 77–86.

Scott, Janelle, and Huriya Jabbar. 2014. "The Hub and the Spokes: Foundations, Intermediary Organizations, Incentivist Reforms, and the Politics of Research Evidence." *Educational Policy* 28 (2): 233–257. https://doi.org/10.1177/0895904813515327.

Scott, Janelle, Christopher L. Lubienski, and Elizabeth DeBray. 2009. "The Politics of Advocacy in Education." *Educational Policy* 23 (1): 3–14. https://doi.org/10.1177 /0895904808328530.

Scott, Janelle, Christopher L. Lubienski, Elizabeth DeBray, and Huriya Jabbar. 2014. "The Intermediary Function in Evidence Production, Promotion, and Utilization: The Case of Educational Incentives." In *Using Research Evidence in Education: From the Schoolhouse Door to Capitol Hill*, edited by Kara S. Finnigan and Alan J. Daly, 69–89. New York: Springer.

Seashore Louis, Karen. 2005. "Knowledge Producers and Policymakers: Kissing Kin or Squabbling Siblings?" In *International Handbook of Educational Policy*, edited by Nina Bascia, Alister Cumming, Amanda Datnow, Keith Leithwood, and David Livingstone, 219–38. New York: Springer. https://www.springer.com/gp/book/9781402031892.

Seashore Louis, Karen, and Lisa M. Jones. 2002. "Dissemination with Impact: What Research Suggests for Practice in Career and Technical Education." St. Paul, MN: National Research Center for Career and Technical Education.

Shonkoff, Jack P. 2000. "Science, Policy, and Practice: Three Cultures in Search of a Shared Mission." *Child Development* 71 (1): 181–187. https://doi.org/10.1111/1467-8624.00132.

Snow, C. P. 1959. *The Two Cultures and the Scientific Revolution*. Cambridge: Cambridge University Press.

Staff. 2016. "State Board Votes to Replace Common Core Standards." *Eastern Arizona Courier*, December 27. https://www.eacourier.com/news/state-board-votes-to-replace-common-core-standards/article_d291898c-c965-11e6-8a9f-6351e655992a.html.

Staff. 2019. "A Year after the Teacher Walkout, a Timeline of Arizona's 'RedforED Movement.'" *Arizona Republic*, April 11. https://www.azcentral.com/story/news/local/arizona-education/2019/04/11/arizona-teacher-walkout-timeline-red-for-ed/3337757002/.

Stedman, Lawrence C. 1994. "The Sandia Report and U.S. Achievement: An Assessment." *Journal of Educational Research* 87 (3): 133–146. https://www.jstor.org/stable/27541911.

Steele, Colin. 2008. "Scholarly Monograph Publishing in the 21st Century: The Future More than Ever Should Be an Open Book." *Journal of Electronic Publishing* 11 (2). https://doi.org/http://dx.doi.org/10.3998/3336451.0011.201.

Stone, Deborah. 2012. *Policy Paradox: The Art of Political Decision Making*, 3rd ed. New York: Norton.

Sundquist, James L. 1978. "Research Brokerage: The Weak Link." In *Knowledge and Policy: The Uncertain Connection*, edited by Laurence E. Lynn, 191. Washington, DC: National Academies Press. https://www.nap.edu/catalog/19941/knowledge-and-policy-the-uncertain-connection.

Task Force on American Innovation. 2009. "Basic Research: Tackling America's 21st Century Challenges." Washington, DC: National Academy of Sciences.

Thompson, Genevieve N., Carole A. Estabrooks, and Lesley F. Degner. 2006. "Clarifying the Concepts in Knowledge Transfer: A Literature Review." *Journal of Advanced Nursing* 53 (6): 691–701. https://doi.org/10.1111/j.1365-2648.2006.03775.x.

Tseng, Vivian. 2012. "The Uses of Research in Policy and Practice." *Social Policy Report* 26 (2): 1–24.

Utah State Legislature. N.d. "Office of the Legislative Auditor General." Accessed on July 9, 2019. https://olag.utah.gov/olag-web/.

Walgrave, Stefaan, and Yves Dejaeghere. 2017. "Surviving Information Overload: How Elite Politicians Select Information." *Governance* 30 (2): 229–244. https://doi .org/10.1111/gove.12209.

Weber, James R., and Charlotte S. Word. 2009. "The Communication Process as Evaluative Context: What Do Nonscientists Hear When Scientists Speak?" *BioScience* 51 (6): 487–495.

Weible, Christopher M. 2008. "Expert-Based Information and Policy Subsystems: A Review and Synthesis." *Policy Studies Journal* 36 (4): 615–635. https://doi.org/10.1111 /j.1541-0072.2008.00287.x.

Weible, Christopher M., Tanya Heikkila, Peter deLeon, and Paul A. Sabatier. 2012. "Understanding and Influencing the Policy Process." *Policy Sciences* 45 (1): 1–21. https:// doi.org/10.1007/s11077-011-9143-5.

Weible, Christopher M., and Paul A. Sabatier, eds. 2018. *Theories of the Policy Process*, 4th ed. New York: Routledge.

Weick, Karl E. 1976. "Educational Organizations as Loosely Coupled Systems." *Administrative Science Quarterly* 21 (1): 1–19. https://doi.org/10.2307/2391875.

Weiss, Carol H. 1972. *Evaluating Action Programs: Readings in Social Action and Education*. Boston, MA: Prentice Hall.

Weiss, Carol H. 1976. "Symposium on 'The Research Utilization Quandry': Introduction by the Symposium Co-Editors." *Policy Studies Journal* 4 (3): 221–224.

Weiss, Carol H. 1977. "Research for Policy's Sake: The Enlightenment Function of Social Research." *Policy Analysis* 43 (4): 531–545.

Weiss, Carol H. 1979. "The Many Meanings of Research Utilization." *Public Administration Review* 39 (5): 426–431. https://doi.org/10.2307/3109916.

Weiss, Carol H. 1980. "Knowledge Creep and Decision Accretion." *Science Communication* 1 (3): 381–404.

Weiss, Carol H. 1989. "Congressional Committees as Users of Analysis." *Journal of Policy Analysis and Management* 8 (3): 411–431. https://doi.org/10.2307/3324932.

Weiss, Carol H, and Michael J. Bucuvalas. 1977. "The Challenges of Social Science Research to Decision Making." In *Using Social Research in Public Policy Making*, edited by Carol H. Weiss and Michael J. Bucuvalas, 213–224. Lexington, MA: Lexington Books.

Wherry, John H. 2004. "The Influence of Home on School Success." *Principal*, September–October. https://www.naesp.org/sites/default/files/resources/2/Principal /2004/S-Op6.pdf.

Whitty, Geoff. 2006. "Education(al) Research and Education Policy Making: Is Conflict Inevitable?" *British Educational Research Journal* 32 (2): 159–176. https://doi.org/10.1080/01411920600568919.

Wildavsky, Aaron. 1979. *Speaking Truth to Power: The Art and Craft of Policy Analysis.* Toronto, Canada: Brown and Company.

William T. Grant Foundation. 2019. "Research Grants on Improving the Use of Research Evidence." http://wtgrantfoundation.org/grants/research-grants-improving-use-research-evidence.

Wilson, James Q. 1981. "'Policy Intellectuals' and Public Policy." *Public Interest* 64 (Summer): 31–46.

Wirt, Frederick M., and Douglas E. Mitchell. 1982. "Social Science and Educational Reform: The Political Uses of Social Research." *Educational Administration Quarterly* 18 (4): 1–16.

Wiseman, Alexander W. 2010. "Chapter 1: The Uses of Evidence for Educational Policymaking: Global Contexts and International Trends." *Review of Research in Education* 34 (1): 1–24. https://doi.org/10.3102/0091732X09350472.

Wong, Kenneth K. 2008. "Considering the Politics in the Research Policymaking Nexus." In *When Research Matters: How Scholarship Influences Education Policy*, edited by Frederick M. Hess, 219–237. Cambridge, MA: Harvard Education Press.

Wye, Lesley, Emer Brangan, Ailsa Cameron, John Gabbay, Jonathan H. Klein, and Catherine Pope. 2015. "Evidence Based Policy Making and the 'Art' of Commissioning—How English Healthcare Commissioners Access and Use Information and Academic Research in 'Real Life' Decision-Making: An Empirical Qualitative Study." *BMC Health Services Research* 15 (1): 1–13. https://doi.org/10.1186/s12913-015-1091-x.

Yorkshire Medical Marketing. N.d. "How to Use Social Media Effectively When Lobbying." Accessed March 12, 2019. https://yorkshiremedicalmarketing.com/2019/03/12/how-to-use-social-media-awareness-days-in-your-healthcare-marketing/.

Zuiker, Steven J, Neils Piepgrass, Adai Tefera, Kate T Anderson, Kevin Winn, and Gustavo Fischman. 2019. "Advancing Knowledge Mobilization in Colleges of Education." *International Journal of Education Policy and Leadership* 15 (1): 1–19. https://journals.sfu.ca/ijepl/index.php/ijepl/article/view/808.

INDEX

Note: page numbers followed by *f* and *t* refer to figures and tables, respectively.